Snowshoe Hikes in the
White Mountains

Snowshoe Hikes
in the
White Mountains

Steven D. Smith

Bondcliff Books · Littleton, New Hampshire

Snowshoe Hikes in the White Mountains

Copyright © 2000 by Steven D. Smith
2nd Printing, February 2002

Library of Congress Card Number 1–931271–00–3

ISBN 00–109845

DISCLAIMER: Every effort was made to ensure that the information in this book was
accurate at press time. However, trail conditions are subject to change. We would
appreciate hearing of any changes.

Also, readers should note that snowshoeing in the mountains is a potentially hazardous activity. Weather and trail conditions can change rapidly. Proper gear, clothing,
conditioning and knowledge are prerequisites for a safe winter journey. Readers are
responsible for their own actions and safety, and are urged to exercise caution and
sound judgement. Use of this guide is at the reader's own risk. The author and pub-
lisher assume no liability.

Text composition by Passumpsic Publishing, St. Johnsbury, Vt.

Printed in the United States by Sherwin Dodge Printers, Littleton, N.H.

PHOTOGRAPH CREDITS
Ken Stampfer: pages 6, 13, 17, 62, 68, 158, 168, 204, 210, 220, 242
Mike Dickerman: pages 77, 132, 153
Carol Smith: pages 31, 120
All other photographs by the author.

FRONTISPIECE: Approaching the South Ledges of Moriah

Additional copies of this book may be obtained directly from:
Bondcliff Books
P.O. Box 385
Littleton, NH 03561

To Carol

My Favorite Snowshoer

Contents

For updates and additional snowshoe hikes, visit
www.mountainwanderer.com and click on "Paths & Peaks".

Acknowledgments

I'd been exploring the trails in the White Mountains for five years in summer and fall before it ever occurred to me that you could hike them in winter, too. My first thanks go to John Dickerman, who sparked my interest in snowshoeing with his tales of frozen ponds and frosty peaks. He loaned me his Sherpa Featherweight snowshoes for my first real winter hike, up the Crawford Path to Mt. Pierce on a luminous February day in 1983. I've been hooked ever since.

Mike Dickerman, John's brother, has been a stalwart hiking companion for nearly two decades now. We did most of the winter 4000-footers together, and many other snowshoe treks in all kinds of weather and snow. It's a special pleasure to team up with Mike, the owner of Bondcliff Books, to publish this guide. His strong support and expert guidance are most appreciated.

Richard Curry, perhaps the most enthusiastic hiker I know, has contributed greatly to this book with his thoughtful suggestions and heartfelt opinions. If you need convincing to climb Kearsarge North, talk to Richard. He gives it a 5+ on his view rating system from 1–5. He also provided information on several trails I was not able to return to in winter.

Ken and Ann Stampfer were delightful companions on several "research trips" for this guide. Ken never saw a camera he didn't like, and a number of his artful photos grace these pages. He also reviewed part of the manuscript. Special thanks to Ann for toughing it out up to Bicknell Ridge after losing a snowshoe—we won't say how. The Stampfers also furnished reports on several other snowshoe hikes.

Thanks also to family and friends who have accompanied me on winter trips through the years, many of which have ended up in this book: my brother Drew, with whom I've shared some special snowshoe hikes and exciting bird sightings; his wife, Kate; my nieces, Rachel and Rebecca Smith; my nephews, David and Michael Meguerdichian; Roger and Peter Doucette; Bill Vecchio; Harry & Barb Cunningham; Cathy Goodwin; Cindy DiSanto; Steve Martin; Sue Johnston; Al & Jean LaPrade; Ginger Lang; peakbagging guru Gene Daniell; Jeff Tirey, who introduced us to hot liquid Jell-O; and especially fellow bushwhacking nut Creston Ruiter.

Helpful information was provided by Dave Govatski, Kathy Didier and the folks at the touring centers around the Whites. P. Thompson Davis kindly reviewed several parts of the manuscript and made many helpful suggestions.

Thanks to Tom Ekman and the folks at TOPO!/National Geographic Maps for permission to use their excellent product to create the maps.

I would also like to thank Scott Cahoon of Passumpsic Publishing for his outstanding layout and production work, and the folks at Sherwin Dodge Printers for a fine printing job.

A special acknowledgment is owed to Laura and the late Guy Waterman, whose words and deeds have been an inspiration to me and many other hikers. We miss you, Guy, but your spirit lives on amidst these forests and these crags.

Every guidebook writer owes a debt to the dedicated professionals and volunteers who tend to our marvelous White Mountain trail system, and to the search and rescue folks who willingly risk their lives to help hikers in need.

Most of all I thank my wife, Carol, without whose unwavering support this book would not have happened. In addition to snowshoeing a number of trails with me, she typed sizeable chunks of a scribbled manuscript and patiently endured my many late nights at the computer as both the deadline and our wedding approached. This book is dedicated to her.

*Snowshoe Hikes in the
White Mountains*

Introduction

Cold as the peak was on which I stood, and the only way to prevent freezing at midday was to keep up a constant movement on snowshoes, it seemed as if I could not descend into the valley while such a glimpse of ethereal beauty was before me. —Julius H. Ward on Doublehead Mtn., "Under the Winter Solstice" in *The White Mountains: A Guide to Their Interpretation*, 1896

Why Winter?

When I asked my good friend Richard Curry, a recent and enthusiastic convert to hiking, why winter was his favorite season to roam the trails of the White Mountains, his answer was simple: "It's so beautiful it makes you want to cry!"

A bright winter day, with temperatures in the twenties and the woods and peaks draped in a fresh cloak of snow, can, indeed, induce a boundless exhilaration. The leafless hardwoods on the lower slopes are expansive and inviting, offering long views through the forest. Higher up the evergreens are molded into platoons of fantastic snow sculptures. Break out onto an open ledge and you see waves of rime-frosted ridges rolling to the horizon. Winter's clear, crisp air allows maximum visibility for mountain vistas. Some days it looks like the whole world's been washed clean.

There are other advantages in taking to the trails on snowshoes. As one winter tramper put it, "No bugs, no bears." If you despise heat and humidity, this is your season. If downhill pounding makes your knees cry out in protest, you'll appreciate the forgiving surface of a packed snowshoe track. This is also the prime season for animal tracking.

With a new generation of high-tech snowshoes and clothing, it's more comfortable to explore the winter trails than ever before. The basics of snowshoeing are easy to pick up. The old adage goes that "If you can walk, you can snowshoe," and a snowshoeing lesson is on the order of, "Strap 'em on and go!" You'll be pleasantly surprised by how well modern snowshoes can handle mountain terrain. Snowshoers can travel with ease where all but the most hardcore skiers would throw in the towel.

It's not all peaches and cream in winter, of course. It's cold out there, at least most of the time. Winter's chill makes every simple act on the trail more difficult. Benumbed fingers fumble with straps and zippers. Water

*Deep winter in
Crawford Notch*

bottles freeze solid. Summit stays and other rest stops are, by necessity, short and to the point.

This is the season when White Mountain weather is at its most wildly changeable. There are those rapturous bluebird-sky days, yes, but you may just as easily encounter flesh-freezing blasts of polar wind, a cold, soaking rain, or cloudbanks that shroud the ridges in gloom for days on end, granting you nothing but "gray air" at a hard-earned viewpoint.

The other major factor you deal with in winter is snow, in all its forms. You may slog through powder deep enough to swallow a ski pole, or clatter across crust hard enough to break glass. Travel times may be much slower or faster than in summer, depending on the snow surface. Happily, today's snowshoes are capable of handling a wide range of conditions.

It's obvious that snowshoe hikes require more planning, equipment and caution than a summer afternoon lark. In this introductory section I'll offer some admittedly subjective pointers based on my experiences snowshoeing in the White Mountains. For more information on the "how-to" end of things, I'll refer you to the books on snowshoeing and winter hiking listed in the *Recommended Reading* section. Among the best are Dan Allen's *Don't Die on the Mountain*, John Dunn's *Winterwise*, Gene Prater's *Snowshoeing*, and Larry Olmsted's *Snowshoeing: A Trailside Guide*.

This guide is primarily a "where-to" book, intended to show you some of the best places to snowshoe in the White Mountains. The trips selected here run the gamut from easy jaunts of an hour or less to strenuous climbs up 4000-foot summits, and all-day probes into remote valleys. All of the trips are described as single day hikes. The majority are of the intermediate, half-day variety, within the capabilities of the great majority of snowshoers.

I've included plenty of trails that lead to views of the Presidentials (always a spectacular sight in winter) and other high peaks, plus a variety of treks to ponds, waterfalls and other points of interest. Along the way I've tried to relate some of the fascinating history of these places. For those who enjoy surveying the views, there are fairly detailed descriptions of what you can see from the best outlooks, a tradition that goes back to the guidebooks of the late 1800s, when vistas were to be "appreciated."

With the proper gear, clothing and attitude, you'll find snowshoeing in the White Mountains an exhilarating pastime. I wish you many safe and happy journeys.

A WORD FOR BEGINNERS

If you're just starting out on snowshoes, you're about to discover a wonderful new world out in these snowy mountains. I urge you to start slowly, with the shortest, easiest trips described in this guide, ideally on trails you've hiked in summer. Don't attempt a trip beyond your capabilities and experience. Read up on equipment, clothing and winter safety. Better yet, go out with friends who are experienced in the winter woods, or join a club that sponsors organized trips led by knowledgeable snowshoers. Several chapters of the Appalachian Mountain Club (AMC) have extensive winter trip schedules in the White Mountains. Visit *www.outdoors.org* and click through to the chapter website of your choice. The AMC and other organizations also offer winter hiking and snowshoeing workshops.

Snowshoeing Tradition in the White Mountains

The White Mountains have been a renowned center for summer hiking since the early 1800s, when the stalwart Ethan Allen Crawford and his father Abel built trails to Mt. Washington for use by guests staying at their Crawford Notch inns. It took a little longer for recreational hiking to take hold in winter, but in the early 1880s members from the fledgling Appalachian Mountain Club formed a special "Snow-Shoe Section." Snowshoeing in the mountains soon became a popular pastime.

Each February, a group of "Appies" would spend a week or two at a hotel in Randolph, Waterville, or especially Jackson, climbing as many nearby mountains as time and weather permitted. First winter ascents of many White Mountain peaks were engineered by these groups in the 1880s, 1890s and early 1900s. Women, wool skirts and all, were prominent and active in the Snow-Shoe Section, making up twenty of the forty-six charter members. These were thoroughly sociable gatherings—one climb of Mt. Pierce (Clinton) in 1902 drew a throng of 54 snowshoers to that semi-alpine summit.

In 1915 this AMC group published its own 25-page "Snow-Shoe Manual," offering tips on clothing, equipment, snowshoes, technique, first aid, and trail etiquette. The authors recommended snowshoe sizes of 12" × 42" for men and 11" × 38" for women—huge and awkward by today's standards.

In the 1920s an elite group of AMC climbers, including the estimable Miriam O'Brien and Robert Underhill (who later married), formed a group called the "Bemis Crew" for the purpose of tackling a more adventurous climbing agenda. Each winter for the next several years, they took on some of the most challenging terrain in the White Mountains on snowshoes. In a typical week, this energetic bunch might record a total of 20,000 feet of elevation gain—equivalent to climbing Mt. Washington five times.

Skiing became all the rage in the mountains in the 1930s and 1940s, though a devoted cadre of snowshoers continued plodding up the mountain trails. Improvements in equipment and clothing during World War II led to a new era of snowshoeing in the 1950s and 1960s. The squat oval "bearpaw" and the Westover brand "modified beavertail" became the snowshoes of choice for mountain ascents. Winter trampers were bedecked in army surplus gear, including olive-drab wind pants and later the insulated rubber "Mickey Mouse" boots. They lugged huge packs with sleeping bags, tent, and ample emergency supplies even for day trips. There were still relatively few snowshoers afield in the '50s and '60s, so trailbreaking was often an arduous task. Trips to the remote summits were multiday adventures requiring a firm commitment to safety and self-reliance. One of the shining snowshoers of this era was Robert Collin, an AMC leader who in the early 1960s undertook such epics as a six-day jaunt through the Pemigewasset Wilderness and an attempted traverse of the AMC hut system.

Soon after the formation of the AMC's "Four Thousand Footer Club" in 1957 (the goal being to climb all of the 4000-foot summits in the White Mountains, then numbering 46, in a practice called "peakbagging"), a small, hardy band of climbers assaulted the list in winter. On a bitter December day in 1960, Miriam and Robert Underhill, eminent mountaineers then 62 and 71 respectively, scaled their 46th winter peak, Mt. Jefferson. The temperature on top was –8 degrees F, with an invigorating breeze of 70 mph. In the ensuing four decades, a couple of hundred hikers have followed their snowshoe tracks to bag the "winter 48" (two new peaks have since been added), but this is still only a fraction of those who have climbed them in summer. The late Guy Waterman crafted the most wondrous feat in the annals of White Mountain snowshoeing by ascending the forty-eight 4000-footers from each of the four points of the compass. From north and south, from east and west, mostly without trails, through untold numbers of spruce traps and blowdowns, he did them all.

Winter hiking and snowshoeing have seen boom times in the last thirty years. Many more people are out on the trails, and the popular routes are often packed out to the point where snowshoes are superfluous (except for traction) and "bare-booting" is possible. The Kancamagus Highway is plowed year-round, making more trailheads accessible, and the AMC keeps two of its backcountry huts open year-round on a caretaker basis. Fleece, Gore-Tex, plastic boots and aluminum snowshoes have displaced army surplus garb, Mickey Mouse boots, and wooden bearpaws. The late 1990s saw snowshoeing go mainstream, with more people than ever taking it up as a leisure pursuit. Some veterans feel that winter hiking has become almost too easy, that a spirit of adventure and commitment shared by earlier generations of winter trampers has been lost. For a fascinating perspective on the recent evolution of winter hiking, see the piece "Five Winter Trips—The End of Adventure?" in Laura and Guy Waterman's *A Fine Kind of Madness*, published by The Mountaineers. Even today, though, on the lesser-used trails, or anyplace after a big dump of snow, there's still plenty of adventure and even solitude to be found.

For a more complete history of winter hiking and snowshoeing in the White Mountains, see the Watermans' epic and engaging *Forest and Crag*: Chapters 32, 47, 49, 59, and 60. The brief narrative above draws liberally from this authoritative source.

Gear and Clothing

SNOWSHOES

If your idea of snowshoes is four-foot wooden monsters straight out of a Jack London novel, there is good news. Today's high-tech snowshoes are comfortable, durable and able to handle a variety of terrain and snow conditions. Though some traditionalists mush on with the venerable wooden snowshoe, most 'shoers on White Mountain trails use one of the modern aluminum-frame variety. The first such snowshoes were developed out west in the 1960s and became known as the "Western" model. A narrower profile, upturned toe, solid neoprene decking, pivot-rod binding and aggressive traction device distinguished them from wooden snowshoes. Some of the better-known manufacturers of aluminum frame snowshoes today are Tubbs, Sherpa, Atlas, Yuba, Redfeather and MSR.

I've used Sherpas since I first started snowshoeing in 1983, but I have friends who are equally loyal to other brands. The best advice I can give you

Packs always seem larger in winter

is "try before you buy." Rent a couple of different pairs, or borrow them from friends, and try them out on the trail. A number of outdoor stores and touring centers in the White Mountains have snowshoes available for rent.

TYPES OF SNOWSHOES

Snowshoes suitable for trail use in the White Mountains break down into two general categories: **recreational** and **mountaineering**. Recreational snowshoes are less expensive and are designed for more casual use on easier trails. They are fine for snowshoeing many of the beginner and easier intermediate trips in this guide. As of this writing you can snag a pair of these for under $150.

Mountaineering snowshoes are sturdier and have more aggressive traction devices. They will serve you better on steep terrain and in crusty or icy conditions. If you plan to tackle the steeper intermediate or advanced treks, the one time investment in solid mountaineering 'shoes—over $200 to $350 or more—will be money well spent. When weighing a purchase, consider what type of snowshoeing you're most likely to do.

SIZE

The "flotation" of a snowshoe—how well you stay on top of the snow—depends on the size of the frame and the weight that it's bearing. In the White Mountains you'll rarely need humongous pickerel snowshoes designed for bottomless Minnesota powder. Many of the trails in this book are consistently tramped out, and our New England weather brings us hardpack as often as powder, so smaller snowshoes are the rule here. You'll appreciate their maneuverability and ease of walking. Common sizes and recommended weight ranges (you plus your pack) for aluminum frame snowshoes are:

8" × 25"	up to 150 lbs. for powder / up to 175 lbs. for packed track
9" × 30"	150–200 lbs. for powder / 175–225 lbs. for packed track
10" × 36"	over 200 lbs. for powder / over 225 lbs. for packed track

I weigh 180 lbs., carry a 25-lb. pack, and wear 9 × 30s. My wife does wonderfully with the 8 × 25s. Choose a pair in the size that best fits your weight and intended use.

BINDINGS

No one has yet come up with the perfect binding, one that goes on and comes off easily with numb fingers, has a smooth hinging action, and is secure on the toughest sidehills. There's a wide variety of binding systems out there, using various configurations of straps, buckles, hooks or clips. If testing a snowshoe, make sure the bindings fit snugly and put them through their paces at various angles of ascent, descent and sidehill.

TRACTION DEVICES

In crusty old New England, more traction is better. Today's aluminum snowshoes come with some type of crampon attached under the insteps of your feet. Additional crampons under heels and toes or around the edge provide extra surefootedness. Test snowshoes out at different angles and on different surfaces to see how they grip. Buy the most traction you can afford. Your feet may look like inverted Stegosauruses, but with well-armored snowshoes you can tackle all but the iciest conditions on the trails in this book.

SKI POLES

I heartily recommend using one or two ski poles when snowshoeing backcountry trails. Many snowshoers swear by adjustable-length poles, which can be shortened or lengthened to suit snow depth and terrain. Regular ski poles of a comfortable length are fine, too. Poles are invaluable for balance coming down a slope, for pushing off on climbs, and for rhythmic 'shoeing on easy ground. Other uses are for knocking snow from overhanging branches, banging clumps of wet snow off your snowshoes, and testing ice at stream or pond crossings. Don't leave home without 'em.

BOOT CRAMPONS

When rain and thaw followed by arctic cold turn all the snow in the mountains to boilerplate, you'll find boot crampons an invaluable addition to your winter arsenal. They're also useful early in the season when snow cover is thin and water on the trail freezes into ice flows. Even in good snow times they can come in handy for a tricky pitch or an ice-encrusted summit ledge.

Simplest, lightest and least expensive are "instep crampons" that attach under the middle of your boots. You must buy the proper size to fit the width of your boot—shoepacs have a wider base than mountaineering boots. Make sure they fit snugly. Insteps are fine when moderate trails get icy. They don't perform as well on steep terrain and aren't suitable for above-treeline travel.

Full crampons attach under the length of your boot and provide more security than instep crampons. I have a pair with 8 points (spikes), but most come with either 10 or 12 points. Twelve-pointers have two front points that stick out ahead of your toes; they are intended for use on seriously steep ice and are overkill for the hikes in this book. The front points can be a hazard for inexperienced users. Most snowshoers would do well to stick with 8- or 10-point crampons. Make sure the points of your crampons are not exposed when carrying them in or on your pack. I carry mine in a thick canvas bag.

Crampon frames are hinged or rigid. The hinged variety can be used, with care, on flexible boots such as shoepacs. Rigid frame crampons can only be used on stiffer mountaineering boots. Crampon bindings may be of the strap-on or step-in variety. Since you'll be fussing with them in the cold, user-friendly bindings are desirable. Make sure they fit properly.

Walking with crampons requires focus. It's all too easy to catch a point and trip. Practice with them on level ground before attempting climbs and descents. On a slope keep crampons flush against the icy surface rather than edging them like a ski. Cramponing for long distances is tiresome. I'll use them only when confronted with a stretch of ice that's just too nasty for my snowshoe crampons, or in that dreaded thaw/freeze pattern when the entire trail has no snow to speak of and is just one long ice flow. They do give you a nice feeling of security in these situations, when the only alternative is to stay home. At such times I'd suggest shorter, easier trips.

One warning: *never* slide down a trail with crampons on—you could easily catch a point and break your leg.

ICE AXE

Some snowshoers regularly use this classic tool of the winter mountaineer. If you're climbing Mt. Washington, a Northern Presidential peak, or the upper Franconia Ridge (trips beyond the scope of this book), an ice axe is an important safety item that can stop a potentially deadly slide down a steep icy slope with a technique called "self-arrest." It can also be used to cut steps in hard snow or ice, as a prop to push or pull yourself up in steep terrain, and as a secure support when descending a hardpacked slope. A longer ice axe can be used as a walking staff in gentler terrain. For several winters I used an adjustable-length axe in such a manner and found it quite handy, though it tended to slip if I put my full weight on it.

It's my feeling that in reasonable snow conditions an ice axe is not needed for the majority of trips in this book. The only exceptions might be when some of the higher summits (e.g. Mt. Moosilauke, Mt. Pierce, Mt. Jackson) and a handful of the other most difficult trips described here are very icy at the top. It's a matter of individual choice. Use your judgement. If your group is axeless and encounters a dangerous open slope, turn back.

You need training and practice to make an effective self-arrest. A quick, instinctive reaction is needed to stop a slide. In unpracticed hands an ice axe could be more of a hazard than help, impaling the user or a companion. If you feel you should bring one, obtain instruction on how to carry it and use it.

CLOTHING

Layering is the all-important principle of dressing on the winter trail. Through the course of your trip you should try to regulate your temperature—wear fewer layers when exerting and add layers when you stop for a break. This will help prevent you from getting overly soaked with perspiration, which can chill you dangerously. Also, several thin layers provide more insulation than one thick layer. Brush snow off your clothes frequently.

Before suggesting what to wear, I'll start with one thing *not* to wear: cotton, including blue jeans. Once it gets wet, cotton will chill you to the bone. Avoid it!

For a first layer I wear a polypropylene long-sleeved shirt and long johns. Polypro becomes quite rank after an hour or two of sweating, but it does a fine job of wicking perspiration away and it dries quickly. When climbing steeply through deep snow some snowshoers will strip their upper body down to the polypro layer no matter how cold it is. I always bring several spare polypro shirts. Though a gust of wind always seems to kick up just when I'm changing at the top, a fresh dry shirt feels heavenly once it's on.

Good choices for an insulating second layer include a wool or synthetic shirt or sweater for the upper body and wool or synthetic pants. Bringing an extra shirt or sweater along is a good idea. As for pants, I've always been partial to old-fashioned baggy, scratchy woolies.

Outer layers include a pile / fleece jacket, a down or fiberfill vest, a windproof and rainproof shell, a warm down or fiberfill parka for rest stops on cold days or emergencies, and wind / rain pants. Fiberfill garments will retain warmth far better when wet than down vests or jackets.

Gloves and mittens are, of course, essential. Layering can be used with liner gloves, regular wool or synthetic gloves / mittens, and mitten overshells. When climbing, you may find that liners are enough to keep your hands warm. Mittens are warmer than gloves, though clumsier. I always carry two or three extra pairs of mittens and gloves in my pack—often enough your first pair will get wet partway through your trip.

Warm headwear is also critical for snowshoeing. On warmer days, or when climbing, an earband may do the trick, but you should always bring at least one warm wool or synthetic hat of the balaclava variety, which covers your neck as well as the top of your head. Better yet, bring two in case one gets lost or blown away. Everyone knows that if you're cold, put on a hat—major heat loss occurs from the head. If you're too hot while climbing, take your hat off—it makes a great thermostat. If you're traversing a windy pond or exposed summit, a facemask may come in handy. On warm, sunny spring days a baseball hat is de rigeur.

FOOTWEAR

The adaptability of modern snowshoe bindings allows you to use just about any kind of footwear. Although some snowshoers use summer leather boots, I don't recommend it. They're just not warm enough. Most of my snowshoeing has been done with traditional **shoepacs**. These boots have rubber bottoms, leather uppers, lug soles and removable felt liners. They're toasty, loose-fitting and reasonably comfortable. On the downside, they're not as secure as a rigid boot for crampon use, and the rubber bottoms tend to wear through where the bindings rub against them. Shoe goo will hold this problem at bay for a while.

Many snowshoers prefer **double plastic mountaineering boots**. These have a warm insulating inner boot and a semi-rigid waterproof outer shell. I've been using a pair for the last few winters and though I found them stiff and uncomfortable at first, they have proven to be warm and durable. They're the only choice for rigid crampons and clip-on snowshoe bindings. Their narrow soles make them less appealing to me for "bare-booting" than my bigfoot-size shoepacs.

In recent years several manufacturers have come out with insulated "**winter utility boots**" specifically designed for active winter outdoorspeople. These are said to have a snugger fit than shoepacs, and are more comfortable than plastic double boots. I've never tried them, but they sound like a good option.

For **socks** I prefer a thin inner layer of silk or polypropylene for wicking and a thick wool outer sock for insulation. Don't try to cram too many sock layers into your boots—you'll end up with restricted circulation and cold feet. Some snowshoers use "**vapor barrier**" socks that prevent the sweat from your feet soaking the outer insulating layers. Your feet wallow in sweat, but they stay warmer because your insulation is dry. Being a frugal Yankee, I use small plastic bags as vapor barriers for my feet on cold days, placing them over my liner socks. They can be re-used several times if stored discreetly.

Gaiters should be a part of every snowshoer's wardrobe. These nylon sleeves cover the tops of your boots and lower pant legs, serving a double function of keeping snow out of your boots and off your pants, and adding another layer of insulation to your lower legs. I prefer a full length pair that comes up to the knee. Make sure they fit easily over your boots. If you wear thick wool pants, get your gaiters a size larger so you don't feel like you're wearing tourniquets on your legs.

Sunglasses should always be carried. The sun is doubly bright in winter when it reflects off snow. On a sunny March day you can sustain a stinging burn if you don't have UV protection, especially in open hardwood forest and ledgy areas. **Goggles** may be in order on windy or snowy days in exposed places such as ponds or summits.

PACKS

For snowshoeing you'll need a bigger **day pack** than you use in summer— mostly for all those extra clothing layers. Mine goes 25–30 lbs. and close to 4000 cubic inches in capacity, but then I'm infamous among my hiking friends for carrying monster day packs, even in summer. You may not need to haul quite as much, but in winter spacious is better. Cramming too much stuff into a small pack leads to frustration when your hands are numb and you need something that's stuck at the bottom.

I always line the main compartment of my day pack with a double layer of thick garbage bags—this ensures that extra clothing will be dry when it's needed. Smaller bags can be used to line pack pockets.

Among the essential items to carry in your pack are:

- A **flashlight** or **headlamp** with extra batteries and spare bulb. I usually bring a headlamp and two small flashlights. Reverse the batteries or tape the switch "off" to prevent the light from turning on and draining the batteries.
- **Trail map** and **guidebook**. A ziplock bag is handy for carrying these. Every member of a snowshoeing party should have a map and be familiar with the route.
- **Compass.** I usually carry two. There's no space to go into it here, but every snowshoer should know how to use a map & compass. One of the best of the many books on the subject is *Wilderness Navigation*, by Bob Burns and Mike Burns. Remember that in the White Mountains the compass needle points about 16½ degrees to the west of true north (magnetic declination). An **altimeter** is also a handy device—either of the pocket variety or on a multi-function sports watch. This should be checked at known elevation points and reset if barometric pressure changes. I have zero experience with **GPS units**, but they are very popular and some snowshoers will want to bring them along. They do run on batteries, so it will pay to keep a GPS unit close to your body and warm.
- **Waterproof matches** and **firestarter** or **candle**.
- **Pocket knife.** The trusty old Swiss Army Knife is just fine.
- **Watch.** This is critical for determining turn-around time and available daylight. Have at least two with your group in case one fails.
- **First Aid Kit.** There are many good packaged kits available designed specifically for backcountry use. These can be customized to your specific needs. Such kits also come with a small first aid manual, and there

are many good books on the subject. Better yet, take a basic first aid course.

- **Bivouac sack** or **space blanket.** Worth its weight in gold in an emergency.
- **Sunscreen.** I prefer SPF 30 or higher for the best protection. Apply liberally to your nose, especially.
- **Heat Packs.** Chemically activated, these are light and inexpensive and are great for warming cold hands or feet.
- **Toilet Paper.** You haven't lived until you've answered the call of nature on snowshoes. See the section on *Protecting the Mountain Environment.*
- **Rope, Cord** or **Wire.** For emergency snowshoe repair or other unforeseen uses. Can also be used to attach snowshoes to packs. Many snowshoers carry a small repair kit and duct tape.
- **Whistle.** For drawing attention in emergency situations.

Optional items include:

- **Camera.** Great for recording ice-laden beards, snowshoers floundering in spruce traps, and an occasional mountain vista. Remember that bright sun on snow will throw off your exposures. It's best to bracket several different settings if you really want the shot. Keep your camera close to your body so the batteries stay warm.
- **Binoculars.** Handy for scanning views and identifying peaks.
- **Cell phone.** This is not the place to get into the great cell phone debate. It can be a lifesaver in a dire situation, but in winter the batteries may fail unless you keep them warm. In many trail locations there will be no signal at all, especially in low-lying areas. Also, note that under recent New Hampshire legislation, unnecessary or frivolous rescue calls will result in a hefty search and rescue bill for the calling party.

FOOD AND DRINK

Snowshoers should bring a **trail lunch** and plenty of **high energy snacks.** Choice of foods is a matter of personal taste; I happen to like PB&J sandwiches, peanuts, animal crackers and M&Ms. Some snacks such as Snickers bars and Powerbars become rock hard in the cold and are liable to break your teeth. You must eat through the day to keep your engine going in the cold, even if you don't feel that hungry.

It's equally important to drink lots of **water** through the trip. Bring at least two quarts on an all-day venture. You must make a concerted effort to drink before you get thirsty. Dehydration is a real problem in the cold, dry air, and can contribute to hypothermia. If your urine is dark, you need to drink more water.

Wide-mouth water bottles are more practical in winter. If frozen, they're easier to crack open than a narrow-mouth model. On very cold days your water may freeze into slush. If the thermometer is hovering around

Mt. Hight is a prized objective for advanced snowshoers

zero in the morning, I'll warm up my water to a moderate temperature on the stove before dumping it in the bottle, then I'll insert each bottle into a wool sock for insulation. One trick to keep the cap from freezing is to place the bottle upside down in a pack pocket. That way the ice forms first at the bottom of the bottle. Just make sure the cap's on tight.

A **thermos** of hot tea, soup or other liquid will win you praises from the other snowshoers in your group. A veteran winter camper once turned us on to hot liquid Jell-O. It sounds odd, but it's guaranteed to warm your innards.

Weather, Season and Snow Conditions

WEATHER

The weather forecast may be the single most important piece of information you need to plan a snowshoe hike. Weather can change quickly in the White Mountains, and even more so in winter. During the course of the season you may encounter blizzards, rainstorms, freezing rain, sleet, arctic cold, high winds, balmy thaws, and those wonderful, sunny days when you have to get up high for a view. Temperatures can range from 30° below to 60° above Farenheit.

Sometimes a pattern will take hold for several days: bitter cold with fierce winds bringing "wind fog" to obscure the peaks; a series of flurries floating over the mountains, piling up a foot or more of snow in small increments; interminable rain-spattered thaws that open the brooks and turn the snow to slush; or the snowshoer's dream, a big Canadian high with day after glorious day of bright sun and 30-degree highs.

Plan your snowshoe hike with the weather in mind. The weather *before* your trip can affect your choice of routes. For example, if it's rained recently and opened up the streams, pick a trail that doesn't have unbridged crossings. A recent heavy snow means you'll be doing some laborious breaking and you'll have to scale down your mileage expectations.

Check the forecast for the day *of* your hike one last time the night before you go. Take note of projected temperatures, wind speed and direction, cloud cover and possible precipitation. If there's going to be low clouds or gusty winds, there's not much point in seeking a lofty outlook—try a valley, waterfall or pond hike instead. Outings should be shorter and less exposed on cold days. Wait for a forecast of sunny skies and light winds for trips to the higher, more exposed mountains. If you're in for sub-zero temperatures, high winds, a raging blizzard or a driving rain, stay home by the fire—some days a snowshoe hike is just not meant to be.

Whenever you go, note that temperatures will usually drop 3–5°F for every 1000 feet of elevation gain, though sometimes there are inversions where the valleys are colder than the summits. Higher places are almost always windier. TV meteorologists love to hype the "wind chill"—the combined cooling effect of temperature and wind. Snowshoeing across an exposed ledge or pond gives new meaning to the term. A 20 mph wind at 20°F feels like ten below. Plan your trips accordingly. Another consequence of going to higher elevations is that you're more likely to be "socked in" by clouds, erasing any chance for a view.

Good sources for weather information include **weather phones** in Littleton (603–444–2656) and Conway (603–447–5252). On the web check the Mount Washington Observatory site (*www.mountwashington.org*) or the National Weather Service (*iwin.nws.noaa.gov/iwin/nh/zone.html*).

SEASON

The snowshoeing season generally extends from mid to late December into late March, and sometimes early April in shaded locations. Early in the winter there's often thin cover with no base at lower elevations. It takes about 8–12" of snow to get things started, though you could snowshoe on less with firm snow. More cover is needed on rough, rocky trails. In December and early January the days are short (darkness comes shortly after 4:00 PM) and likely to be cold. January sometimes brings better snow cover and the start of a firm base, but may also be a month of thaw, freeze and ice.

February and March are the best snowshoeing months, with warmer temperatures, longer days, brighter sun, and firmer, deeper snow. By the beginning of March it doesn't get dark until almost 6:00 PM. Warm, sunny March days will melt snow cover on south-facing trails; in late winter the best snowshoeing is found on shaded north and east-facing slopes. Once

<table>
<tr><td colspan="5" align="center">MEAN MAXIMUM AND MINIMUM TEMPERATURES (F)
FOR BETHLEHEM, NH, 1985–1994</td></tr>
<tr><td></td><td>December</td><td>January</td><td>February</td><td>March</td></tr>
<tr><td>Mean Maximum</td><td>28</td><td>25</td><td>27</td><td>39</td></tr>
<tr><td>Mean Minimum</td><td>10</td><td>5</td><td>6</td><td>17</td></tr>
</table>

Bethlehem is at the NW edge of the White Mountains, elevation 1380 ft. *Source*: U.S. Historical Climatology Network

---

"mud season" begins in April, it's time to put the snowshoes away and to leave the trails alone until they dry out.

SNOW CONDITIONS

> *There is no royal way of ascending mountains at any time, and least of all in the winter. If the crust is too hard you are constantly slipping down hill, and if the snow is too soft, you plunge into it so deep that the legs become weary before the climb is over.* —Julius H. Ward, "Snow-Shoeing on Osceola," in *The White Mountains: A Guide to Their Interpretation*, 1896

The range of snow conditions during a White Mountain winter is enough to befuddle any snowshoer. You may encounter fluffy powder, heavy powder, wet glop, a packed powder track, breakable crust, windpack, a hard packed track, corn snow, boilerplate and glare ice. You may even deal with several of these surface types in one day—e.g. in late winter the snow may be frozen hard in the valley from morning cold, deep and powdery up on a ridge, then soft and wet in the afternoon sun back down below. The type of snow you find will depend on the amount of snowfall, the type of snow that falls, weather patterns between snowstorms, forest cover, the amount of use a trail receives, aspect to the sun, and elevation.

That last factor is key—throughout the winter, snow depths increase the higher you go. On wooded ridges above 3000 feet there's likely to be a three or four foot snowpack by late winter. Blazes seen at eye level in summer may be down at your ankles in March, and trail signs can be buried to the hilt. It's a wondrous thing to snowshoe across a high wooded ridge where the snow lifts you several feet above the ground. Even if there's just a thin crust at the base of the mountain, you can count on cover up high. Hikers who ascend without snowshoes sometimes discover this to their regret, especially in early or late winter when cover is deceptively sparse in the lowlands.

Generally, through the course of a winter there will be a series of thaws and freezes, resulting in a consolidation of snowpack by late winter. Devo-

	MEAN SNOWFALL			
	December	*January*	*February*	*March*
Berlin, NH	18"	23"	23"	21"
Elevation 1030 ft.				
Pinkham Notch	27"	35"	30"	33"
Elevation 2020 ft.				

tees of off-trail snowshoeing enjoy their arcane pursuit most when the snow gets firm and deep in February and March.

On the most popular trails you'll often find a hardpacked snowshoe track that renders snowshoes superfluous, though they do provide extra traction when a patch of ice bulges through the snow cover. Some winter hikers actually prefer to "bare-boot" the trails and either don't bring snowshoes, or carry them strapped to their pack for the day. I've done it myself at times when the trail was smooth as a city sidewalk.

Problems occur when hikers bare-boot a soft track or unbroken trail. This leads to "postholing," one of the most miserable forms of locomotion known to man. This lurching gait not only wears out the postholer, it ruins the trail for all who follow. I've never understood why some hikers do this. On all but the most firmly packed trails, snowshoes provide easier passage. Please be considerate of your fellow winter travelers. Even if there's a packed trail leading from the trailhead, you should bring your snowshoes along in case you need them higher up. In the High Peaks of New York's Adirondacks, winter hikers are *required* to bring either snowshoes or skis.

There are times every winter when the snowshoeing is just plain lousy. A rainy thaw followed by a bony freeze may turn a solid snowshoe track into a glaze of boilerplate and ice. Hemlock-wooded areas at low elevations are especially prone to this. Then it's crampon time. You *might* find better conditions on seldom-used trails. Two other brands of snowshoe misery are a breakable crust, where the surface layer holds you for a second, then lets you drop through, and a gloppy top layer that clumps on your crampons and frames until you feel like you're walking with footballs attached to your snowshoes.

Often enough, though, you'll be plowing through fresh powder atop a firm base, and all will seem right with the winter world.

Snowshoeing Tips

ON THE LEVEL

- Although you may need to widen your stance slightly, with today's narrow snowshoes there's no need for an exaggerated straddle and waddle.

Setting out on the Caribou Trail

Proceed as if you were walking normally, with just a little extra lifting, and the snowshoes will come along.
- On level, packed-out trails your inbound and outbound times will be about the same.
- Ski poles will help you establish a good rhythm.

GOING UPHILL

- Your ascent time will usually be considerably longer than it would be up the same trail in summer—especially when you're breaking trail through deep snow, in which case it could take you three times as long. Snowshoeing uphill is hard work! With the labor of Hercules, you advance at the ponderous pace of a dinosaur. Sometimes you're lucky to make a mile an hour.
- In unbroken snow, snowshoers proceed single file, with the leader "breaking out" the trail. This laborious task should be rotated frequently—in heavy conditions three to five minutes, or 100 steps, may be a long enough turn. When the leader hands over the job, he or she should drop to the back of the line and let the next breaker take over. In this way you always have reasonably fresh legs in the lead, and your group advances faster as a whole. Those following the leader can pack down the snow between the tracks. Bring friends—there's strength in numbers!
- Use your energy effectively rather than bulling your way up the hill. An energy-saving trick is the "rest step," a momentary locking of the rear knee that gives your leg muscles a quick break. This can be combined with "stamping," where after placing your forward snowshoe you pause

for a split second before applying your full weight. In that brief instant powder snow will compact somewhat and you won't sink in as far. This makes for a slower, more sustainable pace.

- Ski poles are a great asset for pushing off while climbing.
- When breaking trail up a steady incline you may need to lengthen your stride to create a "step" in the snow. If the steps are too close together they will undermine and you'll do some floundering. Snowshoers who follow should try to preserve these steps as much as possible on slopes, corners, and around obstacles.
- If the trail is wide enough, switchbacking is easier than a direct ascent up a steep grade. Even the littlest zig-zags or windings can help you follow the easiest line up a trail corridor. Some snowshoers resort to the skier's "herringbone" maneuver for a moderate climb.
- For the steepest trail pitches you may need to *kick* steps into the snow with the toe of your snowshoe. If the snow is too hard to kick into, short steps and a vigorous application of your snowshoe crampons will be needed. Keep your weight centered on your traction devices for maximum grip.

GOING DOWNHILL

- Descent times are often much faster than summer, especially if you have a softly packed snowshoe track. A joyful swoop down in these conditions can take half as long as picking your way down a rocky, rooty trail in summer.
- The easiest downhill technique is a slide step where you let gravity do the work. It's best to stand straight with knees slightly bent and your weight over your feet. Lean too far forward and you could take a header; too far back and your feet may come out from under you.
- Some hikers like to "glissade" on their snowshoes. This can be done in a standing fashion, with the back knee bent telemark skiing style; good balance is required. Or you can actually sit back on your snowshoes and slide—best done with water-repellent pants as your rear will get covered with snow. Glissades should be carefully controlled—you don't want to run into a tree, rock or snowshoer at the bottom!
- If snow is crusty or icy, sliding is not a good idea. You can take small steps directly downhill, keeping your weight over your snowshoe crampons for maximum grip, and using your poles for balance.
- Snowshoers sometimes sidestep carefully down steeper spots—this is easier with smaller 'shoes.

SIDEHILLING

- Many trails traverse across a slope, especially those that follow streams on the side of a valley. "Sidehilling" can make an easy summer trail very difficult in winter. Looking ahead the trail is an unbroken smooth slope of snow, and often there's open forest on the downhill side that is not particularly reassuring in the event of a slip. If the snow is soft you can use your snowshoes in an edging technique to stamp out a platform across the slope. If the snow is hard and smooth, a steep sidehill section may be difficult and even dangerous to traverse. You'll have to apply your snowshoe crampons with vigor, flush against the slope; if you try to edge them they may slip. A few of the hikes in this book have some sidehill sections, and I've tried to note them in the descriptions. I avoided including some of the notoriously difficult sidehill routes, such as the middle section of Hale Brook Trail up Mt. Hale and the stretch of Nancy Pond Trail alongside the Nancy Cascades.

IN GENERAL

- Your snowshoe frames and traction devices can take some abuse, but try to avoid extensive use on rocks. It's better for the rocks, too.
- Wet snow balling up on your frames and crampons can be a real problem on warm days. Some traction devices have a nylon covering beneath to help prevent this.
- Watch out for rocks, branches, or other obstacles under the snow.
- Use caution on ledgy areas, where it may be crusty or icy.
- Sidestepping is often the best way to cross narrow footbridges.
- Use your ski poles to knock snow off evergreen branches that hang over the trail. It beats getting a profoundly refreshing shower down your neck. When you do get snow on your clothes, take care to brush it off—you'll stay alot drier.
- One unique winter hazard is the "spruce trap," a fluffy pocket that forms when unconsolidated snow covers small conifer trees. Spruce traps can swallow snowshoes and snowshoers alike, and disentangling your 'shoes from the clinging branches is an act that rivals Houdini—a good reason not to hike alone. Spruce traps are more common at higher elevations, but can bedevil you in the lowlands as well if you wander off the trail.
- It's difficult to back up on snowshoes. To turn around, you can swing around with side steps, or employ a 180-degree kick turn, using your poles for balance.

FOLLOWING THE TRAIL

In the "old days" of snowshoeing, say up to the early 1970s, most trails were seldom traveled in winter, and the simple act of following the trail was one of the biggest challenges facing the snowshoer. Snow does an admirable job of hiding the signs of a cleared trail. The trodden footway is covered, and blazes and cairns may be obscured. Trying to trace a lightly-blazed trail requires serious focus in open hardwood forest, where potential corridors may spin off in several directions. The cut swath of a trail is more obvious in dense coniferous growth up on the ridges, but paths trimmed to a height for summer passage may be crammed with snow-laden fir branches when you're walking atop a three or four foot snowpack. And at any elevation, winter blowdown can obliterate a stretch of trail until it's cleared the next spring.

With the recent surge in winter hiking, many trails are broken out regularly and route-finding skills are less often brought into play. However, the less-traveled trails still require your undivided attention, and the same can hold true for any trail if you're the first to head in after a snowfall. For that reason I've made some of the trail descriptions in this book a bit more detailed than the norm.

Here are a few tips that will help you keep your snowshoes on the trail. For a thorough discussion on route-finding, consult Dan H. Allen's excellent book, *Don't Die on the Mountain*.

- It's easier to follow a trail you've hiked in summer. When hiking in any season, take time to consult your map and compass, comparing the trail route and topography on the map to the surrounding terrain. Does the trail follow a ridge, run along a stream, or switchback up a steep slope? The better you get at relating map to terrain, the more successful you'll be at following an unbroken trail.
- Continually look ahead for what Dan Allen calls the "trail carpet"—a smooth corridor of unbroken snow that portends the trail route. Where the corridor is not obvious, keep a sharp eye out for blazes, cut branches and other signs of trail maintenance. If there are no blazes ahead, look behind you—there may be one facing in the opposite direction. Unless the snow is very deep, there will often be branches of hobblebush or other shrubs/small trees poking up through the snow on either side of the trail. Areas of ledge and scrub, where blazes are mostly on the rocks and thus covered, present a special challenge in route-finding. Sometimes you just have to *sense* where the trail should go. Allow extra time. Two or three pairs of eyes are better than one.
- If a blowdown blocks the apparent trail corridor, skirt around it and see if you can pick up the route in the same direction on the far side. Climbing over a blowdown on snowshoes may involve comical contortions.
- If new snow has fallen over a track beaten out by previous snowshoers, the trail route may show as a slight depression leading through the woods. Often you can feel the firmness of the old track underfoot—step off to the side and you plunge in to your knees.
- Pay special attention at stream crossings, sharp bends in the trail, and junctions.
- Even if you're following a snowshoe track, check the map often to make sure you're on the trail. Other snowshoers may veer off the trail to bushwhack or camp, or because they themselves have lost the route.
- Should you truly lose the trail, normally all you need do is follow your

tracks back until you pick it up again—a big advantage of snowshoeing. Exceptions might occur on very windy days, when your tracks could be blown in or whiteouts reduce visibility, or when the snow is so firm you hardly make a track at all. Above treeline, an area beyond the scope of this book, the trick is to follow cairns carefully. In whiteouts this can be nearly impossible—thus mountaineers should venture up into that wild, woolly world only on the most favorable winter days.

MOONLIGHT SNOWSHOEING

Seeing the winter world by moonlight is a special treat that may be enjoyed only a handful of times each season. You can snowshoe through a hushed hardwood forest flooded with light, trees casting long shadows on the snow, or amble across a frozen mountain pond where moonbeams glint off the icy crags above.

Moonlight trips require careful planning, and of course, clear skies. Though experienced trekkers sometimes ascend high peaks by the light of the moon, most snowshoers should stick to shorter outings on trails where moonlight will shine through unobstructed (e.g. in open hardwoods or along a wide trail corridor; avoid dense, dark spruce forests!). Bring flashlights and plenty of batteries in case the moon ducks behind a cloud, and bundle up for nighttime cold. Some moonlit evenings will be well below zero and too cold for comfortable travel.

Some of the places where I've enjoyed moonlight snowshoeing include Lost Pond, Echo Lake (North Conway), the lower Champney Falls Trail, Lincoln Woods Trail and Lonesome Lake.

Life in the Winter Forest

Winter is the best of all seasons for studying animal tracks, especially with a light dusting of snow atop a firm base. The tracks of the snowshoe hare are perhaps the most frequently spotted. Whole areas of the forest may be pockmarked by their furry feet. You might steal a glimpse of a hare in its ghost-white winter coat.

You'll often come upon moose tracks and other signs of the region's largest mammal. We once followed a moose's postholings for a mile or more down the Sabbaday Brook Trail. In winter moose scat takes the form of pellets about 1½ inches long, sometimes deposited in great heaps. Look for small deciduous trees marked by incisor scrapes where moose have stripped the bark.

You may happen upon various other tracks along the winter trails, including red squirrel, red fox, coyote, mouse, fisher, bobcat, deer and even an occasional black bear awakened by a thaw from its semi-hibernation.

Birds are not seen in great numbers during the White Mountain winter, but those that stick around bring cheer to the forest. You may hear the chat-

Moose scraping in the forest

ter of chickadees (black-caps down low, boreals up on the ridges) and "winter finches" such as white-winged crossbills, common redpolls, pine siskins and evening or pine grosbeaks. Nuthatches, golden-crowned kinglets, woodpeckers, blue jays and a few other birds also wander through the winter woods. You may even happen upon wintering robins—we were once startled to see a group feeding on mountain ash berries along the Crawford Path in February.

On other occasions we've been jolted by ruffed grouse blasting out of the snow. When conditions are right, grouse fashion winter roosts beneath the surface, taking advantage of the insulating qualities of snow. Tracks, wing prints and cylindrical scat can be found at a grouse's snow roost. On the higher wooded ridges you may encounter the absurdly tame spruce grouse. Around cliffs and ledges you'll often hear the croaking of ravens; sometimes you can observe their dazzling aerial acrobatics.

Surely the most entertaining denizen of the winter forest is the Gray or Canada Jay, also known as "Camp Robber" and "Whiskey Jack." This tame bird resembles an oversized chickadee and may glide in for a handout anywhere in the high country. They will happily partake of as much of your lunch as you care to offer.

If you'd like to learn more about what you see along the snowshoeing trails, *A Guide to Nature in Winter*, by Donald Stokes, is an excellent resource covering animal tracks, birds, trees and even the nature of snow itself.

Winter Driving and Parking

New Hampshire's roads are very well-kept in winter. Even the lofty Kancamagus Highway is plowed and open except during the very worst storms. If you live in the Northeast you're used to driving in snow; I'll just remind you to "take it slow," whether or not you have 4-wheel drive.

Make sure your car is winter-ready before you go—check oil, antifreeze, washer fluid, wiper blades, tires, belts and battery. Gas up the day before heading out to save time. Good items to have in your car include a couple of ice scrapers, a snow brush, jumper cables, a snow shovel, a can of sand or cat litter for traction, dry gas for cold days, extra washer fluid, towels, and perhaps a sleeping bag in case you get stranded. A change of dry clothes in the car will make the post-hike drive more comfortable.

Trailhead parking is a major consideration in winter. Most Forest Service access roads are unplowed or closed to public vehicular use. These include the Zealand, Haystack, Gale River Loop, Sawyer River, Tunnel Brook, Wild River, Bog Dam, Mill Brook (Stark) and Crocker Pond Roads. Some roads such as Slippery Brook and Rocky Branch are plowed partway in. Through roads that are closed in winter include Bear Notch, Tripoli, Sandwich Notch, Dolly Copp (Pinkham B), North and South, Hurricane Mtn., Deer Hill, Cherry Mtn., Mt. Clinton and Jefferson Notch Roads, and the section of NH/ME 113 through the central part of Evans Notch.

There are plowed lots or pulloffs for nearly all the snowshoe hikes in this guide. Details are given in the "Trailhead" information. After storms they may be the last places to be plowed, and some may occasionally go unplowed between snowfalls. Always have a snow shovel in the car in case you need to clear out a parking space. Do not block roads or driveways when you park. If safe parking is unavailable, consider an alternative hike nearby.

WMNF PARKING PASS

In 1997 Congress directed the White Mountain National Forest (WMNF) and other Forests to establish a parking permit program to provide recreation funding. Moneys raised go towards repair and maintenance of campgrounds, trails and shelters, wildlife habitat enhancement and interpretive programs. You *must* have a parking pass to park at trailheads on WMNF land. The section at the beginning of each featured hike tells you whether or not you need a pass there. You have four options:

Daily Pass	$3.00	Purchased at trailhead—self-service tube
7-Day Pass	$5.00	Purchased at stores or ranger stations
Annual Pass	$20.00	Purchased at stores or ranger stations
Household Pass	$25.00	Purchased at stores or ranger stations, good for 2 cars

Protecting the Mountain Environment

In general, day-trip snowshoeing has less impact on the mountains than summer hiking, simply because a mantle of snow cushions our steps. No matter what the season, though, hikers should consider what their impact could be, and practice the "Leave No Trace" (LNT) ethic.

- Carry out what you carry in, and pick up any litter left behind by other winter travelers.
- Limit the size of your group to 10 persons or fewer.
- Avoid stomping on shrubs or small trees that are buried in the snow.
- In ledgy areas, take care to stay on the trail and off the fragile, low-lying vegetation, especially when snow cover is thin. This is extra important on the few trips in this guide that take you to the edge of treeline.
- Try to avoid scratching rocks and ledges with snowshoe or boot crampons. It's easier on the gear, too.
- Do not mark your routes with surveyor's tape or other flagging—that's tantamount to littering the woods.
- Avoid disturbing wildlife unnecessarily—they have enough stress in winter.
- Answer the call of nature at least 200 feet from trails and even farther, if possible, from streams or ponds. When choosing a spot, remember that winter deposits are uncovered when snow melts in spring. Try to find a site where no one is likely to visit or camp. Decomposition occurs best in direct sunlight—experts recommend using a cathole just below the surface of the snow. Burn or pack out your toilet paper (in double ziploc bags). Some LNT enthusiasts use snow in place of T.P.! Cover urine stains with fresh snow.
- Keep off the trails during the spring "mud season," when the trails are highly susceptible to erosion. The same holds true if a midwinter thaw bares the trails.

For more information on low-impact hiking and other important wilderness issues, see *Backwoods Ethics* and *Wilderness Ethics*, both by Laura and Guy Waterman (Backcountry Publications), and *Soft Paths*, by Bruce Hampton and David Cole (Stackpole Books).

You can give something back to the mountains by joining the Adopt-A-Trail program, a cooperative project of the WMNF and AMC. Adopters take over the basic maintenance for their chosen trail: cleaning drainages, brushing, blazing, removing litter, and taking out blowdown. The work is performed in summer. For information contact AMC Trails, Box 298, Gorham, NH 03581 (*www.outdoors.org*), or WMNF Adopt-A-Trail Program, PO Box 638, Laconia, NH 03247.

Winter Trail Etiquette

Many lower elevation snowshoeing trails are shared with backcountry skiers. (WMNF cross country ski trails are generally excluded from this guide.) These two forms of winter locomotion create very different kinds of tracks. Wherever possible, snowshoers should avoid trampling existing ski tracks. Snowshoe alongside them if there's space, or use the designated middle lane (as at Lincoln Woods). This is a hard-and-fast rule on track-set trails at commercial touring centers. If there are no tracks on a trail that is also used by skiers, snowshoe along one edge, leaving enough room for a ski track. Many trails are too narrow for two tracks, so all that can be asked is that you be aware that skiers are out there looking for fun too, and do the best you can.

Avoid postholing the trail by "bare-booting" in soft snow. This is a snow-shoeing guide—if you're sinking in, use 'em! Postholing is a sure way to antagonize and possibly endanger fellow winter travelers.

You may also encounter snowmobilers along a few trails. Yield the trail and give a friendly wave—they enjoy winter, too, and they're laying down a nice track for you to snowshoe on.

Winter Safety

The consequences of a mistake or mishap on the trail are more serious in winter. Help may be a long time coming in an emergency, and the cold leaves a much smaller window for survival. Highly dedicated and competent search and rescue folks—many of them volunteers—will give up their time and risk their lives to help you. You can help them by using common sense and following some basic safety practices. This will go a long way towards ensuring a safe and happy snowshoe trip.

Trip planning, clothing, gear, snowshoe travel, route finding and other subjects are discussed elsewhere in this introduction. A few points deserve emphasis.

- Check the weather forecast and snow conditions.
- As veteran snowshoer Dan Allen emphasizes, "There is no adequate substitute for an early start!" This is especially true in winter, when days are short and travel is slower. Establish a turn-around time—1:00 PM, or 2:00 PM at the latest—and stick to it.
- Four is a safe minimum for group size, though experienced snowshoers often go in smaller groups or even solo (not recommended for beginners).

- Don't attempt a trip beyond the capability or desire of any member of the group. Make sure all in your party have suitable clothing and gear. Set a reasonable pace that all can enjoy.
- Good physical conditioning is an important prerequisite for a strenuous snowshoe hike.
- Leave word of your itinerary and expected exit time with family or friends.
- Every snowshoer should have a map and be familiar with the route.
- Keep your group together on the trail. Wait up for everyone at trail junctions.
- Inexperienced snowshoers should not plan on loop hikes—better to follow your tracks out the way you came.
- Turn back if the weather goes bad.
- Eat food and drink water!
- Hiking at any time of year is a sport of self-reliance, and therein lies much of its appeal. You're on your own out there in the winter woods. Common sense, a positive attitude, and good decision-making will go a long way towards making your snowshoe hike a safe and enjoyable experience.

Several safety matters specific to winter merit special mention.

HYPOTHERMIA

Hypothermia is the "silent killer" that causes a potentially lethal lowering of the body core temperature. It occurs when the body loses more heat than it generates. If not corrected, it can be fatal. Indeed, a large number of mountain fatalities can be attributed to hypothermia (sometimes called "exposure"), and not just in winter.

Contributing factors to hypothermia are external, in the form of cold, wind and wetness from precipitation, and internal via dehydration, fatigue, hunger, and wetness from perspiration. Cold, wet, windy days are real hypothermia-breeders. The first signs are shivering, clumsiness, slurred speech, apathy, forgetfulness, confusion, fatigue and cold extremities. In later stages victims stop shivering and lose the ability to rewarm themselves. Without treatment, coma and death will result.

The best treatment for hypothermia is prevention! Regulate your body temperature carefully with the layering system, have proper clothing, put on a hat if cold, make sure you eat and drink frequently, stay as warm and dry as possible, avoid getting overtired, turn back if the weather is wet and windy. Be alert for the first signs of hypothermia in yourself or other members of your party. If these symptoms are detected, act immediately before they get worse. Replace wet clothes with dry garments and add layers to reduce any further heat loss, especially from head, neck and trunk. (Thus the importance of carrying extra clothing.) Get the victim out of the wind and into a sheltered location. Give him or her liquids (warm if available) and high-energy foods. After a short rest, if possible, get moving again and head down to the trailhead. Exercise will help keep the person warm.

FROSTBITE

Frostbite is the freezing of body tissue. It's most likely to occur in exposed terrain on very cold, windy days. Ears, nose, face, fingers and toes are the most susceptible parts of the body. As with hypothermia, prevention is of prime importance, starting with clothing that gives adequate protection from cold and wind—mittens, balaclava or face mask, warm boots and socks. Do not make your boots too tight or you will restrict circulation in your toes. Don't touch skin to bare metal. Wiggle your hands and toes continuously if cold, make faces, and do jumping jacks or other activities to stay warm. Drink plenty of water and snack often.

Snowshoers should keep a careful eye on each other for white skin patches. Frostnip is the mildest form of frostbite, involving only the outermost layer of the skin. It usually occurs on the cheeks or ears, showing as a gray or white patch. Tingling may be the first sign. If detected quickly, it can be thawed with the palm of a hand. Superficial frostbite goes deeper into the skin and appears as patches of white or waxy skin that are hard at the surface but soft underneath the area. Treatment is to rewarm the affected areas against warm skin. Do not rub the frostbitten skin—this could cause serious tissue damage. Deep frostbite, where the underlying tissue is frozen hard, necessitates immediate evacuation. Do not try to thaw the frozen flesh—this is extremely painful for the victim and should only be done in a sterile situation. Experts say it's best to walk out on severely frostbitten feet; once the feet are thawed, the victim will have to be carried out.

RESCUE

In the event of an emergency, self-rescue is your best option if at all possible. If you're very far in, there will be a long, cold wait for help to arrive. Search and rescue personnel are willing to risk their lives to bring someone to safety, but they should not be asked to do so unless absolutely necessary. If a call for rescue is the result of reckless actions or gross unpreparedness, New Hampshire legislation allows for the billing of the calling party for rescue services. If assistance is necessary, two persons from a party of four should proceed to the trailhead with information on the exact location, the nature of the emergency, and the condition of the victim. A key emergency number is the NH State Police Line: 1–800–852–3411.

STREAM CROSSINGS

Approach all winter stream crossings with caution. In deep winter, when the snow has piled up and it's been consistently cold, solid ice and snow bridges make many brook crossings relatively simple. Still, it's best to place your snowshoes where rocks are likely to be underneath (look for humps in the snow) and avoid stepping on ice bridges with air and running water

Deep drifts on the Crawford Path

beneath. Each crossing is a puzzle to be solved, and the safest route may involve some winding about. Cross single file and keep your group spaced apart. Probe carefully with your ski pole. Solid ice will respond with a good "thunk." Avoid ice that gives back a hollow sound.

In early and late winter and during thaws, stream crossings can be a real problem. Ice coated rocks are extremely treacherous. There are some times when brook crossings should be avoided altogether. Then you could try one of the snowshoe hikes in this guide that have no unbridged crossings. If crossing suspect ice, unbuckle your pack waistband and loosen your snowshoe bindings. A fall through the ice can be a life-threatening matter—use caution and good judgement.

CROSSING POND ICE

Several of the hikes in this guide lead to ponds and suggest that you snowshoe across the ice for the best views. The traverse of one of these open white expanses can be a rewarding experience on snowshoes, but it is not without risk. You should approach any pond ice with respect. The keys to a safe visit are caution, common sense, awareness and experience. If in doubt, don't go out on the ice.

Five inches is considered a minimum thickness of ice for general use. Higher ponds, say above 2000 feet, are generally well-frozen from New Year's through mid-March, varying from year to year at either end of the season. Lower elevation ponds may have a shorter period for safe passage. Be aware of recent weather patterns. Midwinter ice can be well over a foot thick and has a hard, gray look when not buried in windpacked snow.

Look for recent snowshoe, ski or snowmobile tracks on the pond. If there are no tracks, use a ski pole to tap and test the ice ahead of you. A solid "thunk" is good; a hollow sound is a signal to retreat. Keep your group spread out. Skirt any ice that appears discolored, dark or slushy. Avoid ice around inlet and outlet brooks, where it may be much thinner. Other potential danger spots include springs under the ice and places where beavers are active. Avoid the ice after a heavy rain and thaw—there may be a deep layer of slush and water on top. Beware of deep, heavy snow over ice early in the season. In late winter avoid honeycombed ice, which may look thick but is very weak.

If crossing ice that is at all suspect, one recommended precaution is to loosen your bindings; if you do break through it will be easier to get out of your snowshoes quickly. If you do fall in, spread your arms on the ice, kick free of the water, and roll onto firmer ice. Rescuers should crawl spread-eagled on the ice and extend a ski pole, rope or hand to the victim. Anyone who has fallen in should immediately be led out of the wind and changed into dry clothes.

AVALANCHES

The greatest avalanche danger in the White Mountains is in the ravines of the Presidential Range and in steep gullies elsewhere in the mountains. The snowshoe hikes in this book do not lead you into known avalanche danger areas (with the exception of Hermit Lake and Spaulding Lake). Avalanches are much less common outside the ravines but it is possible that with certain conditions any slope of 25 to 45 degrees with low brush or widely spaced trees could have a snowslide. The greatest danger occurs immediately after heavy snowfalls, high winds, rain and major thaws. Avalanche danger ratings for the major ravines are posted daily at Pinkham Notch (603–466–2721) and on the Mount Washington Observatory website (*www.mountwashington.org*). Detailed information on avalanche safety can be found in several winter hiking, mountaineering and backcountry skiing manuals.

How to Use This Guide

This book describes over 100 snowshoe trips in the White Mountains, presented in 45 chapters. In each chapter there is a featured snowshoe hike, or series of short hikes, described in detail. Most chapters also have "Additional Option" hikes—extensions or loops off the featured routes, or separate trips in the vicinity. These excursions are outlined in less detail.

The hikes are organized into twelve regions across the White Mountains. Most are located on trails within the White Mountain National Forest (WMNF). Several are in state parks and a handful are partly or wholly on private land. All are on regularly maintained trails.

Included are hikes suitable for every level of snowshoer, from never-evers to peakbaggers. The book is weighted towards the middle, with many intermediate trips within the capabilities of the average backcountry snowshoer. Many of these trips will be familiar to summer hikers. In winter they take on a whole new look!

The summary information at the beginning of each featured hike includes:

- General **location**
- A thumbnail **description**
- What **trails** the route follows
- Round trip **distance** in miles
- **Starting** and **highest elevations**
- Total **elevation gain** for the trip, includes all ups and downs along the way
- Difficulty **rating**
- The **USGS maps** used to create the trail map
- Directions to the **trailhead**
- Whether a **WMNF parking pass** is required

For **Additional Option** hikes, I've listed *round trip distance, elevation gain* and *difficulty rating*. There are no maps in this guide for these trips; use one of the trail maps described in the Maps section below.

Because winter trail conditions are so variable, I have chosen not to give time estimates for the hikes. If you're breaking trail the whole way it could take two or three times as long to reach your destination than if you find a packed snowshoe sidewalk when you arrive at the trailhead.

DIFFICULTY RATINGS

See the Key to Snowshoe Hikes (pp. 33–37) for a listing by category.

Beginner: Short and easy, mostly level or gentle gradient. Good choices for introducing kids to snowshoeing.

Beginner/Intermediate: Still generally easy, but longer and/or more elevation gain. Fine for energetic kids.

Intermediate: Moderate and occasionally steep climbing with over 1000 feet of elevation gain, or a shorter but steeper trek. May feature an occasional ledgy scramble. Most can be done in a half day with ordinary snow conditions; a few are closer to ⅔ day.

Intermediate/Advanced: Longer or steeper than intermediate hikes;

Before the climb

⅔ day to all day in duration. Some have elevation gain of 2000 feet or more, and there may be steep, challenging sections. These are for snowshoers with mountaineering 'shoes and considerable experience.

Advanced: These are the most difficult trips in the book. Most involve long and fairly steep climbs, some with ledgy pitches and a bit of exposure to weather. A few trips trace long, relatively gentle routes into isolated corners of the WMNF and are rated as advanced due to their remoteness and potential route-finding difficulties. The advanced trips are all-day journeys for well-seasoned winter trampers equipped with sturdy mountaineering snowshoes. Caution is required, especially in icy or windy conditions, for the more exposed destinations such as Mt. Pierce, Mt. Liberty, Mt. Moosilauke, Mt. Hight, Madison Hut, Mt. Moriah, Mt. Jackson, Mt. Flume and Mt. Garfield. Crampons should be carried on these trips. Long trips above treeline to the higher Presidentials or Franconias are beyond the scope of this guide. An ascent of a peak such as Washington, Jefferson or Lafayette is on another order of difficulty, with great exposure to weather and traverses of potentially dangerous open slopes of hard snow and ice. That's winter mountaineering, not snowshoeing. A few of the advanced trips do let you poke your head above treeline without making a full commitment.

THINGS TO CONSIDER WHEN CHOOSING A TRIP

- Your group's experience level, fitness, equipment and ambition.
- The weather forecast.
- Distance and elevation gain.
- Overall difficulty of the trail—steepness, stream crossings, how hard it is to follow.
- Features of the hike—views, ponds, riverside scenery, nice forest.
- Length of drive to trailhead.
- Length of available daylight.
- Snow conditions—if you can, know before you go.
- In general, you must set your sights lower in winter. Travel is slower on snow and the days are shorter.

MAPS

The maps in this book show trail routes on USGS 7½-minute (scale 1:24,000) and 7½-minute × 15-minute (scale 1:25,000) quadrangles. These have 20-foot, 40-foot, or 6-meter contour intervals. The routes of featured hikes are shown with thick lines; where appropriate, some "additional option" hikes are depicted with thin lines. Stars indicate scenic views or points of interest. The quadrangles covering featured hikes are listed at the beginning of each chapter. For older USGS maps some trail locations were corrected on the maps prepared for this guide.

The maps were created using TOPO! Interactive Maps on CD-ROM from National Geographic Maps. TOPO! CD-ROMs are designed specifically for outdoor enthusiasts and feature USGS maps along with tools for elevation profiling and for exploring, customizing, and printing seamless topographic images. For this book, we used TOPO! New Hampshire and The White Mountains, a two-CD set that covers the entire Granite State. National Geographic Maps also offers interactive map products for many recreational and metropolitan areas around the U.S. For more information, contact National Geographic Maps at 415–558–8700 or *www.topo.com*.

For digital versions of the trip maps in this book, visit *www.topo.com*.

Every snowshoer should also carry a White Mountains trail map. To go with its 1200 miles of trails, the White Mountains are blessed with some excellent hiking maps:

- *Map Adventures White Mountains Trail Map* This waterproof map is the clearest and easiest to read of the region's trail maps. One side covers most of the western half of the National Forest at a 1:75,000 scale; the other spans most of the eastern half (including the Presidentials) at a 1:50,000 scale. Contour interval is 20 meters (65 feet). Outstanding features include mileages between points and notation of viewpoints along the trails. The map can be purchased separately or with the 60 page *White Mountain Map Book*, which includes 76 hike descriptions, 5 close-up maps, and useful general information on hiking, camping, etc.

- *Appalachian Mountain Club White Mountains Trail Maps* The AMC's fine trail maps are printed on tyvek and folded to pocket size. A set of four maps covers the entire White Mountain National Forest. Most are at a 1:95,000 scale; the Presidentials map is 1:47,500. Contour interval is 100 feet. These maps are clear and easy to use, with very accurate GPS-surveyed trail locations. The maps also come in a paper version with the 26th edition (1998) of the venerable *AMC White Mountain Guide.* This authoritative guide describes every mile of trail in the White Mountains and belongs in any hiker's library. Most of the mileages used in the trail descriptions in this book were obtained from the AMC Guide.
- *Delorme Trail Map and Guide to the WMNF* This 1:100,000 scale map covers nearly the entire White Mountain region on one large sheet. It is not as clear or as easy to read as the Map Adventures or AMC maps, but is valuable for an overview of the Whites. It's printed on regular paper with 100-foot contours.

There are several other excellent maps that focus on specific regions:

- *Wonalancet Out Door Club Trail Map and Guide to the Sandwich Range*, a colorful map with mileages between points and viewpoints.
- *Randolph Mtn. Club Map of Randolph Valley and the Northern Peaks*, which comes with a guidebook, *Randolph Paths.*
- *White Mountains Hiking Map* by Map Adventures; covers Franconia Notch, Mt. Chocorua, North Conway, and the Presidentials/Crawford Notch.
- *Chatham Trails Association Map of Cold River Valley and Evans Notch*, includes elevation profiles for Evans Notch trails.
- *Mount Washington and the Heart of the Presidential Range*, an exquisite AMC map crafted by Bradford Washburn—the best map ever made of the Presidentials.

Key to Snowshoe Hikes

Featured Hikes in bold; for locations of Featured Hikes, see key map (p. 35).

Hike	Mileage/ Elevation Gain (ft.)	Page	Comments
BEGINNER SNOWSHOE HIKES			
1. **Lost Pond**	1.2/80	39	View of Mt. Washington
9. **Short Trips Around Crawford's**	Varies	71	Waterfalls, ponds, viewpoint

Hike	Mileage/ Elevation Gain (ft.)	Page	Comments
BEGINNER SNOWSHOE HIKES (CONT'D.)			
13. Dry River Trail	1.8/200	89	Riverview option
14. Diana's Baths	1.2/100	94	Frozen cascades
21. Champney Falls	3.6/650	118	Waterfalls & view
24. Greeley Ponds	4.4/450	133	Cliff-shadowed ponds
25. Lincoln Woods Trails	Varies	137	Easy riverside 'shoeing
26. Flume–Pool Loop	2.2/400	146	Gorges & cascades
38. Mt. Moosilauke Trails	3.4/500	192	To Ravine Lodge
Appalachia Waterfalls	2.6/650	64	5 cascades
Sam Willey Trail	1.0/0	92	Along Saco River
Echo Lake	1.0/0	99	Views of cliffs
Easy Trails along the Kancamagus Highway	Varies	126	Lowland rambles
Pemi Trail	Varies	149	Explore Franconia Notch
Dickey Notch	3.6/500	172	Beaver ponds
Smarts Brook Trail	3.0/300	173	Cascades & beaver meadow
Basin Pond/Hermit Falls	4.2/150	217	Pond with views
Mt. Prospect	3.2/650	226	Road with views
BEGINNER/INTERMEDIATE SNOWSHOE HIKES			
10. Mt. Willard	3.2/900	75	Great view of Crawford Notch
15. Cathedral Ledge	2.8/650	96	Clifftop vistas
23. Hancock Notch	5.2/800	129	Remote spruce-woods pass
25. Lincoln Woods Trails	Varies	137	Pond, waterfall or river scenery
35. Three Ponds	5.5/550	181	Secluded ponds
Allen's Ledge	2.2/600	125	View of Albany Intervale
Bridal Veil Falls	5.0/1100	168	Gentle gradient
INTERMEDIATE SNOWSHOE HIKES			
2. Lowe's Bald Spot	4.4/950	41	View of Northern Presys
5. Lower Great Gulf	5.4/950	52	Vista at The Bluff
6. Lookout Ledge	1.6/950	57	Dramatic Presidential views
12. Ethan Pond	6.0/1800	85	High mountain pond
16. South Doublehead	3.0/1500	99	Wide views in Jackson
17. Peaked Mountain	4.2/1200	104	Ledges, pines, vistas
19. East of Chocorua	4.8/1150	112	Fine woods & partial views
20. Boulder Loop Trail	3.0/900	116	Clifftop panorama
22. East Ledges–Hedgehog Mtn.	4.0/1100	123	View of Sandwich Range

MN ↑TN
16½°

0   5   10   15   20   25 miles
0   5   10 15 20 25 30 35 40 km
Printed from TOPO! ©2000 Wildflower Productions (www.topo.com)

Hike	Mileage/ Elevation Gain (ft.)	Page	Comments
INTERMEDIATE SNOWSHOE HIKES (CONT'D.)			
27. Mt. Pemigewasset	3.6/1150	151	View atop Indian Head
29. Lonesome Lake	3.0/1000	157	Pond with gorgeous vista
30. Old Bridle Path	4.0/1620	161	Close-up of Franconia Ridge
31. Bald Peak	4.6/1450	165	Open knob on Kinsman
32. Dickey Mtn. Ledge	2.4/1150	169	Big rock slab
34. The Kettles and The Scaur	4.0/700	177	Glacial hollows, views of Waterville
36. Rattlesnake Mtn.	2.5/1000	185	View of Baker River Valley
37. Blueberry Mtn. (Benton)	4.8/1300	187	Gentle slabs, Moosilauke view
38. Mt. Moosilauke Trails	7.8/1950	192	First outlook on Gorge Brook Tr.
39. Blueberry Ledges	4.0/1000	199	Lower slope of Whiteface
40. Mt. Israel	4.6/1700	202	Sandwich Range panorama

Hike	Mileage/ Elevation Gain (ft.)	Page	Comments
INTERMEDIATE SNOWSHOE HIKES (CONT'D.)			
41. Bicknell Ridge	5.8/1600	209	Baldface vistas
42. Blueberry Mtn. (Evans Notch)	3.8/1300	213	Evans Notch views
Mt. Surprise	4.0/1400	70	Carter-Moriah Trail
Doublehead Loop	3.9/1850	102	Double viewing pleasure
Middle Mtn.	4.2/1300	107	Green Hills viewpoint
White Ledge	3.6/1300	115	East spur of Chocorua
Hedgehog Mtn. summit	3.8/1300	125	Views in two directions
Potash Mtn.	4.4/1450	125	Sandwich Range & Kanc views
Cedar Brook Trail	6.2/1000	132	High, remote plateau
Livermore Pass	4.2/850	133	Wild, isolated place
Lower Georgiana Falls	1.6/300	152	Scramble at end
Welch Mtn. Ledge	2.6/850	171	Flat slabs with views
Timber Camp Trail	5.8/1050	180	Old log road with vistas
Tunnel Brook Notch	6.6/950	190	Beaver ponds & slides
Wachipauka Pond and Mt. Mist	5.8/1200	191	Pond and a view
Al Merrill Loop	8.0/1250	196	Unique Moosilauke view
Cherry Mtn.	3.8/1900	227	Views east & west
INTERMEDIATE/ADVANCED SNOWSHOE HIKES			
3. Carter Notch	7.6/2000	45	Craggy pass with ponds
4. Imp Face	4.4/1900	49	Huge view of Presys
7. Inlook Trail	3.2/1426	61	Steep & ledgy with views
13. Dry River Trail (Mt. Washington view)	3.0/500	89	Tough sidehill leads to neat vista
18. Kearsarge North	6.2/2600	108	Commanding viewpoint
21. Champney Falls Trail (upper)	7.0/2000	118	Ledges with wide views
25. Lincoln Woods Trails	Varies	137	Long loop or remote beaver ponds
43. Caribou Mtn.	6.8/2050	217	Wilderness vistas
44. Mts. Starr King and Waumbek	7.8/2850	222	Presidential views and a 4000-footer
Raymond Path and Tuckerman Ravine	7.8/2100	44	Loop from Lowe's Bald Spot
Inner Great Gulf	Varies	57	Awesome valley
Mt. Crescent	4.0/1400	60	Views South & North
Mt. Hayes	7.4/1800	70	Lower Mahoosuc vantage
Mt. Avalon	3.8/1550	78	Above Crawford Notch

Hike	Mileage/ Elevation Gain (ft.)	Page	Comments
INTERMEDIATE/ADVANCED SNOWSHOE HIKES (CONT'D.)			
Mt. Tom	5.8/2150	78	Surprising Pemi views
Mt. Crawford	5.0/2100	93	Rock knob with 360 view
East Pond	7.4/1900	136	Seldom visited in winter
Hi-Cannon Trail to outlook	3.2/1600	160	Steep ending, view of Franconia Ridge
Flat Mountain Pond	8.6/1400 or 9.6/1300	206	Two approaches to long, isolated pond
ADVANCED SNOWSHOE HIKES			
8. **South Ledges of Moriah**	8.2/2650	66	Views of Wild River and Presidentials
11. **Mt. Pierce**	6.4/2400	80	Taste of treeline
28. **Mt. Liberty**	8.0/3250	154	Great Pemi views
33. **Jennings Peak**	7.0/2100	173	Sharp, rocky knob
38. **Mt. Moosilauke Trails**	Varies	192	Two routes to high out-looks or summit
45. **Rogers Ledge**	8.4/1500	227	Remote Kilkenny trek
Mt. Hight	8.8/3200	48	Spectacular viewpoint
with Carter Dome	10.4/3600	48	More views
Spaulding Lake	13.0/3000	57	For strong & experienced only
Madison Hut	7.6/3350	65	Poke above treeline
Gray Knob viewpoints	8.0/3500	65	Winterized cabin
Mt. Moriah summit	10.0/3150	69	Continuation of #8
Mts. Field and Willey	8.4/3100	79	Two 4000-footers
Mt. Jackson	5.2/2150	83	Rocky cone, fine views
Shoal Pond	11.2/2250	88	Remote trip into Pemi
Perkins Notch	10.4/1150	103	Deep into Wild River Valley
Mt. Hancock	9.8/2650	131	Steep loop over two peaks
Mt. Flume	10.2/4250	156	Extension from Liberty
Kinsman Pond	7.2/2200	161	Above Lonesome Lake
Greenleaf Hut	5.8/2450	163	Treeline on Lafayette
Mt. Garfield	12.4/3100	164	Look down into Pemi
Gordon Pond	7.2/2250	168	Roly-poly ridge route
Sandwich Dome	9.2/2750	176	Add-on to Jennings Peak
Mt. Passaconaway	9.2/2950	201	Sandwich Range 4000-footer
Kilback Pond	9.6/1500	231	With Rogers Ledge
Unknown Pond	6.6/1550	231	Sidehill to remote tarn

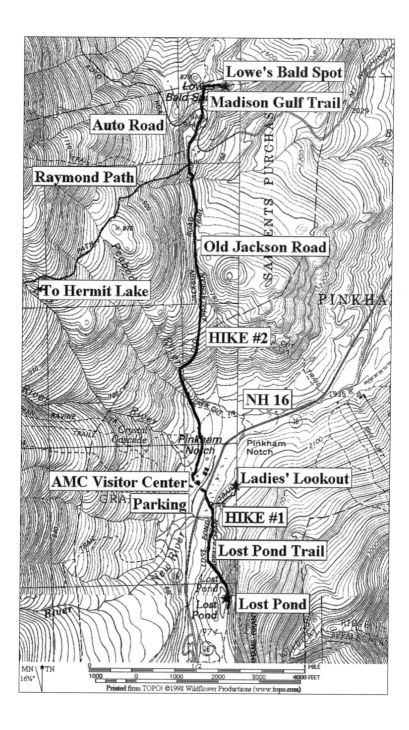

Lowe's Bald Spot

Madison Gulf Trail

Auto Road

Raymond Path

Old Jackson Road

To Hermit Lake

HIKE #2

PINKHA

SARGENTS PURCHASE

NH 16

AMC Visitor Center

Ladies' Lookout

Parking

HIKE #1

Lost Pond Trail

Lost Pond

Pinkham Notch

Crystal Cascade

MN \ ★TN
16½°

1000   0   1000   2000   3000   4000 FEET

0   ½   1 MILE

Printed from TOPO! ©1998 Wildflower Productions (www.topo.com)

1. Lost Pond

LOCATION: Pinkham Notch

DESCRIPTION: Short, easy trip to a small frozen pond with views of Mt. Washington

TRAIL: Lost Pond Trail

DISTANCE: 1.2 miles round trip

STARTING ELEVATION: 2032 ft.

HIGHEST ELEVATION: 2070 ft.

ELEVATION GAIN: 80 ft.

RATING: Beginner

USGS MAPS: Mt. Washington, Stairs Mtn.

TRAILHEAD: Parking for the Lost Pond Trail is in the large lot at the AMC's Pinkham Notch Camp on NH 16, 10.6 miles south of US 2 in Gorham and 11.3 miles north of US 302 in Glen. At a few peak times the lots may be full, in which case you'll have to park at Wildcat Ski Area a mile north. Parking on the shoulder of the highway is strictly prohibited.

WMNF PARKING PASS: Not required, but requested by AMC on a voluntary basis.

The trip to Lost Pond is one of the easiest snowshoe jaunts in the White Mountains, with a nice reward at the end. The alpine-flavored view across the pond to the east side of Mt. Washington is worthy of a much greater effort. Lost Pond is perfect for first-time snowshoers, young children, or experienced winter trekkers looking to take a break from more strenuous outings.

From the parking area at Pinkham Notch Camp, walk out the entrance to Rt. 16 and cross carefully to the east side of the road. A few yards right (south) you'll find the sign for Lost Pond Trail, which forms a short link in the Georgia-to-Maine Appalachian Trail. Strap your snowshoes on here. In a few yards the trail crosses a snow-buried bridge over the outlet of an open bog on your left. You swing right and up into the woods and quickly come to the junction with Square Ledge Trail on the left.

Go right (south) here, climbing over a rise and dipping to the shore of the Ellis River, which flows south from the notch. The next 0.2 mile is a delightful easy shuffle through corridors of fir along the bank of the stream. The way is marked with white blazes (for the A.T.) and blue diamonds. Picturesque yellow birches lean out over the river.

At 0.3 mile you pull left away from the river, cross a small tributary on a bridge, and climb moderately through white and yellow birch. The grade soon eases and at 0.5 mile you approach the north end of the pond. A few

Across Lost Pond to the Gulf of Slides

steps to the right a clearing opens a long view down the four-acre pond with a steep slope rising on the left.

Two hundred feet farther along the trail you come to the first outlook westward across the pond to the huge snow-draped bulk of Mt. Washington, with its trademark ravines cut deeply into its flanks. Left to right you see the Glen Boulder ridge, the wide Gulf of Slides, Boott Spur, Lion Head, the summit cone with its antennae peering over, the ravine of Raymond Cataract, the craggy gouge of Huntington Ravine, and Nelson Crag. (The famous Tuckerman Ravine is hidden by the east ridge of Boott Spur.) The view is dazzling on a sunny winter day.

The trail continues along the shore under gnarled yellow birches, passing more outlooks, then leads through a tunnel of firs to a large open area with a fortress-like boulder on the left. Here Huntington Ravine takes center stage in the view. If the pond is securely frozen, this is a convenient spot from which to amble out onto the ice for more views, including gleaming icefalls on the steep slope to the east.

The return to your car is along the same route. For a short diversion to another viewpoint on the way back, turn right on Square Ledge Trail and climb steadily for less than 0.1 mile. At a sign for "Ladies' Lookout," turn left on a side path and climb slightly for 150 feet to a wooden railing and a tree-framed view of Mt. Washington and the buildings of Pinkham Notch below. For safety's sake, don't venture beyond the railing. This side trip will add 0.2 mile round trip and 75 feet of climbing to the Lost Pond trip.

(*Note*: Square Ledge, a rock outcrop 0.5 mile and 500 ft. up from Lost Pond Trail, offers an impressive view across the notch to Mt. Washington. However, the upper section of this trail shoots up a steep gully and is quite difficult and often icy in winter. It's not recommended for snowshoeing.)

2. Lowe's Bald Spot

LOCATION: Pinkham Notch

DESCRIPTION: Moderate trip with several short, steep pitches leading to an open knob with spectacular views of Presidential Range and surrounding mountains

TRAILS: Old Jackson Road, Madison Gulf Trail

DISTANCE: 4.4 miles round trip

STARTING ELEVATION: 2032 ft

HIGHEST ELEVATION: 2875 ft.

ELEVATION GAIN: 950 ft.

RATING: Intermediate

USGS MAP: Mt. Washington

TRAILHEAD: This trip starts at the Appalachian Mountain Club's Pinkham Notch Camp on NH 16, 11.3 miles north of US 302 in Glen and 10.6 miles south of US 2 at Gorham. There is ample parking here. At a few peak times the lots may be full, in which case you'll have to park at Wildcat Ski Area a mile north. Parking on the shoulder of the highway is strictly prohibited.

WMNF PARKING PASS: Not required, but requested by AMC on a voluntary basis.

Some hikers maintain that the view of Mts. Adams and Madison—the second and fifth highest peaks in the Northeast—from Lowe's Bald Spot is one of the finest single outlooks in the White Mountains. This is your reward for a generally easy snowshoe trek through pleasant woods, with just a few short, steep scrambles thrown in. If conditions are icy, the last clamber up to the ledges of this little rocky knob can present a challenge.

The trip starts right behind the Trading Post at Pinkham Notch Camp. This busy spot is information central for the Presidential Range. Here you can obtain the latest weather and trail conditions as well as maps, guidebooks, gear and advice. Don't be discouraged by the bustle—most folks here are heading up to Tuckerman Ravine or other destinations high on Mt. Washington. On a sunny January Saturday we encountered only one other party on the trip to Lowe's Bald Spot, even though there were dozens of cars in the parking lots.

Bear right behind the Trading Post onto the Tuckerman Ravine Trail. For bragging rights, you can weigh your packs on a scale-and-hook contraption at the start of the trail. A few yards farther a large sign posts avalanche dangers in the various ravines on Mt. Washington—not a concern on the hike to Lowe's Bald Spot. Beyond the sign, bear right onto the Old Jackson Road (OJR)—a link in the Appalachian Trail—as the Tuck's trail goes left.

The white-blazed OJR undulates gently northward through open hardwoods, crossing a service road and small brook. At 0.3 mile you cross the Blanchard Ski Loop, and at 0.4 mile you bear left onto the actual bed of the Old Jackson Road as the Link ski trail goes to the right. Built in 1885, the OJR was used as a connecting route to the Mount Washington Carriage Road (now the Auto Road) for horse-drawn carriages heading up from the town of Jackson south of Pinkham Notch. The road was eventually abandoned, but it was reopened as a foot trail in 1920. Today it is also used as a cross-country ski trail. Try not to trample existing ski tracks, and yield to descending skiers.

You cross a brook on a plank bridge; on the far side the Crew-Cut Trail departs on the right. Now the OJR begins a steady climb through hardwood and birch forest, with several minor brook crossings. Look left up the largest brook to see a pretty frozen waterfall. At 0.8 mile the grade eases amidst hardwoods with tops broken off by the 1998 ice storm. The George's Gorge Trail leaves right at 0.9 mile and OJR proceeds across a level divide between two knolls. Farther on the trail descends gently, crossing several more little streams. The ragged knob of Lowe's Bald Spot can be seen ahead.

At 1.6 miles, where the old roadway continues ahead across another brook, the relocated trail goes sharp left up a steep scrambly pitch, then turns right and contours to a junction with Raymond Path, a connecting link to Tuckerman Ravine. You meander across a softwood plateau and over two more brooks to the junction with Nelson Crag Trail at 1.7 miles. The OJR leads up a spruce-covered hogback ridge to a short rocky scramble, where there's a glimpse up to the barren slopes of Nelson Crag. You may have to take your snowshoes off to get up this little pitch. Soon you emerge into a scrubby opening amidst ledges—a long-abandoned gravel pit. A climb up to the right opens a good view up to Nelson Crag and back to Boott Spur.

A short distance beyond, at 1.9 miles, the OJR ends at the Mt. Washington Auto Road. Cross the road, marked with the tracks of sno-cats bringing Mt. Washington Observatory crews to and from the summit. Enter the woods on the far side at a sign for Madison Gulf Trail. In 100 yards another sign announces that you're entering the Great Gulf Wilderness. The trail climbs steadily, and 0.2 mile from the Auto Road the 0.1-mile side trail up to Lowe's Bald Spot departs on the right. The snow on the ledges can be crusty

Mts. Adams and Madison from Lowe's Bald Spot

or icy, so good snowshoe or boot crampons will be useful here. It's a good place to layer up, as you'll be exposed to the elements above.

The first short scramble is best negotiated on the left side. Bear right along the base of the second ledge pitch and cut back left across the top. Now the going is easier over the crest of the scrubby, semi-alpine knob to the first view ledge. Proceed a few yards farther to a flat open area with the widest views. (Please take care not to trample any fragile vegetation poking up through the snow.) Look NW across the lower Great Gulf to the gigantic snowy peaks of Mt. Adams (5799 ft.), the pointed peak on the left, and Mt. Madison (5366 ft.), a bulky rock pile with serrated Osgood Ridge trailing off to the right. Between them is the glacial scoop of Madison Gulf. With binoculars you can admire picturesque ice cliffs on the headwall. It's a memorable view.

To the SW and close at hand is the huge bulk of Nelson Crag, an outlying peak that blocks out the actual summit of Mt. Washington. Farther south is the great snowy buttress of Boott Spur. Looking northward there's a striking vista down the broad valley of the Peabody River to the distant jumble of the Mahoosuc Range. Old Speck, highest of the Mahoosucs, rises far back in the center. Eastward across the valley is the great wooded Carter Range. Left to right you see North & Middle Carter, with the cliff of Imp Face below; shapely South Carter; bare-topped Mt. Hight; slide-scarred Carter Dome; and the multiple summits of ski-trailed Wildcat Ridge. If the day is not bitterly cold, these are views to savor for a while.

Return to your car by the same route, using caution on the descent off the ledges.

ADDITIONAL OPTION

Intermediate/advanced snowshoers can fashion a longer loop back to the AMC camp via the **Raymond Path** and **Tuckerman Ravine Trail**, with a side trip to **Hermit Lake**. On the return along OJR from Lowe's Bald Spot, turn right on Raymond Path and climb steadily across the lower slopes of Nelson Crag. At 0.8 mile, at the crest of a small ridge, there's a good view up to the crags of Lion Head and Boott Spur. You continue climbing, with some easier stretches, passing another view of Boott Spur, and reach Huntington Ravine Trail 1.8 miles from OJR. Just beyond, there's a steep drop to a book crossing (use caution if icy). Next, you cross the brook coming down from Raymond Cataract. At 2.1 miles, you cross the Huntington Ravine Fire Road, and after a steady climb, you come to Tuckerman Ravine Trail at 2.4 miles.

Turn right here and proceed 0.3 mile to the Hermit Lake area at the foot of Tuckerman Ravine. There are impressive views up to the famous headwall, notorious for its challenging spring skiing, and the surrounding crags —Lion Head on the right and Boott Spur, with its jagged Hanging Cliffs, on the left. In winter, when the lofty battlements are plastered with snow, it's one of the most alpine settings in the White Mountains. This can be a wild and windy place on a midwinter day. Around the area there are ten lean-tos and a WMNF ranger's building. Tiny, solidly frozen Hermit Lake itself is worth a visit while you're here.

For the return trip, you descend the wide, hardpacked Tuckerman Ravine Trail, which winds steadily downward for 2.4 miles to the AMC Camp. About 0.3 mile from the bottom, you pass frozen Crystal Cascade on the left. The loop to Lowe's Bald Spot and back via Raymond Path and Tuckerman Ravine Trail is 7.8 miles with 2100 ft. of elevation gain—a full day's trip.

The climb up to Hermit Lake via Tuckerman Ravine Trail makes a fine, intermediate snowshoe trip from Pinkham Notch by itself, though you won't lack for company on this popular, well-beaten trail. It's a 4.8-mile round trip with an 1850-ft. elevation gain.

The upper floor of Tuckerman Ravine is not recommended for snowshoeing unless you're prepared to travel in avalanche-prone country. Snow rangers post avalanche danger ratings each day at Pinkham Notch Camp—read them!

3. Carter Notch

LOCATION: Carter Range, east of Pinkham Notch

DESCRIPTION: A long, moderate snowshoe up an attractive valley to a wild notch with rugged mountain scenery, frozen ponds and an AMC hut

TRAIL: Nineteen Mile Brook Trail

DISTANCE: 7.6 miles round trip

STARTING ELEVATION: 1487 ft.

HIGHEST ELEVATION: 3388 ft.

ELEVATION GAIN: 2000 ft.

RATING: Intermediate / advanced

USGS MAP: Carter Dome

TRAILHEAD: A plowed parking area for the Nineteen Mile Brook Trail is found on the east side of NH 16, 1 mile north of Mt. Washington Auto Road and 2.3 miles south of the entrance to Dolly Copp Campground (closed in winter).

WMNF PARKING PASS: Yes

This day-long snowshoe venture leads you up the scenic Nineteen Mile Brook Trail to the desolate gap of Carter Notch, where the tiny Carter Ponds open views up to the steep, crag-hung faces of Wildcat Mtn. and Carter Dome. The notch can be a wild and wonderful place in winter, with deep drifts, biting winds and a real sense of isolation. A light civilized touch is provided by the AMC's Carter Notch Hut, which remains open on a caretaker basis throughout the winter.

Because it's the access route for the hut, this trail often has a packed snowshoe track. In thin snow conditions a couple of spots along the brookbank can be icy and tricky to negotiate, so make sure you have good snowshoe crampons for this one.

From the parking area and kiosk, the Nineteen Mile Brook Trail follows a wide, easy-graded old road through hemlock forest for 0.7 mile. Nineteen Mile Brook is close by on your right. In deep winter it's muffled in snow and ice, its many boulders transformed into softly molded sculptures.

About a mile in you traverse two potentially icy spots along the edge of the brookbank. Use caution and dig in with your snowshoe crampons. To bypass the spot you can scramble steeply through the woods above or down along the edge of the brook below. The trail continues climbing gradually beside the brook, passing a small dam and pool at 1.2 miles. Beyond, you traverse rolling streamside terrain through picturesque yellow birches. At 1.9 miles the Carter Dome Trail diverges left, bound for Zeta Pass and the high summit of Carter Dome.

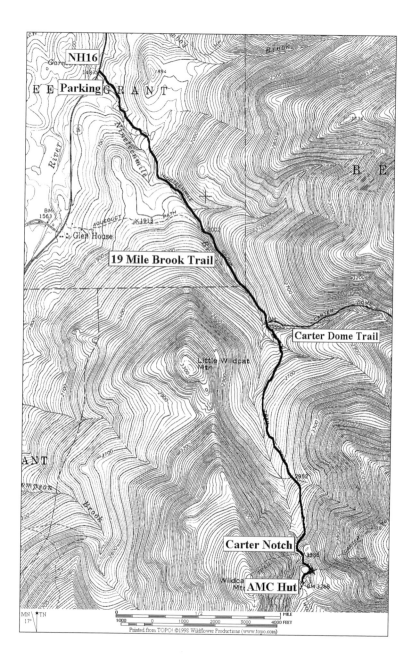

NH16

Parking

E E G R A N T

B E

19 Mile Brook Trail

Glen House

Carter Dome Trail

Little Wildcat
Mtn

ANT

Carter Notch

Wildcat
Mtn AMC Hut

Past the junction you climb moderately up the valley through a lovely forest of white and yellow birch. The north ridge of Wildcat Mtn. rises across the valley. You tightrope across two log footbridges over tributary brooks. The trail becomes rougher as you ascend higher, with some short, steep pitches. At 3.1 miles, after crossing a small brook, you begin a stiff upward pull through snow-caked conifers, aiming for the top of Carter Notch. If the trail is unbroken there may deep windblown powder. You'll want to rotate the job of breaking trail on this sustained climb. At 3.6 miles you attain the height-of-land (elevation 3388 ft.) on a wild, windswept flat of fir woods. The Wildcat Ridge Trail splits right for the summit of Wildcat Mtn.

Keep ahead on Nineteen Mile Brook Trail, which descends rather steeply to the south and swings left and down to the NW shore of Upper Carter Pond. The rugged scenery of Carter Notch bursts upon you when you emerge at this opening. The trail tracks around the east shore, but the frozen surface of Upper Carter Pond is the best vantage point for viewing the notch. From this magnificent spot you can look up at the great wall of Wildcat Mtn. (4422 ft.) looming on the west and the craggy shoulder of Carter Dome (4832 ft.) shooting up on the east. The jagged Pulpit Rock juts out wildly from the side of the Dome.

The mountainscape here was created by continental glaciers, and from afar Carter Notch presents the U-shape characteristic of ice-carved passes. The frozen pond you stand on is just over an acre in area but drops off to a depth of 15 feet. A huge boulder on the west shore is a notable landmark that can be visited in winter. If a bitter breeze is blowing you'll appreciate the original name applied to these ponds by an exploring party in 1853: "Lakes of the Winds."

If you opt to follow the trail around the east shore, you'll still find excellent views up to Wildcat Mtn. By the SE corner of Upper Carter Pond the Carter–Moriah Trail diverges left to begin a very steep climb to Carter Dome. (This section of the Carter–Moriah Trail, and the Wildcat Ridge Trail leading from the height-of-land to the summit of Wildcat, are very steep and difficult to snowshoe and are best left to experts. The Wildcat Ridge Trail crosses an icy slide partway up that requires crampons, ice axe and great caution; falls and injuries have occurred there in winter.)

From the south end of Upper Carter Pond, a few snowshoe shuffles through stunted firs will bring you to diminutive Lower Carter Pond, rimmed by a jumble of snow-covered boulders. The area south of the pond is known as The Rampart, a wild labyrinth of rocks that have tumbled down from the towering cliffs on the side of Carter Dome.

The trail continues south from the Lower Pond and rises slightly to the AMC Carter Notch Hut, open all winter on a self-service basis for up to 40 guests. Day-trippers will find limited refreshments here. The hut and outlying bunkhouses aren't heated so if you're planning an overnight bring a winter-rated sleeping bag and plenty of warm clothes along with food and

*Upper Carter Pond
in Carter Notch*

other necessities. The first AMC cabin was built here in 1904. In 1914 it was replaced by a stone hut that's still in use today.

To return your car, follow the Nineteen Mile Brook Trail back up over the notch height-of-land and down the long valley.

ADDITIONAL OPTION

Mt. Hight & Carter Dome *Mt. Hight only: 8.8 miles round trip, 3200-ft. elevation gain, advanced. Both summits: 10.4 miles round trip, 3600-ft. elevation gain, advanced* Experienced snowshoers with the stamina for a long climb can enjoy a real high mountain adventure on Mt. Hight (4675 ft.) and Carter Dome (4832 ft.), the two tallest peaks in the Carter Range. The bare summit of Hight is in the top rank among White Mountain viewpoints, and in winter deep ridgetop snow transforms scrubby Carter Dome into a stellar vantage point as well. This all-day trip calls for an early start and involves a section of steep climbing below Mt. Hight. Crampons may be needed for traversing Hight's exposed, rocky peak.

The trip starts at the Nineteen Mile Brook trailhead on NH 16. Follow

Nineteen Mile Brook Trail for 1.9 miles, then turn left on the moderately-graded Carter Dome Trail, which once served a firetower atop the Dome. The trail climbs steadily alongside a brook, crossing at 2.4 and 2.7 miles. You then begin a series of switchbacks leading up to Zeta Pass (3890 ft.), the col between Mt. Hight and South Carter, at 3.8 miles. As you climb there are glimpses of the Dome's rime-frosted summit towering up to the right.

At Zeta Pass, where the snow lies deep in open fir forest, turn right on the combined Carter Dome/Carter–Moriah Trails. After 0.2 mile of easy climbing bear left on Carter–Moriah Trail as Carter Dome Trail stays straight. The climb is very steep for 0.4 mile until you emerge on the bare, windswept summit of Mt. Hight at 4.4 miles. Bundle up if you want to enjoy the dazzling 360-degree view: west to the snow-capped Presidentials and their great ravines; north up the Carter Range with the Mahoosucs and distant Maine peaks beyond; east over the remote valley of Wild River, dotted with beaver ponds, and out to the snowy Baldfaces and the lowlands of western Maine; and south to the rounded, slide-streaked crown of Carter Dome. This is one of the great panoramas in the Whites.

By continuing to the Dome you'll enjoy an exciting ridge traverse and an expanded view to the south, and you'll bag an "official" 4000-footer. The Carter–Moriah Trail makes a sharp right turn on the snow-crusted rocks of Hight's summit, then descends easily into rime-frosted scrub that crowds the trail. In 0.4 mile you reach a col and junctions with the Carter Dome Trail (right) and Black Angel Trail (left). Then you snowshoe steadily up the scrubby north ridge of the Dome. In mid and late winter the scrub is buried in snow on the upper part of this climb, creating an open ridge effect with huge views across to the Presidentials. You attain the flat summit of Carter Dome 0.8 mile from Mt. Hight. Continue to the south end of the plateau for a great vista SW over waves of blue ridges leading out to the peaks of the Sandwich Range and Pemigewasset Wilderness.

For the return trip you can retrace your steps across the ridge and over Mt. Hight (the trail makes a sharp left turn at the summit), or you can take the Carter Dome Trail back to Zeta Pass. The latter option avoids the steep descent off Hight and is 0.2 mile shorter, but presents its own challenge in the form of a long sidehill section as it slabs the slope — very tiring in crusty conditions.

4. Imp Face

LOCATION: Carter Range, north of Pinkham Notch

DESCRIPTION: A fairly challenging climb to a clifftop with a huge panorama of the Presidentials

TRAIL: Imp Trail (north loop)

DISTANCE: 4.4 miles round trip

STARTING ELEVATION: 1270 ft.

HIGHEST ELEVATION: 3165 ft.

ELEVATION GAIN: 1900 ft.

RATING: Intermediate / advanced

USGS MAP: Carter Dome

TRAILHEAD: This trip follows the northern leg of the Imp Trail, which makes a 6-mile loop including the top of the Imp Face cliff. The northern trailhead for Imp Trail is on the east side of NH 16, 5.4 miles south of US 2 in Gorham and 5.2 miles south of the AMC's Pinkham Notch Camp. (The south trailhead for Imp Trail is 0.2 mile south along NH 16.) Park at the plowed shoulder by the trail sign.

WMNF PARKING PASS: Yes

The Imp, a sheared-off cliff on a western spur of North Carter Mtn., is a prominent landmark when driving north from Pinkham Notch on Rt. 16. When viewed from Dolly Copp Road at the site of the Dolly Copp Homestead, the cliff presents a profile of a misshapen human face—a "grotesque colossal sphinx" according to one 19th-century writer. For strong snowshoers, the ledges atop the Imp cliff are a rewarding objective for a vigorous half-day outing. Some sidehill traversing and steep climbing make this a fairly difficult route. On a clear day the views across the valley to Mt. Washington and the Northern Presidentials are astounding.

From the roadside the north link of the yellow-blazed Imp Trail makes a short climb up to a powerline swath, turns left along it, then quickly leaves it and enters a beautiful forest of tall hemlock and spruce. You climb easily along a high bank on the south side of Imp Brook, with frequent views down to the snowbound stream. Father along you draw closer to the brook. At 0.7 mile you cross a small tributary, pass a frozen cascade, and after a brief

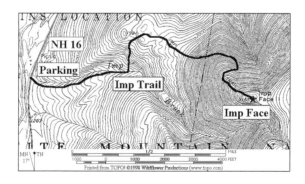

Taking in the huge Presidential view from Imp Face

climb cross Imp Brook. With good snow cover the pretty woods traverse to this point makes a nice beginner's trip. After thaws or in times of snow drought, this section tends to ice up.

On the far side of the brook you angle up at a steady grade through hardwoods for 0.3 mile. At the top you swing right and level out on a 1920-ft. plateau. The going is easy as you meander across this shelf of open hardwoods. Through the trees you can see the steep knob behind the Imp cliff rising ahead. At 1.4 miles the trail bears left and starts to climb more steeply into darker woods. There's one set of wooden steps to negotiate. As you loop around the NW side of the ridge you get peeks out through the trees towards Pine Mtn., the city of Berlin and the Mahoosuc Range.

At about 2400 ft. there's a section of sidehill trail through white birches along the brink of the ravine to the north. This could be a difficult stretch in crusty conditions—good snowshoe crampons are useful here. At 1.8 miles / 2600 ft. the trail makes a sharp right and climbs steeply up the slope, then makes a swing around to the left, rising steadily through birch and dense conifers. This sustained climb will leave you huffing! Eventually you bear right and the grade slackens. One last little pitch brings you up to the spacious ledgy area atop the cliffs, 2.2 miles from the trailhead.

The cliff faces south, so on a calm, sunny winter day it can be a comfortable spot—the better to take in the top-notch view. The star attraction here is the vista across the valley of Peabody River to the majestic snow-capped peaks of the Presidentials. Left to right, you see Boott Spur and Mts. Washington, Clay, Jefferson, Adams and Madison. Between Washington and its

Northern Presidential neighbors is the vast glacier-carved chasm of the Great Gulf. The fields at the base of Mt. Washington mark the start of the Auto Road, whose windings can be followed up the mountain. Parts of Rt. 16 can be seen in the valley.

To the south, on the left of Mt. Washington, you look into Pinkham Notch, with Wildcat Mtn. on the east side. Looming close by on the SE is the great wooded wall of the Carter Range, topping out over 1500 ft. higher than your vantage point. The snow-speckled crest of Carter Dome peers over the ridge of South Carter.

To the NW, right of the Presidentials, there's a distant view to the Pliny and Pilot Ranges, including Mts. Starr King, Waumbek, Weeks and Cabot, The Bulge, and The Horn, with the Crescent Range in front. One of the most impressive aspects of this viewpoint is the deep drop-off in front, down into the ravine of Imp Brook. The cliff is several hundred feet high—don't venture too close to the edge!

The return to your car is down the route you came up on the north leg of Imp Trail.

5. Lower Great Gulf

LOCATION: Great Gulf Wilderness on east side of Presidential Range

DESCRIPTION: A moderate trip into the lower reaches of the Great Gulf, with river scenery and views up to the high peaks of the Presidentials. Option to return via loop or extend trip farther into the Gulf.

TRAIL: Great Gulf Trail

DISTANCE: 5.4 miles round trip

STARTING ELEVATION: 1350 ft.

HIGHEST ELEVATION: 2278 ft.

ELEVATION GAIN: 950 ft.

RATING: Intermediate

USGS MAPS: Carter Dome, Mt. Washington

TRAILHEAD: The starting point for this hike is a spacious plowed parking area for the Great Gulf Wilderness on the west side of NH 16, 6.5 miles south of the junction with US 2 in Gorham and 4.1 miles north of the AMC Pinkham Notch Camp. There are toilets at the trailhead.

WMNF PARKING PASS: Yes

The Great Gulf is a huge glacier-carved valley that sprawls for five miles between Mt. Washington and the Northern Presidentials—Mts. Clay,

Looking up to Mt. Adams from The Bluff

Jefferson, Adams and Madison. It's the largest cirque in the White Mountains, with steep soaring ridges, a broad floor and a craggy headwall twice as high as the more notorious Tuckerman Ravine. The Great Gulf Trail, an excellent snowshoeing route in its lower and middle reaches, runs up the length of the valley.

A snowshoe venture into Spaulding Lake in the very heart of the Gulf can be an awesome experience, but that arduous 13-mile round trip is suitable only for veteran winter trampers. The easier trip described here penetrates far enough into the lower reaches of the valley to give you a sampling of its charms, and perhaps inspire you to explore further another time. This pleasant route follows the gently rising Great Gulf Trail along the West Branch of the Peabody River and climbs to a small outlook called The Bluff, where you can gaze up at the snowy, craggy high peaks. Snowshoers seeking a longer trip can extend their day by continuing farther up the Great Gulf Trail, or returning from The Bluff via a longer loop over the Osgood Cutoff and lower Osgood Trail.

The Great Gulf Trail begins at the north end of the loop road around the parking area. There's a large kiosk with a map and information about the Great Gulf Wilderness. Following an old road, the trail descends gently for 0.1 mile, then turns left, with a glimpse of Mt. Adams high above, and drops to cross the Peabody River on an impressive suspension footbridge.

On the far side of the river you climb a short pitch and at 0.3 mile come to the junction with the Great Gulf Link Trail from Dolly Copp Campground. Turn left here for scenic snowshoeing under tall spruces along the

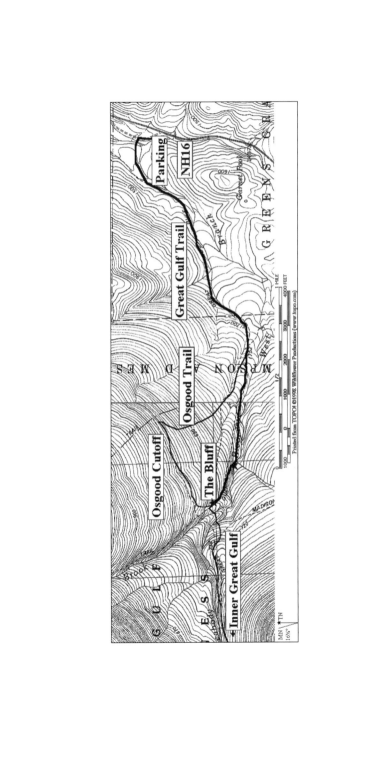

wide, easy trail. This and other parts of the trail farther ahead are shared with cross country skiers. Down to your left is the West Branch of the Peabody River, a big watercourse here just above its confluence with the main river.

At 0.6 mile the Great Gulf Trail splits left off the old road, which continues as a ski trail to the right. You meander through spruce and hemlock on a bank above the icebound river. At 0.7 mile the trail bears right at a bend in the river. From the bank there's a nice view upstream to the high, frosted cliffs of Boott Spur. You can drop down a short side path here to explore snowy ledges beside the stream.

The trail now wanders away from the West Branch through mixed woods. At 1.0 mile bear left onto the old road as the ski trail comes in from the right. You pass two more ski trail junctions and cross several small brooks on plank bridges. Rising gently, the trail makes a swing to the right (west).

At 1.6 miles the Hayes Copp Ski Trail splits right. Just beyond, the Great Gulf Trail enters the Great Gulf Wilderness. Snowshoers should sign in at the trail register. This helps the Forest Service monitor use of this popular area, which sees over 30,000 visitors a year, mainly in summer. You continue upward through a nice hardwood forest. At 1.8 miles, amidst darker woods, the Osgood Trail leaves on the right.

The Great Gulf Trail drifts back towards the West Branch, climbing at easy grades parallel to but mostly set back from the river. At 2.4 miles you come right by the stream—a very scenic spot. If you carefully make your way out to the big snowy rocks you'll be rewarded with an interesting view upstream to Mt. Jefferson.

The trail now climbs up a high bank above the river and swings right up a steep pitch of rock steps—the toughest snowshoeing of the trip. After a bit more climbing the trail levels in a dense stand of young conifers.

At 2.7 miles you break out of the woods into the opening known as The Bluff—a high gravelly bank rising above the lower part of Parapet Brook, a tributary of the West Branch. As you emerge from the woods the rime-frosted cone of 5799-ft. Mt. Adams towers to the NW, with the rough hump of John Quincy Adams (5410 ft.) to the right. At the base of Adams is a broad forested spur ridge with a sharp dropoff on the left, a route traversed by the Buttress Trail.

A few yards farther there's a view left (west) to the summit of 5716-ft. Mt. Jefferson and the northern of two sharp ridges known as "Jefferson's Knees." This stupendously steep spur is ascended by the rugged Six Husbands Trail.

From the most open spot at The Bluff, in front of a tall boulder, there's a clear view SW across the lower valley to snowy Chandler Ridge, the massive NE spur of Mt. Washington. With a close look you can pick out the route of the Mt. Washington Auto Road as it winds up the side of the mountain and around a rocky knob known as The Horn. An even wider view can be obtained by scrambling up to the top of the boulder—not an easy feat in winter. The open area in front of the boulder is a nice lunch stop, with good sun exposure into early afternoon. After that, at least in early winter, the sun drops behind the huge mass of Mt. Washington. The clearing behind the boulder is one of several designated tentsites in the Great Gulf.

The views from The Bluff give a hint of the grandeur of the Gulf. This striking valley was first noted in 1642 by Darby Field when, accompanied by two Native American guides, he made the first recorded ascent of Mt. Washington. It was once called the "Gulf of Mexico," but received its present name in 1823 when a hiking group led by Ethan Allen Crawford, the famed trail-builder, innkeeper and guide, were disoriented in the fog above treeline and "wandered about until we came near the edge of a great gulf . . ."

Relatively few trampers penetrated deep into the valley until the first trail was blazed in 1881. From 1908–1910 an energetic band of volunteers led by AMC trailman Warren Hart built a network of steep and spectacular trails connecting the floor of the gulf with the surrounding high peaks. In 1959 the Forest Service declared 5,400 acres of the Great Gulf as a "Wild Area," and it became the East's first Congressionally designated Wilderness area in 1964.

From The Bluff, the 2.7-mile return trip down Great Gulf Trail is an easy ramble that can be accomplished in an hour and a half or less. Remember to bear right near the end where the Great Gulf Link continues ahead.

ADDITIONAL OPTIONS

Loop Option   Experienced snowshoers may enjoy the slightly longer and more strenuous return via Osgood Cutoff and Osgood Trail. Continue a few yards beyond the clearing at The Bluff to the junction with Osgood Cutoff, a short link in the Appalachian Trail. There's a view back to Wildcat Ridge and the Wildcat ski slopes as you exit the clearing.

Turn right at the junction, where the Great Gulf Trail drops steeply left to cross Parapet Brook. Osgood Cutoff climbs steadily for 0.1 mile, then makes a horseshoe bend to the right. You continue to climb through conifers for another 0.1 mile, then make a 90-degree right turn and traverse for 0.4 mile on the 2500-foot contour through an attractive forest with many yellow birches. If the trail is not broken out, you'll have to look carefully for the white blazes. You cross several minor brooks and catch occasional glimpses SE to Carter Dome (marked by a large slide), deep Carter Notch, and Wildcat Mtn.

At 0.6 mile from The Bluff the Osgood Cutoff ends at the Osgood Trail, a popular but very exposed route up to Mt. Madison. Turn right on the Osgood Trail (a spur path leads 100 yards ahead to the Osgood Tentsite). The Osgood Trail descends at a moderate grade through open hardwoods —a delightful snowshoe descent. Through the trees there are peeks at Mt. Washington and the Carter Range. In 0.8 mile from Osgood Cutoff the

Osgood Trail comes down to the Great Gulf Trail. Turn left here for the easy 1.8-mile ramble back to your car. The trip in to The Bluff and back via this loop is 5.9 miles with 1150 ft. of elevation gain.

Inner Great Gulf   Experienced snowshoers prepared to break trail can follow the Great Gulf Trail farther through wild forests up into the heart of the valley. From the junction with Osgood Cutoff just beyond The Bluff, the Great Gulf Trail drops steeply left to cross Parapet Brook, then climbs a bit to meet Madison Gulf Trail atop a narrow hogback ridge. By following Madison Gulf Trail a short distance right to an open scrubby area you can obtain views of Mts. Jefferson, Adams and Madison.

From this junction the Great Gulf Trail drops steeply again and spans the West Branch on a suspension bridge. After a scramble up the far bank the Madison Gulf Trail splits left and Great Gulf Trail drops down and right to the bank above the river. The snowshoeing is smoother now as the trail rises easily alongside the West Branch through deep coniferous woods. In a short distance a side path right leads out to snow-topped rocks in the river with a view up to Mt. Adams. At 3.1 miles (0.4 mile beyond The Bluff) you pass Clam Rock, a huge overhanging boulder, on the left. In another 0.2 mile there's a spot where you can snowshoe out onto riverbed rocks for a picturesque view up the snowbound stream to the steep façade of Jefferson's Knee. Part of the Carter Range can be spotted downstream. This spot is a good turnaround point for an extended intermediate-level outing beyond The Bluff—6.6 miles round trip, 1250 ft. of elevation gain.

Advanced snowshoers can continue up the valley at generally moderate grades, with a few tricky sidehills, enjoying many views of the frozen river in a setting of supreme winter isolation. Possible turnaround points include the junction with Wamsutta and Six Husbands Trails (9.0 miles round trip, 1850-ft. elevation gain), Weetamoo Falls (11.4 miles, 2450 ft.), and the ultimate prize, Spaulding Lake (13.0 miles, 3000 ft.). Buried in huge snowdrifts at an elevation of 4228 ft., this tiny pond occupies one of the most spectacular settings in the mountains below the imposing headwall of the Gulf. From its vicinity there are striking views back down the valley to Mts. Adams and Madison. Avoid this upper area if avalanche danger is moderate or high—check with the AMC Pinkham Notch Visitor Center (603–266–2721) for current conditions.

6. Lookout Ledge

LOCATION: Randolph/Crescent Range

DESCRIPTION: Short, steep climb to a south-facing ledge with outstanding views of the Northern Presidentials and the Carter–Moriah Range

TRAIL: Sargent Path

DISTANCE: 1.6 miles round trip

STARTING ELEVATION: 1310 ft.

HIGHEST ELEVATION: 2260 ft.

ELEVATION GAIN: 950 ft.

RATING: Intermediate

USGS MAPS: Mt. Washington, Pliny Range

TRAILHEAD: This trip follows the Sargent Path, one of several possible routes to Lookout Ledge in the Randolph Mountain Club's excellent trail network. From US 2 at Lowe's Store in Randolph, turn north on a short side road that leads to Durand Rd., which parallels the highway. Turn right (east), drive 1.3 miles, and look for the white RMC trail sign for Sargent Path, facing east on the left (north) side of the road, across from a red summer residence. A sign on the other side of the trail entrance reads "1916." Park as tight as you can to the snowbank by the trailhead. (Durand Rd. is lightly traveled.) *Note*: This trip is entirely on private land. Camping and fires are not allowed.

WMNF PARKING PASS: No

The clifftop perch at Lookout Ledge offers one of the most dramatic of all Presidential Range vistas, looking across the Randolph valley at the great towering masses of Mts. Madison and Adams. The view into King Ravine, the great glacial gouge in the north side of Adams, is especially grand.

Several trails lead to Lookout Ledge, a break of granite on the south side of the Crescent Range. The most popular route, and the one originally intended for this guide, is the Ledge Trail from Durand Rd. However, the lower part of this trail was temporarily closed due to logging operations in winter 2000, so we'll take you up the shorter and steeper Sargent Path instead. This lightly used trail provides an attractive route—steep in places, but not overly so, and short enough to be done in a couple of hours. The trail is named for George A. Sargent, a doctor, businessman and trail-builder who frequented Randolph in the late 1800s and early 1900s and had a summer home below Lookout Ledge.

From Durand Rd. the Sargent Path quickly leads into the woods, bearing left at a fork 50 feet in and commencing a steady climb through mixed woods. The way is well marked with orange blazes. (Don't follow the red property line blazes that are seen along the lower part of the trail.) At 0.2 mile you emerge into open, ice-damaged hardwoods and bend right, then left. Beyond a small brook crossing the grade eases on a gently sloping plateau. Ahead you can see Lookout Ledge on the side of a spruce-wooded knob. The trail winds across this shelf, then takes aim at the steep slope beyond.

At about 0.5 mile the climb resumes, moderate at first, then quite steep, twisting up through a wild, open spruce forest. Though the pitch will test

The Northern Presidentials loom large before Lookout Ledge

your snowshoeing technique, it's a straightforward climb with no tricky ledge scrambles. It could be tough in very crusty or icy conditions. A jog to the right slackens the grade, then you swing left and go up directly again.

Atop this pitch, at 0.7 mile, you veer to the right for an easier traverse, with an occasional short scramble to spice things up. You start to see ledges off to the right, and one last bit of easy climbing deposits you on the snowy shelf atop Lookout Ledge.

This is one of the great viewing perches in the Whites, facing south to the sun and the immense snowy peaks of Madison (L) and Adams (R), seen across the broad Randolph valley. King Ravine appears like a giant scoop taken out of the side of Adams, its headwall seamed with slides and its floor strewn with gigantic boulders. Other features include the broad Nowell Ridge and sharp Durand Ridge on Adams, the winding Snyder Brook valley between the peaks, and the Gordon and Howker Ridges on Madison. Mt. Jefferson peers over the brawny shoulder of Adams, displaying its spiny Castellated Ridge. Mt. Bowman is the wooded hump to the far right.

To the left, east and SE, is another fine vista looking down the spacious valley, across open fields and frozen Durand Lake, to rugged little Pine Mtn. and the Carter–Moriah Range beyond. All three Moriah summits stand out clearly, along with pyramidal Imp Mtn. and bulky North and Middle Carter. On the far left you can see ledgy Mt. Hayes and other peaks in the lower Mahoosucs, and the Bear Mtn. range farther east. Perhaps the only draw-back of this wonderful vantage is the traffic noise that wafts up from Rt. 2 — but the vistas are so compelling that you'll hardly notice it.

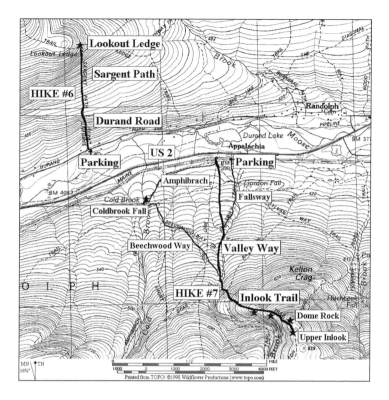

The return trip down Sargent Path is quick indeed. Watch your footing on the steeper ptiches lest it be *too* quick—some sidestepping may be in order.

Note: If the Ledge Trail is open, it provides a longer route to Lookout Ledge that is somewhat less steep. Park by a clearing on Durand Rd. two miles east of Lowe's Store marked by a sign, "Ravine House Site"—from 1877–1961 a summer hotel stood here. The trail starts at the west end of the opening and climbs, rather steeply at first, to a junction with Notchway Trail at 0.6 mile. Bear left here and ascend steadily to Pasture Path at 1.2 miles. A short, steep pitch and a traverse through wild spruce forest leads to the Crescent Ridge Trail at 1.3 miles, just above the ledge. Drop down a few yards left for the view. Round trip by this route is 2.6 miles with elevation gain of 950 ft.

ADDITIONAL OPTIONS

Mt. Crescent *4.0 miles round trip, 1400-ft. elevation gain, intermediate/advanced* This 3251-ft. peak has outlooks south to the Presidentials and north over the Kilkenny area. Take Randolph Hill Rd. 1.9 miles up from US 2 and park at a small plowed area on the right. The Mt. Crescent Trail starts a few yards ahead. Bear right at 0.2 mile with Mt. Crescent Trail and embark on a steady climb up the mountain, passing junctions with Boothman Spring Cut-off, Castleview Loop and Crescent Ridge Trail. Follow markings with care in logged areas. Above the latter junction the snowshoeing is quite steep in places. At the top take in the great view of the Northern Presidentials and Carter Range, then proceed over the south summit and on to the north knob, meeting Crescent Ridge Trail again. The north view is a few yards ahead here. The peaks of the Pliny and Pilot Ranges—Pliny, Waumbek, Weeks, Cabot, The Bulge, The Horn, Unknown Pond Ridge, Rogers Ledge, Deer Ridge—are arrayed in a long chain beyond the broad basin of the Upper Ammonoosuc River. Among many distant mountains the snowy Percy Peaks are prominent. There's really no other view quite like it in the Whites.

Easy RMC Trails   A number of easy snowshoe rambles can be concocted using the extensive RMC trail network on either side of Randolph Hill Rd. Consult the RMC's *Randolph Paths* guide and its excellent trail map. One nice destination is **Castleview Ledge**, an opening with a partial view of the Northern Presidentials—a 2.1-mile loop from the parking spot with a 400-foot elevation gain, using Mt. Crescent Trail, Castleview Loop and Carlton Notch Trail.

7. Inlook Trail

LOCATION: Randolph / Northern Presidentials

DESCRIPTION: A short but steep climb up a series of ledges with views of Mts. Madison & Adams and mountains to the north

TRAILS: Valley Way, Brookside, Inlook Trail

DISTANCE: 3.2 miles round trip

STARTING ELEVATION: 1306 ft.

HIGHEST ELEVATION: 2732 ft.

ELEVATION GAIN: 1426 ft.

RATING: Intermediate / advanced

USGS MAP: Mt. Washington

TRAILHEAD: This trip departs from the spacious "Appalachia" parking area for trails on the Northern Presidentials, located on the south side of US 2 in Randolph 5.5 miles west of NH 16 in Gorham and 7.2 miles east of NH 115 near Jefferson. It's 2 miles east of Lowe's Store, a Randolph landmark.

WMNF PARKING PASS: No

The Randolph Mountain Club's Inlook Trail traverses the lower NW end of Mt. Madison's Gordon Ridge, where a string of open ledges culmi-

*Steep and deep on
the Inlook Trail*

nates in the viewpoints known as Dome Rock (2662 ft.) and Upper Inlook (2732 ft.). Bared by a 1921 forest fire, these vantages present good views "in" to the towering peaks of Madison and Adams (hence the name, "Inlook"), and "out" to the Pliny, Crescent and Mahoosuc Ranges to the north. The first mile of this trip is easy, while the upper half mile is quite steep and will test your snowshoe technique in a few spots. With good snow conditions, this is an exhilarating half-day excursion.

From the Appalachia parking area, climb over the snowbank beside the kiosk and follow the Valley Way across a wide railroad bed now used as a snowmobile trail. Beyond you come to a powerline clearing and trail junction. Bear left on Valley Way as Air Line branches right. The blue-blazed Valley Way ascends easily into open hardwood forest, passing junctions with Maple Walk (just into the woods) and Sylvan Way (0.2 mile).

At about 0.4 mile large hemlocks start to mix into the forest, and soon you're into deep hemlock woods with Snyder Brook, hushed in winter, off to your left. This is a small stand of old-growth forest that survived the era of heavy logging a century or more ago. The yellow-blazed Fallsway comes in on the left at 0.5 mile, splits left on a loop past Tama Fall, and rejoins at 0.6 mile. Valley Way now runs close by the snowbound brook—a scenic stretch of snowshoeing. You rise to a junction with Beechwood Way on the right at 0.8 mile.

In another 100 feet diverge left on the yellow-blazed Brookside, which crosses a small streambed and hops up on the bank of the brook opposite a house-sized boulder. The trail turns right, crosses a small gully, and quickly meets the Randolph Path beside a railinged footbridge, 0.9 mile from your car. The elevation here is 1900 ft. Turn left to cross the bridge, and at the three-way fork on the east bank continue straight ahead on the Inlook Trail, marked by an RMC sign. (Randolph Path goes left here and Brookside diverges right.)

After its first 75 feet the Inlook Trail commences serious, straightforward climbing through a forest of small birches and conifers. The grade is relentless for about 0.3 mile and 300 feet of elevation gain. There's a level breather, then you meander upward and make a quick left and right, scrambling up to the first outlook ledge (elevation 2275 ft.). To your right you look up to the great snowy hulk of Mt. Madison, towering 3000 feet above you, with the wooded end of Durand Ridge on its right.

The trail ducks left into the scrub, then climbs up to the flat-topped second outlook. Here you can look back (west) down the Randolph valley to distant horizons, and NW to Mt. Waumbek, highest in the Pliny Range, looming darkly behind Mt. Randolph, the westernmost summit of the Crescent Range. You climb gently through scrub again and emerge on the third ledge, where the notched summit of Mt. John Quincy Adams (an Adams sub-peak) pops out beside Madison. The view is good to the west here also. Looking ahead you can see some of the upper ledges on this ridge.

Now you snowshoe steeply up through scrub and ledgy areas with occasional vistas. The trail may be hard to follow, but generally keeps a bit back from the steep south edge of the ridge. Good snowshoe crampons are essential if the snow is hardpacked on the more exposed ledges. Snow may drift deeply in places, and the wind can come howling in from the west. Just over a mile from the road this little trail gives you weather, terrain and views worthy of a much higher climb!

About 0.5 mile above the footbridge, elevation 2525 ft., you emerge on a large exposed ledge, perhaps the best viewpoint on the trail. If the snow is crusty or icy here, stay back from the edge as you traverse this open stretch.

The view is commanding, looking straight up the twisting valley of Snyder Brook to the whitened crests of Madison, John Quincy Adams and Adams itself. The broad view west is guarded by Cherry Mtn. and Owls Head on the left and Mts. Waumbek and Randolph on the right. On clear days the Worcester Range and the tops of Camel's Hump and Mt. Mansfield can be spotted far off in Vermont.

Above here you rise 200 feet through scrub, then claw your way right and left up a steep ledge and continue climbing through a swath behind a sloping face on the right. The grade eases atop this steep pitch and you pass a view to the right, then wind up through semi-open terrain to a left turn. A level 200-foot stretch through snow-laden spruces leads you to Dome Rock, 1.5 miles from your car.

This snow-crusted ledge provides a good view north to the wooded Crescent Range across the valley—left to right, Mt. Randolph (with the snowy patch of Lookout Ledge on its side), Mt. Crescent, and Black Crescent Mtn. To the left of the Crescents is Mt. Waumbek, a long ridge bordered by Mt. Starr King on its left and the three summit tips of Mt. Weeks on the right. Distant North Country peaks can be seen to the right of the Crescent Range. To the NE is the sprawling Mahoosuc Range, spotted with many snowy ledges. Old Speck, the highest, is on the left and the sharp peaks of Goose Eye Mtn. rise from the center of the range. Farther right and closer is the low mass of Pine Mtn. with cliffs on its south end, and on the far right the three Moriah summits close in the horizon.

The Inlook Trail reenters the woods to the SE behind Dome Rock— look for a white "PATH" sign. You climb moderately a short way, then snowshoe along a corridor through spruces whose snow-weighted branches may hang over the trail. A right turn and short pitch hoist you to the Upper Inlook, just 0.1 mile above Dome Rock.

This high perch opens a wide view west beyond the ledgy ridge you've come up. Looking left you gaze up at the mighty summits of Madison and Adams from another perspective, with lower ridges trailing out to the Randolph valley. When the wind blows from the NW this is a cold spot to hang out for long, but the view is superb.

A few yards behind Upper Inlook, the Inlook Trail ends at a junction with the Kelton Trail. This is the normal turnaround point for this snowshoe trek, though there is the option to go left on the Kelton Trail and descend slightly for 0.2 mile to another crag called "The Overlook." Located just right of the trail, this perch affords a striking vista of the Mahoosucs, Pine Mtn. and the Moriahs with more valley foreground than you see from scrub-grown Dome Rock.

The trip back down the Inlook Trail will have you whooping with delight if the snow conditions are good—but use caution if there's crusty snow or ice. Once back down on Valley Way, you can vary your descent by following the parallel Fallsway alongside Snyder Brook, viewing the frozen cascades at Tama Fall, Upper and Lower Salroc Falls, and Gordon Fall. Fallsway will bring you out at the east end of the Appalachia parking area.

ADDITIONAL OPTIONS

Appalachia Waterfalls Loop *2.6 miles, 650-ft. elevation gain, beginner* This pleasant snowshoe ramble weaves through the web of RMC trails on the lower slopes of the Northern Peaks and brings you past five frozen waterfalls. From the east end of the Appalachia parking area, follow Fallsway across the old railroad grade and powerline and into the woods. Climbing at easy grades, you pass Gordon Fall at 0.2 mile and Lower and Upper Salroc Falls at 0.5 mile. At 0.6 mile Fallsway briefly merges with Valley Way, then departs left and ascends past Tama Fall before rejoining Valley Way at 0.7 mile. Follow Valley Way up for 0.2 mile, then turn sharp right and descend on Beechwood Way through open hardwoods. In 0.3 mile you cross Air Line.

Continue another 0.5 mile to Sylvan Way; turn left here and snowshoe 0.1 mile to Coldbrook Fall, which has a nice rocky basin at its foot. Below the waterfall Sylvan Way meets Amphibrach at the Memorial Bridge over Coldbrook—from the bridge there's a nice view up to the cascade. Follow the gentle Amphibrach east for 0.7 mile to the Air Line. Turn left on Air Line for the 100-yard walk across the powerline and railroad grade to the Appalachia parking area.

OTHER TRAILS ON THE NORTHERN PRESIDENTIALS

Ascents to the Northern Presidential summits—Madison, Adams, and Jefferson—are serious winter mountaineering treks with lots of above treeline exposure and are beyond the scope of this book. But there are nearly limitless options for snowshoeing below treeline on the extensive network of trails on the northern slopes of these high peaks. Most of these are maintained by the Randolph Mountain Club and date back to the late 1800s, when Randolph was a favorite haunt for the leading trailblazers of the day. RMC also operates the winterized Gray Knob Cabin, high on the side of Mt. Adams.

Some of these trails—Valley Way and Lowe's Path, in particular—are heavily used as access routes to the peaks or to Gray Knob Cabin, and are often packed out to the point of being icy. **Valley Way** provides a sheltered and relatively moderate route, steepest at the top, to treeline at the col between Adams and Madison, where the AMC's Madison Hut (elevation 4825 ft., closed in winter) is located. For experienced and well-equipped snowshoers, the trek up to the hut, where there are good views to the north and up to the neighboring Mts. Adams and Madison, is 7.6 miles round trip with 3550 ft. of elevation gain. Crampons should be carried and may be needed for the last short stretch up to the hut.

Lowe's Path, which starts from US 2 just west of Lowe's Store (the only place where trailhead parking is available; nominal fee), provides a straightforward route to Gray Knob Cabin and several fine viewpoints nearby. Grades are moderate for the first 2.1 miles, then the trail is quite steep as it climbs past the Log Cabin (an open door shelter) at 2.4 miles and on to the crest of Nowell Ridge. Crampons may be needed if the steep section is icy. At 3.2 miles you come to an excellent outlook (elevation 4400 ft.) to nearby Mt. Jefferson and distant Mt. Lafayette. Here a trail named The Quay leads left 0.1 mile to Gray Knob Cabin, which was rebuilt in 1989. It accommodates 15 hikers and is partially heated by a woodstove. A caretaker is in residence and a small fee is charged for overnight use. A short distance beyond on Lowe's Path, the Gray Knob Trail also splits left to the cabin. Elevation gain to this area, which is just below treeline, is 3050 ft. From the cabin, you can snowshoe an easy 0.4 mile east on Gray Knob Trail through snowpacked firs to Crag Camp (4247 ft.), another RMC cabin (not insulated for winter use). Perched on the western rim of King Ravine, this camp looks down into that yawning glacial cirque and up to Adams and Madison. For an even more dramatic view, you can turn right here on the Spur Trail and plug steeply uphill for 0.2 mile to a side path that leads 100 yards left to the Knight's Castle (4588 ft.), a crag with a spectacular view into King Ravine and out to the north. A round trip to Gray Knob, Crag Camp, and Knight's Castle, is 8.0 miles with 3500 ft. of elevation gain, suitable only for experienced and fully equipped snowshoers.

Many other RMC trails are seldom used in winter and often require arduous trail breaking. Numerous below-treeline loops are possible, though views are infrequent on the lower wooded trails. Some trails are very steep, and those in King and Castle Ravines should be avoided due to avalanche danger.

8. South Ledges of Mt. Moriah

LOCATION: Carter–Moriah Range, south of Gorham

DESCRIPTION: A long, moderate climb to open clifftop ledges with spectacular views of Wild River valley, the Carter Range and the Presidentials

TRAILS: Stony Brook Trail, Carter–Moriah Trail

DISTANCE: 8.2 miles round trip

STARTING ELEVATION: 930 ft.

HIGHEST ELEVATION: 3550 ft.

ELEVATION GAIN: 2650 ft.

RATING: Advanced

USGS MAP: Carter Dome

TRAILHEAD: This hike starts at the plowed parking area for Stony Brook Trail on the east side of NH 16, 1.8 miles south of its east junction with US 2 in Gorham. Turn onto a road marked by a hiker symbol, just south of a bridge over the Peabody River, and quickly turn left into the parking area.

WMNF PARKING PASS: Yes

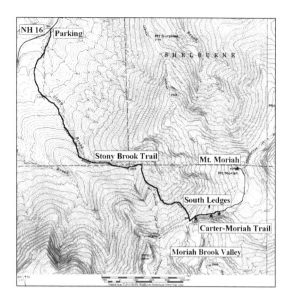

Wondrous wintry views await you on the ledgy perches atop the south cliffs of Mt. Moriah. This full-day trip leads you up the moderately graded Stony Brook Trail—a fine snowshoe route—to the high col between Moriah and Imp Mtn. From here you climb north to a series of outlooks with intimate views of the Moriah Brook valley and the higher summits of the Carter Range, and more distant prospects to the Presidentials and the Pilot Range. Save this one for a day with bright blue skies and reasonable temperatures—the better to savor the vistas. Good snowshoe crampons will be needed up on the ledges.

From the parking lot, the trail starts by crossing a footbridge (with steps) over Stony Brook. Follow the blue-blazed trail gently upward through hemlocks beside a small brook. Soon you swing right to cross another footbridge spanning a miniature flume. You come to the bank of Stony Brook and begin a leisurely meander up beside it through hemlocks and spruce. At about 0.8 mile you join an old logging road and plod up it about 0.2 mile, then make a short, steep drop to the right and cross Stony Brook. Look carefully for blazes on the far bank, where the trail exits up to the right. You make a quick series of turns—left, right, then left again through young hardwoods. Soon you bear left once more on another old logging road, picking up the old trail route. (Up until now you've been on a relocation that avoids private development.)

Now you settle in for a long, gradual climb, with Stony Brook down on your left and the west ridge of Moriah rising beyond. You swing eastward as you progress up the valley. There's a level stretch with a minor sidehill, then you resume the easy ascent. After traversing a lovely glade of birch and hard-

Surveying the Wild River valley from the south cliffs of Moriah

wood you dip left to cross Stony Brook at 2.3 miles. Up to this point you've climbed a mere 900 feet.

Across the brook the ascent steepens; it's a steady grind from here to the ridgetop col. The woods are beautiful—northern hardwoods and white birch mixed with some fir and spruce. Looking left through the trees and across the valley, you see a series of snowy crags fronting the steep slope of Moriah's west ridge. Plow your way upward through groves of birch, gaining glimpses of the col ahead. Snow-draped conifers speckle this winter wonderland forest.

At 3.4 miles the trail makes a brief traverse right, then you tackle the stiffest climb of the day through wiry birches and white-coated firs. The snow may be windblown and drifted in here. At the top the trail abruptly levels out, brushes by a boulder, and meets the Carter–Moriah Trail in the 3127-ft. col. You've come 3.6 miles from your car.

Turn left on the ridge trail, part of the white-blazed Appalachian Trail. Within a few yards you pass the junction with Moriah Brook Trail on the right. (One of the loveliest trails in the mountains, it descends over 5 miles down the valley of Moriah Brook through birch and hardwood forests, ending at the Wild River. Due to unplowed roads, it's an impractical winter approach.)

Heading northward on Carter–Moriah Trail, a short climb lifts you to the first sunny, snowy outlook ledge. The eastward view is a wild one, overlooking the upper fold of the Moriah Brook valley enclosed by a southern arm of Mt. Moriah. Extensive areas of snow-whitened ledge give the ridge a ghostly, barren look. The rock was bared by a forest fire that engulfed the valley when it was being logged in the 1890s from the Wild River to the east. You can see across this spacious Wild River basin to Meader Ridge and the snowy cone of North Baldface on its eastern rim.

This is a good place to layer up before continuing up the trail. You quickly come to a second viewpoint where you can look left and up to the top of the south cliffs—your ultimate objective on this hike. After a short scramble you snowshoe gently up the narrow ridge through a corridor of scrubby firs and birches. The wind can pile the snow deep in here. Though you're in the trees, a westerly breeze can nip exposed skin. You pass a couple of openings with views west to the great snowy pyramids of the Northern Presidentials and NW to the many rounded humps of the Pliny–Pilot Range.

After 0.2 mile the grade steepens through stunted woods, staying left at the base of open ledges. There are a couple of moderately steep pitches, but nothing overly difficult. In another 0.2 mile you huff your way up to the prize of this trip—a series of three ledgy terraces, one above the next, with spectacular flat, open perches atop the south cliffs. The trail passes by each of these, climbing alternately through protected scrub and up moderately sloping ledges marked by cairns. If conditions are crusty or icy, you'll want good snowshoe crampons or boot crampons for traction.

The views here are extraordinary. Down to the east, the wild, winding valley of Moriah Brook, the Wild River valley, Meader Ridge, Baldface, and distant hills in western Maine. To the south, the massive ridges and high wooded peaks of the Carters. To the SW, a stunning portrait of Mt. Washington and the Northern Presidentials—Clay, Jefferson, Adams and Madison. Out to the NW, the extended chain of the Pliny-Pilot peaks (Waumbek, Weeks, Terrace, Cabot, The Bulge and The Horn) and, farther away, the mountains of the Nash Stream area, where the twin white cones of Percy Peaks stand out.

The turn-around point for this trip is the uppermost ledge perch in this group, where, at the far right edge (it's flat, but use caution) you look straight down the cliffs to the birch-clad valley below.

The Carter–Moriah Trail continues another mile to the summit of Moriah (see below), but these are perhaps the best views on the mountain. Return by the same route. With good conditions you'll swoop down to the col in a flash, and the trip is pleasant all the way down.

ADDITIONAL OPTIONS

Mt. Moriah Summit From the ledges atop the south cliffs you can forge northward another mile on Carter–Moriah Trail to reach the 4049-ft. summit of Mt. Moriah. The grades are mostly easy to the junction with Kenduskeag Trail. Most of this section is through beautiful ridgetop fir forest, with occasional ledge breaks opening views north to the Mahoosucs and more distant peaks in western Maine. Where the Carter–Moriah Trail turns left at the junction, a formidable challenge awaits—a difficult scramble up a rock face several feet high. The summit of Moriah is just beyond this spot on a side path left. The small rock knob has a fine 360-degree view. Ascent of Moriah by Stony Brook Trail and Carter–Moriah Trail is 10.0 miles round trip with a 3150-ft. vertical rise.

Carter–Moriah Trail from Gorham   From its north trailhead at the end of Bangor Rd. in Gorham, the Carter–Moriah Trail climbs 4.5 miles to the summit of Moriah at a steady grade, good for snowshoeing, with several views from ledges en route. The first views, looking west to the Northern Presidentials, are from a little hump called Mt. Surprise (2194 ft.). This makes a nice intermediate half-day trip: 4.0 miles round trip, 1400-ft. vertical rise. More ledge viewpoints are found about a half mile farther and several hundred feet higher. The round trip to the summit of Moriah by this route is 9.0 miles with a 3400-ft. vertical rise. Be prepared for several disheartening false summits along the upper mile.

Mt. Hayes *7.4 miles round trip, 1800-ft. elevation gain, intermediate / advanced*
The ledgy summit of Mt. Hayes, the southernmost summit of the 30-mile Mahoosuc Range, offers good views both north and south. The climb from Shelburne up the Centennial Trail (built by AMC during the club's 100th anniversary year in 1976) is fairly long but mostly at easy to moderate grades with several views en route. This is a link in the Appalachian Trail—the white blazes are not always easy to follow in the snow. Drive 3.3 miles east on US 2 from its easterly junction with NH 16 in Gorham and turn left on North Road, which crosses the Androscoggin River on a bridge in 0.3 mile. In another 0.1 mile, look for unplowed Hogan Road leaving on the left, just before North Road makes a sharp right turn. Park on the roadside by this junction and walk 0.2 mile up Hogan Road to the start of Centennial Trail.

   The trail starts out with a moderate climb, then traverses to a pair of ledgy viewpoints looking south to the Moriahs, Carters and Presidentials. A steep climb leads to a third outlook, then you dip down into a small valley at 1.8 miles. You soon head up again steadily through open hardwoods, where care is required to follow the trail. A steep pitch up east-viewing snowy ledges lifts you to an eastern spur of Mt. Hayes at 3.0 miles. Open rock here provides views of the high peaks to the south. A slight dip and climb gets you to the junction with the Mahoosuc Trail at 3.3 miles. To the left (south), the trail leads 0.2 mile to the summit of Hayes and a superb southern viewpoint 0.2 mile beyond. Left to right, the 180 degree view takes in Caribou Mountain, the Moriah and Carter summits, Wildcat, the majestic snow cones of Washington, Adams and Madison, and the Crescent, Pliny and Pilot Ranges. Other ledges just north of the Centennial / Mahoosuc junction offer views NW to the Pilot Range and other North Country peaks, and NE to the higher summits of the Mahoosucs. The moderate slant of Centennial Trail makes for a pleasant snowshoe descent.

9. Short Trips Around Crawford's

The network of trails around Crawford's—the high plateau above the Gateway of Crawford Notch—is perfect for an afternoon of easy, leisurely exploration on snowshoes. For over a century, this was home to the Crawford House, one of the most popular grand hotels in the White Mountains. Although the hotel itself burned in 1977, several of the outlying buildings have been incorporated into the AMC's Crawford Notch Hostel, including the beautifully restored Victorian railroad station (an information center in summer), the carriage barn, and the studio of nineteenth century artist Frank Shapleigh. The studio building and two adjacent cabins provide heated accommodations in the winter.

From the open fields surrounding the hostel buildings and from nearby US 302, trails radiate to several easy, rewarding objectives. You can link all of these gentle excursions with short strolls along and/or across Rte. 302. The plowed parking area for several of these trails is on the west side of US 302, just south of the hostel. A WMNF parking pass is not required, but is requested by AMC on a voluntary basis. A parking pass is required at the parking areas for Crawford Path and Webster–Jackson Trail.

The high elevation of Crawford's—1900 ft.—ensures good snow cover through much of the winter even for these lowland rambles. All of these trips are covered by the USGS Crawford Notch quad.

Ammonoosuc Lake and Red Bench *1.8 miles round trip, 150-ft. elevation gain, beginner* This easy one- to two-hour snowshoe jaunt leads you around Ammonoosuc Lake, a small gem hidden in spruce woods behind the Crawford House site, and out to Red Bench, where a break in the forest opens a view out to the Presidential Range. From the parking area, follow the driveway north to the hostel and a sign for Around the Lake Trail, with views left to the Willey Range. Turn left here and snowshoe 80 feet down to an old road. Turn left here and descend gradually into the woods. Soon you swing left off the road onto a trail (sign) and descend gently to the loop junction, 0.3 mile from your car.

Steer left here, cross Crawford Brook on a bridge, and meander through spruce forest. Soon you drop to Merrill Spring, near the SW corner of Ammonoosuc Lake. Famously pure water was once pumped from here into the lobby of the Crawford House. The trail proceeds through a fringe of woods along the west shore. Up to the left are the tracks for the Crawford Notch Scenic Railroad. To your right there are views across the pond to the wooded ridges of Mt. Pierce (Clinton). Oddly, the pond was nearly drained in the summer of 2000, so ice conditions may be uncertain.

At 0.6 mile, the Around the Lake Trail rises to a junction at the NW corner of the pond. Here the Red Bench Trail splits to the left. This spur rolls through the woods for 0.2 mile, cuts across the railroad tracks to the west side, and crosses a small brook on a bridge. At 0.3 mile from the junction you arrive at the Red Bench—a nice wooden seat in summer, but not as inviting when buried in snow. The fine view of the snowy Presidentials is even better in winter with the leaves down and includes Mounts Jefferson, Clay, Washington, Monroe, and Eisenhower.

Returning to the Around the Lake Trail, turn left and proceed a short distance above the north shore through spiky spruces. A side path branches right and dips to the pond edge. There's a nice view across the snowy opening to Mounts Jackson and Webster (left) and Mt. Willard (right). The trail soon swings around the NE corner of the pond and runs along the base of a steep little glacial ridge, skirting the east shore. As you emerge from the woods by the narrow neck at the east end of the pond, look right for a view up to Mt. Avalon, then cross a footway over the small dam by the outlet. You snowshoe across a small meadow that was once the site of a beach house for Crawford House guests. Continue up an old road, cross a bridge, and bear right on the Around the Lake Trail back to the loop junction. Go left for the slightly uphill trek of about 0.3 mile back to your car.

Beecher and Pearl Cascades *0.8 mile round trip, 200-ft. elevation gain, beginner* A quick jaunt up the Avalon Trail and a spur loop shows you two frozen waterfalls and fine brook scenery along Crawford Brook. From the parking area, traverse the field towards the Crawford Depot railroad station, cross the railroad tracks and follow the Avalon Trail into the woods. A marker reading "P85" by the tracks indicates that Portland, ME is 85 miles away. You pass the junction with Mount Willard Trail at 0.1 mile and rise gradually through slender hardwoods to a crossing of Crawford Brook at 0.2 mile.

On the far side you climb steadily for 100 yards to the Cascade Loop. Bear left here, climbing easily to a sign and a side path that leads 200 feet back down to the left, ending on a bank overlooking frozen Beecher Cascade and its small enclosing gorge. With care you can descend the path to the foot of the waterfall and a view downstream through a small flume. This was a favorite haunt of the abolitionist preacher, Henry Ward Beecher, who summered in the mountains for many years in the 1800s. In another 0.1 mile the Cascade Loop comes to a sign where you drop left to the brookbed and look upstream through another little flume to the snow curtain of Pearl Cascade. In a cold, deep snow spell it's fun to explore the brook bed itself up to the base of the waterfall. A short distance beyond Pearl Cascade the loop trail links back with Avalon Trail. Turn right for an easy 0.4 mile downhill jaunt back to your car.

Gibbs Falls *1.2 miles round trip, 400-ft. elevation gain, beginner* A short climb along the venerable Crawford Path leads to Gibbs Falls, a modest frozen cas-

Crawford Notch from Elephant Head

cade set deep in an old growth forest of red spruce and yellow birch. Parking for the Crawford Path is now located at a plowed area on the left 0.1 mile up the Mt. Clinton Road, which leaves US 302 0.2 mile north of the Crawford Notch Hostel parking area. From the parking area there's a beautiful view of the Willey Range. The Crawford Connector leaves the north end of the parking lot, leading to the right through a strip of woods and across the road. Bearing right, the trail climbs gradually through deep spruce forest, reaching Gibbs Brook at 0.4 mile, just past a side trail left to Crawford Cliff. (This steep, rough, sidehilly trail is not recommended for snowshoeing.)

Cross the brook on a footbridge and turn left on the Crawford Path, renowned as the oldest continuously used hiking path in America. It was cut in 1819 by the legendary pioneer, Ethan Allen Crawford and his father, Abel, and in 1840 it was upgraded to a bridle path. Over the years it has led many thousands of trampers up to the heights of the Southern Presidentials and on to Mt. Washington. The forest along the Crawford Path is one of the few old-growth stands in the White Mountains. Though they don't quite compare to the redwoods of California, the spruce and birch here are impressive by New England standards, and look especially magnificent with a cloak of snow. Note: The intersection with Crawford Connector is 0.2 mile up Crawford Path from the previous trailhead on US 302; there is no parking at this trailhead but it's just a short walk from the AMC Hostel.

You rise moderately up the Crawford Path for 0.2 mile to a sign and side path left leading down to a bank overlooking Gibbs Falls, a cascade of snow and ice that spills over steep ledges to a frozen pool. The falls are secluded at the back of a small wooded grotto, as pretty a forest setting as you can find on snowshoes. The brook and cascade were named for Col. Joseph Gibbs, a prominent hotelier who managed the nearby Crawford House and Notch House in the 1850s and 1860s.

Upon returning to the trailhead, you can indulge in some playful snowshoeing in the open hilly fields below the parking lot. This area was once the golf course for the Crawford House. It's now a designated sledding and sliding area.

Saco Lake Trail *0.3 mile, no elevation gain, beginner*   This trail makes a short semicircle around the east side of six-acre Saco Lake, the source of the Saco River, beginning and ending on the east side of US 302. The south terminus is found at a parking area near the pond's outlet, while the north end begins across from the AMC Hostel. From the south, the trail crosses the outlet on a footbridge, runs briefly through the woods, crosses an inlet brook on a log bridge, then follows closely along the east shore beneath steep ledges, crossing several bog bridges and offering views of the Willey Range. At the north end, you swing left into a hardwood stand, passing a short spur that leads you up to a small canine burying ground. At 0.3 mile the trail ends at US 302. To loop back to the starting point, snowshoe along the roadside and the west edge of the pond where there are views up to Elephant Head and Mt. Webster. The trailheads are 0.2 mile apart.

Elephant Head *0.6 mile round trip, 150-ft. elevation gain, beginner*   From points nearby to the north, the steep ledge that guards the east side of the Gateway of the Notch does, indeed, look like the noggin of a giant pachyderm. The flat top of the ledge offers a good view of the Notch, the Crawford's area, and surrounding mountains. Snowshoeing up to the top of this miniature mountain is a great way to cap off an exploration of the trails around Crawford's.

Access is provided by the Webster–Jackson Trail and a spur path. There's a plowed roadside parking area on the west side of US 302 just north of the Gateway and south of Saco Lake. The start of the Webster–Jackson Trail is diagonally across the road. Snowshoe gradually upward for 0.1 mile on the W–J Trail, then turn right on the marked spur to Elephant Head.

This 0.2-mile side trail starts with a level section over snow-buried bog bridges, then climbs steadily for 100 yards. After a short breather and another little climb, you dip along the backside of the ledge. Turn right for a short, twisting climb, with a couple of little ledgy scrambles, to the flat top of Elephant Head. Out in front are spacious flat ledges with open views.

To the left you look over the Gateway into the Notch. Mt. Webster rises steeply on the left; to the right are the steep slopes of Mts. Willey and Willard. Beyond the Notch you see Mts. Bemis and Nancy. Close by, above and behind you, is the rock face of Bugle Cliff.

To the right you look down on the Crawford's plateau at a large swamp,

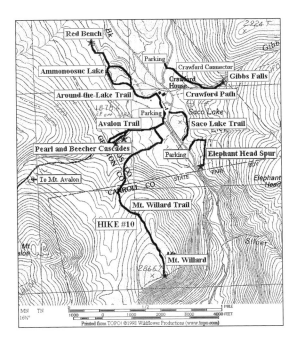

the railroad tracks and station, and Rt. 302 winding around Saco Lake. Mt. Tom looms to the west. Northward is the distant white castle of the Mt. Washington Hotel, backed by broad-spreading Cherry Mtn. Darkly wooded Mt. Deception is on the far right.

The short descent back to the road is a lark on snowshoes.

10. Mt. Willard

LOCATION: Top of Crawford Notch

DESCRIPTION: A relatively easy climb to a summit cliff with a gaping view south through Crawford Notch

TRAILS: Avalon Trail, Mount Willard Trail

DISTANCE: 3.2 miles round trip

STARTING ELEVATION: 1900 ft.

HIGHEST ELEVATION: 2800 ft.

ELEVATION GAIN: 900 ft.

RATING: Beginner/intermediate

USGS MAP: Crawford Notch

TRAILHEAD: This hike begins at the location known as "Crawford's," where the AMC's Crawford Notch Hostel is set beside US 302 on a plateau above the Gateway of the Notch. This area is 8.5 miles east of the stoplight in Twin Mountain and 20 miles west of North Conway. A plowed parking area is provided on the west side of the road, south of the hostel buildings.

WMNF PARKING PASS: Not required, but requested by AMC on a voluntary basis.

Mt. Willard is one of the classic beginner/intermediate snowshoe trips in the White Mountains. The climb of this small mountain is fairly easy, partly following the route of an old carriage road, and the view of Crawford Notch from the top is astounding, inspiring this classic line from earlier editions of the *AMC White Mountain Guide*: "From perhaps no other point in the mountains can so grand a view be obtained with so little effort." It's one of the most popular winter climbs in the region, so you'll often find a well-packed snowshoe track.

From the parking area cross the field towards the beautifully restored old railroad station, which serves as an information center in summer. Cold winds often blow across the open fields here. Cross the railroad tracks behind the station and follow the Avalon Trail into the woods.

After 0.1 mile of level going the Mount Willard Trail splits off to the left opposite a kiosk and traverses southward for 100 yards, crossing a small brook, then bears right and begins a moderate ascent of the mountain's lower slopes. At 0.5 mile you pass a sign for the small "Centennial Pool" in the brook down to your right. Here you steer left for a steeper climb of 0.2 mile.

At the top of this pitch you turn right onto the wide, easy-graded route of the old carriage road, which once led genteel guests from the old Crawford House via horse and wagon up to the summit ledges. The original carriage road was built in 1846 by Thomas Crawford, brother of Ethan Allen Crawford and at that time proprietor of the nearby Notch House. The route soon swerves left and heads south up the slope. Off to the right there are glimpses of Mt. Avalon's craggy face. The long, easy grade leads to a left turn at 1.2 miles. In another 0.1 mile you bend right for the final gentle approach to the summit, cutting through a corridor of snow-caked conifers. A spur trail to Hitchcock Flume (steep and treacherous at the end, not recommended in winter) diverges left at 1.5 miles, and soon you break out from the tunnel of trees to the open clifftop.

The view explodes before you as you emerge from the forest. Mt. Willard blocks the top of Crawford Notch like a huge chockstone and is perfectly positioned for a sweeping vista down the U-shaped trough. It's a classic example of a valley deepened and widened by the grinding power of the continental glaciers. The Webster Cliffs rise on the left in a long line

A rest break atop Mt. Willard

of snowstreaked crags. The steep slopes of Mt. Willey and the nearer Mt. Field loom on the right. Route 302 and the Saco River slither along the broad floor of the Notch, with the parallel cut of the Crawford Notch Railroad up on the lower slopes of Willey. Look closely and you may spot climbers clawing their way up the icy Willey Slide above the tracks.

A few miles south the valley bends left around the wooded backside of Frankenstein Cliff. Distant peaks line the horizon beyond. Mts. Nancy and Bemis are on the right, with the tip of Mt. Tremont peering over an eastern shoulder of Bemis. The spire of Mt. Chocorua rises in the center, over Bartlett Haystack. Bear Mtn., Table Mtn. and West Moat Mtn. are seen to the left.

There's plenty of room to range on either side behind the cliffs, but keep back from the edge. At the left (east) end of the ledges you can peer across at several Presidential peaks to the left of Mt. Webster. Mt. Jackson, with a small snowy cone, and wooded Mt. Pierce loom large and close. Eisenhower's bald dome and the barren, tower-topped crest of Mt. Washington peer over on the left. Mts. Clay and Jefferson can be seen around the corner.

After absorbing the views, point your snowshoes northward for a quick return trip down the Mount Willard Trail. The mountain's gentle north slope presents a sharp contrast to the sheer cliff on the south. The continental ice sheet flowed easily up the north side, then plucked off the rock face on the south as it rode down into the valley beyond. You can thank the glacier for the easy route to these splendid views.

Mt. Avalon *3.8 miles round trip, 1550-ft. elevation gain, intermediate/advanced*
The ascent to 3442-ft. Mt. Avalon, a craggy spur on the side of Mt. Field, is a slightly longer but considerably more challenging alternative to Mt. Willard. Start at the same trailhead at Crawford's and continue straight on Avalon Trail where the Mount Willard Trail goes left at 0.1 mile. You soon cross Crawford Brook and ascend easily past a side loop to Beecher and Pearl Cascades (see chapter on "Short Trips at Crawford's"). At 0.8 mile you cross back over the brook and climb more steadily to a junction with A-Z Trail at 1.3 miles (elevation 2700 ft.). Turn left here with the Avalon Trail.

For the next 0.5 mile the climbing is quite steep through coniferous woods, requiring vigorous use of your snowshoe crampons. At 1.8 miles the grade eases and a side trail splits left for a steep, scrambly climb of 0.1 mile to the open summit of Mt. Avalon. The views here are superb. Looking SE you see the Webster Cliffs and the winding trough of Crawford Notch from a higher perspective than Mt. Willard. The snow-shrouded Presidentials are a striking sight to the NE, and you look straight down at frozen Saco Lake at the base of Mt. Pierce. To the north is the Dartmouth Range beyond the broad plain of Bretton Woods. Close by on the west are Tom, Field and Willey, the high, wooded peaks of the Willey Range.

Before negotiating the steep descent below the summit side trail, it's worth turning left on Avalon Trail and snowshoeing a short distance to an interesting flat area of snow-crusted ledges with views of the upper Willey Range and out to Mts. Pierce, Jackson & Webster.

Mt. Tom *5.8 miles round trip, 2150-ft. elevation gain, intermediate/advanced*
The rounded summit of Mt. Tom, the northernmost peak of the Willey Range, is one of the easier 4000-footers to scale in the winter and provides a nice woodsy climb. The route up has mostly moderate grades. In recent years, the expansion of a blowdown patch has amplified the summit views considerably, especially in winter. After parking at the AMC Crawford Notch Hostel, follow the Avalon Trail on a moderate climb for 1.3 miles to the junction with A-Z Trail (elevation 2700 ft.) Continue ahead on A-Z Trail, going down and up a steep little gully (a potentially tough spot) and ascending steadily up the south side of the ravine of Crawford Brook. The open forest here features some large old yellow birches. At 1.9 miles, after a steep sidehill, you cross the brook and angle steeply up to the right, slabbing the headwall of the cirque-like valley. A left turn elevates you to the col between Mt. Tom and Mt. Field at 2.3 miles (elevation 3700 ft). Turn right here on the Mt. Tom Spur, a narrow, wild trail where you may have to bang snow off overhanging fir branches. As you snowshoe your way gradually upward through the snow-caked forest, you'll find occasional openings with peek-a-

boo views to Crawford Notch, the Presidentials and the Pemigewasset Wilderness. At 2.9 miles you attain the 4051-ft. summit. On the west side, a "fir wave"—a band of dead trees created by the stress of ice, cold, and wind—has created a spacious sunny opening with a fine vista over the Zealand and Pemigewasset Wilderness area. In late winter, with a platform of snow three or four feet deep, the view is even better. It's a wild panorama, a sweep of dark, snow-speckled ridges with few visible signs of man, taking in Mts. Field, Carrigain, Hancock, Bond, Guyot, Zealand, South Twin and North Twin. An hour and a half snowshoe slide should suffice to get you down to your car from the summit.

Mts. Field and Willey *8.4 miles round trip, 3100-ft. elevation gain, advanced*
The two highest summits in the Willey Range, Mt. Field (4340 ft.) and Mt. Willey (4285 ft.) can be linked with Mt. Avalon to create a satisfying all day snowshoe journey. Ascend the Avalon Trail to Mt. Avalon (see below) then continue on the same trail, crossing a ledgy flat with views up to the higher summits. Soon you begin the fairly steep climb up the NE side of Mt. Field, with some limited views back through the trees. Higher up, the grades eases somewhat in close-growing firs, and a long traverse brings you to the Willey Range Trail at 2.8 miles. Turn left for the short climb to the summit of Mt. Field. The former view through a blowdown area west to the Pemigewasset Wilderness is mostly grown up. There is a partial view NE to the Presidential Range and the Bretton Woods area.

Point your snowshoes southward along the Willey Range Trail towards Mt. Willey. Three sharp pitches get you down off the cone of Field, then you enjoy a nice ridgecrest meander through the snowy firs, with several little ups and downs. Follow the blue blazes carefully. The climb up to Willey is quite easy, and at 4.2 miles you emerge at a sunny, west-facing outlook with a wild and powerful view over the eastern Pemigewasset Wilderness. A broad spruce-covered upland extends for miles out to Mt. Carrigain, Mt. Hancock, and the Bond-Twin Range. You look almost straight down at the white splotch of Ethan Pond, 1500 feet below. The summit high point is just a few yards beyond this outlook. Continue a bit farther to the open east outlook for a fabulous view of the Presidential Range and the Webster Cliffs. Willey's summit drops off sharply on three sides—there are few places where you're perched on such a high and detached place. The return trip involves a 350-ft. climb back over Mt. Field, then it's a quick slide down the Avalon Trail.

11. Mt. Pierce (Clinton)

LOCATION: Crawford Notch/Southern Presidentials

DESCRIPTION: A steady climb up the venerable Crawford Path to an open summit at the edge of the alpine zone.

TRAILS: Crawford Connector, Crawford Path, Webster Cliff Trail

DISTANCE: 6.4 miles round trip

STARTING ELEVATION: 1920 ft.

HIGHEST ELEVATION: 4310 ft.

ELEVATION GAIN: 2400 ft.

RATING: Advanced

USGS MAPS: Crawford Notch, Stairs Mtn.

TRAILHEAD: The recently relocated trailhead for Crawford Path is at a plowed parking area 0.1 mile up Mt. Clinton Road, which leaves the east side of US 302 0.2 mile north of the parking lot at the AMC Crawford Notch Hostel. The parking lot is on the left.

WMNF PARKING PASS: Yes

The snowshoe trek to Mt. Pierce offers experienced snowshoers a tantalizing taste of the wild winter world above treeline with only a minimum of exposure. Most of the ascent is on the moderately graded Crawford Path through an endless gallery of snow-plastered evergreens. The route is often well-packed by snowshoes. A short alpine traverse (crampons may be needed for ice and crust) leads to the open summit and excellent views of the higher Presidentials and many other peaks. On a fine winter day, this is an unforgettable adventure—it was my first high mountain in winter, and I've been hooked ever since.

From the parking area, follow the Crawford Connector across the Mt. Clinton Road and easily uphill for 0.4 mile to the Crawford Path, crossing Gibbs Brook on a bridge just before the junction. Turn left here to join a trail that is ancient by American standards. In 1819, Ethan Allan Crawford, the famed innkeeper, woodsman, guide, and all-around mountain man, and his

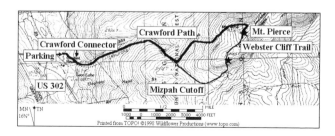

father, Abel, built this path along the ridge of the Southern Presidentials to Mt. Washington—not for pleasure, but to serve the increasing flow of visitors who wished to be led to the top of the greatest White Mountain. Crawford guided many of his inn guests along this route, and even hauled an occasional indisposed tramper along on his back up the more difficult sections. In 1840, the Crawfords upgraded the trail to make it passable for horses.

The trail climbs at moderate, horse-friendly grades for nearly the entire ascent, and in winter, the oft-rocky footing is masked by the usually deep snow cover. After passing the side path left to frozen Gibbs Falls, 0.6 mile from your car, you enter the Gibbs Brook Scenic Area. This designation protects one of the few old-growth forest stands in the White Mountains. Some of the virgin red spruce here are 80 to 90 feet high with trunks two feet thick.

Steady climbing through this deep forest hoists you to the junction with Mizpah Cut-Off at 1.9 miles (elevation 3380 ft.), a good spot to take a breather. Continue straight here on Crawford Path, which slabs up the west side of Mt. Pierce through snow-caked, lichen-tufted firs. Along this stretch you may be visited by Gray (Canada) Jays, tame residents of the north woods that look somewhat like oversized chickadees and will happily partake of any food offerings you present. An occasional peek through the trees reveals distant western horizons.

The trees diminish in stature as you rise past the 4000 ft. mark, and around 2.9 miles the grade eases amidst scrub firs that may be buried in drifted, windpacked snow. If unbroken, the trail may be difficult to follow on this often windswept traverse. On more than one visit, the yellow sign warning of severe conditions above treeline has been completely smothered in snow. A few years back, two hikers lost the trail while descending this section and ended up sustaining serious frostbite after a bitter night in the woods. Note that on windy days your tracks can be blown in very quickly. Also, it's a good idea to bundle up before you get too far along this exposed section.

As you snowshoe through these fantastically sculpted dwarf firs, you have views ahead to the huge snow-dome of Mt. Eisenhower up the ridge, and the giant Washington beyond. The last short stretch to the sign marking the junction with Webster Cliff Trail is completely in the open.

Turn right here for a short, moderate climb through open alpine terrain on the Webster Cliff Trail. There may be just enough snow here for passage with snowshoes. If crusty or icy conditions prevail, you may need to resort to crampons. You'll find that usually there's little snow above treeline—most of it is blown off by the relentless winter winds. Try to stay on the defined trail and off any fragile alpine vegetation. The trail crests the broad summit dome of Pierce amidst ever-expanding views. You reach the actual high spot 0.1 mile from the junction. The summit's name honors New Hampshire's only U.S. President, Franklin Pierce. Before that name was

Packed powder on Mt. Pierce

bestowed in 1913 by the New Hampshire Legislature, the peak was known as Mt. Clinton, after Gov. DeWitt Clinton of New York, who held office in the early 1800s. The Mt. Clinton name still appears on some maps.

The views are wide open most of the way around. Dozens of peaks, valleys, and ridges can be spotted, including 30 White Mountain 4000-footers. The most dramatic winter vignette is looking NE up the ridge to Eisenhower, Monroe, and Washington, with Jefferson on the left and Boott Spur on the right. Montalban Ridge is to the east and the Sandwich Range is prominent to the south. On clear days, Camel's Hump, Mt. Mansfield, and Jay Peak can be seen far off to the NW in Vermont. The summit is hemmed in by high scrub on the west side, but you can still see out to the Willey Range and other peaks around the Pemigewasset Wilderness.

Once down below the scrub line, the Crawford's Path's equable grade provides "no stress" snowshoeing all the way back to the trailhead.

ADDITIONAL OPTIONS

Loop Option   A nice circuit can be made by following the Webster Cliff Trail south to the AMC's Mizpah Spring Hut (closed in winter) and angling back to Crawford Path via Mizpah Cutoff. From the summit of Mt. Pierce, the southbound Webster Cliff Trail eases into scrubby woods, with occasional views SW, and dips to a low point. You climb a bit to the semi-open SW summit of Pierce at 0.5 mile with a view back to Washington looming over the main summit. You soon descend to a nice open ledge with views to Mt. Willey, Mt. Jackson, and many other peaks. The trail now descends very steeply for 0.2 mile—sliding on your snowshoes may be in order at a couple of spots. The hut is reached at the bottom of the downgrade, 0.8 mile from the summit of Pierce. In another 0.1 mile, Mizpah Cut-Off peels off to the right. Follow this moderate trail for 0.7 mile back to Crawford Path and bear left for the 1.9-mile descent to the trailhead. Total distance for the loop option is only 0.5 mile longer than a direct return down Crawford Path, with only a token bit of additional climbing.

Mt. Jackson *5.2 miles round trip, 2150-ft. elevation gain, advanced* The rocky summit of Mt. Jackson (4052 ft.) in the southern Presidentials is a great objective for a fairly short but rugged snowshoe climb. You're in snow-caked evergreen woods from start to finish, including old-growth spruce in the lower part, so this trip is especially attractive in winter. There are several steep pitches in the woods en route, and a final difficult scramble up the ledges of the summit cone that may require crampons. The summit views are excellent in all directions. Park in the plowed space across from the Webster–Jackson Trail on the west side of US 302 just north of the Gateway of the Notch. The blue-blazed Webster–Jackson Trail climbs moderately at first, then lurches up several very steep, rocky pitches interspersed with level stretches. In this section, at 0.6 mile, a short side trail right leads over a rise to the brink of Bugle Cliff and a fine view of the Notch—use great caution here. You climb to a crossing of Flume Cascade Brook at 0.9 mile and reach a fork in the trail at 1.4 miles (elevation 2800 ft.) Bear left on the Jackson Branch for a long, steady climb through a winter wonderland forest of spruce and fir.

At about 3800 ft. the trail swings left through an area of dead trees, where it may be very hard to follow. Then you turn right for the difficult scramble of 200 yards or so up the ledges on the west side of the summit cone. The flat, rocky top is fully exposed to bitter winter winds, but the views are astonishing. Looking NE, the ridge of the Southern Presidentials leads up over the snow-covered peaks of Pierce, Eisenhower, Franklin, and Monroe to the imposing bulk of Washington. On the east, the long, remote valley of the Dry River stretches up to the headwall of Oakes Gulf below Washington, and across to the darkly-wooded Montalban Ridge. To the SW are the mighty Mt. Carrigain and the huddled peaks of the Sandwich Range. The Willey Range looms close by on the west, with the Twins and Franconia Ridge beyond. Northward are the fields of Bretton Woods and the Dartmouth and Pliny Ranges. On the descent, use caution on the steep ledges just below the summit.

Note: Ambitious snowshoers can fashion an attractive snowshoe loop along the ridge-top Webster Cliff Trail in either direction from the summit of Jackson. On both sides, there are steep ledges down off the summit. To the south it's 1.4 miles to the 3910-ft. summit of Mt. Webster, where there are awesome views into Crawford Notch, and then 2.5 miles back down the Webster branch of the Webster–Jackson Trail to the trailhead. Just before

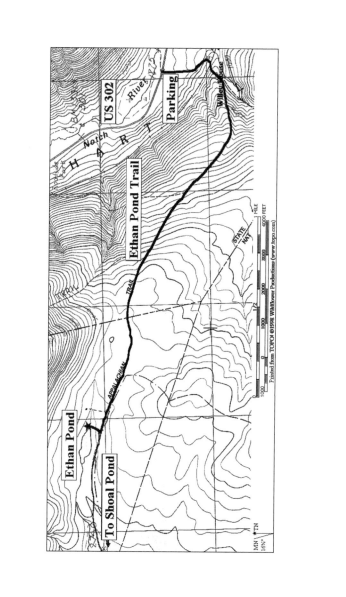

reaching the junction of the two branches, there is a steep down-and-up crossing of Silver Cascade Brook that is difficult on snowshoes. The total loop is 6.5 miles with 2400 ft. of elevation gain.

To the north, it's a nice 1.7-mile wooded deep-snow ridge walk to the AMC's Mizpah Spring Hut (closed in winter), with nice views from an open alpine meadow about 0.4 mile along. To descend, take Mizpah Cut-Off (0.7 mile) and the lower Crawford Path (1.7 miles) to its former trailhead on US 302, then turn left for a 0.2-mile road walk (liable to be cold and windy) back to your car. The total loop is 6.9 miles / 2300 ft.

12. Ethan Pond

LOCATION: Crawford Notch

DESCRIPTION: A steady climb through fine woods to a high, isolated pond with mountain views

TRAILS: Road off US 302, Ethan Pond Trail

DISTANCE: 6.0 miles round trip

STARTING ELEVATION: 1275 ft.

HIGHEST ELEVATION: 2900 ft.

ELEVATION GAIN: 1800 ft.

RATING: Intermediate

USGS MAP: Crawford Notch

TRAILHEAD: In winter, the hike to Ethan Pond starts on US 302 at the Appalachian Trail crossing in Crawford Notch. The spur road that climbs up to the summer trailhead is not plowed. A parking area is usually plowed at the entrance to the side road, across the highway from the Webster Cliff Trail. This is about one mile south of the Willey House Historical Site.

WMNF PARKING PASS: No

Ethan Pond, windswept and desolate in winter, nestles on a high plateau on the edge of the vast Pemigewasset Wilderness. A feeling of supreme wintry isolation and some striking mountain views are your rewards for a moderately strenuous trek up the Ethan Pond Trail, part of the Georgia-to-Maine Appalachian Trail. This is a snowshoe trip that beckons year after year.

From Rt. 302, climb up the side road for 0.3 mile. Often a snowshoe track will already be broken up the middle of the snow-blanketed roadway. At the top there's a wider clearing—the summer trailhead for Ethan Pond Trail.

The white-blazed trail continues up into the woods and quickly crosses the tracks of the Crawford Notch railroad. This line was an engineering marvel when it was pushed through the notch in the 1870s.

During its heyday in the late 1800s and early 1900s, guests travelling up to grand hotels such as the Crawford House, The Mount Washington and Fabyan House would gawk at the dramatic views and trestles along the way. Automobile travel spelled the demise of passenger service on this line by 1960, but in 1995 the Conway Scenic Railroad re-opened this historic rail ride and now runs scenic tours through the notch in summer and fall.

After crossing the tracks, where's there a view of Mt. Willey to the right, the trail traverses a bank and climbs to a junction 0.5 mile from your car. Here the blue-blazed Arethusa-Ripley Falls Trail continues ahead (leading to the base of Ripley Falls in 0.3 mile). Your route, the Ethan Pond Trail, turns right and commences a steep climb up a gullied old logging road— the toughest snowshoeing stretch of the day. For 0.3 mile you slog upward between tall white birches. Then the grade gets progressively easier as you slab NW across a slope of fine hardwood forest. Through the trees there are views across the notch to the long snowy battlement of the Webster Cliffs.

At 1.6 miles the steep Kedron Flume Trail (not recommended in winter) comes in on the right. Ethan Pond Trail continues ahead, climbing roly-poly through darker woods. There's another junction at 1.9 miles. Here the Willey Range Trail proceeds ahead for a very steep climb to Mt. Willey. Turn left here on Ethan Pond Trail for a steady climb of 0.3 mile to the broad, rolling height-of-land (elevation 2900 ft.) that connects Mt. Willey with the trailless, nameless ridge to the south.

The snow piles deep in here amidst wild woods of spruce and fir, with a scattering of heart-leaved birch and mountain ash. You pass by a boggy area and over a couple of rises and dips. A gentle descent, where bog bridges are hidden beneath the snow, marks your entrance into the vast wilderness watershed drained by the East Branch of the Pemigewasset River. Ethan Pond forms the headwater of the East Branch's North Fork, and is sometimes considered the ultimate source of the great Merrimack River. The trail you're snowshoeing is the boundary between two large tracts of protected National Forest land—the Lincoln Woods Scenic Area on the right (north) and the Pemigewasset Wilderness on the left (south).

Descend gently for another half mile through the boggy spruce woods that typify this high plateau. At 2.9 miles a sign marks the side trail to Ethan Pond. Turn right here and meander down this blue-blazed spur, reaching the inlet at the east end of the pond in 0.15 mile. As you approach the frozen pond you may have to clamber over big snowdrifts piled up by the prevailing westerly winds. Look up through the trees and you may be startled by the huge looming bulk of Mt. Willey.

Layer up and don your shades before stepping out onto the white, windswept expanse of the six-acre pond. It's solidly frozen for most of the winter

Mt. Willey strikes a rugged pose above Ethan Pond

and is usually quite safe to traverse—but use caution early and late in the season and avoid the ice at the far west end, where the North Fork flows out from the pond.

From where you emerge at the east end there's a magnificent vista westward to the Twin Range on the horizon. Left to right, you can spot Mt. Bond, Mt. Guyot (a snowy double hump), Zealand Ridge and the rocky crown of South Twin. Close by on your right a long, cliff-faced arm of Mt. Willey encloses the pond. East of the pond a spur trail leads up to a lean-to and tent platforms set back in the woods.

One of the sweetest snowshoeing pleasures in the Whites is a traverse westward across the snowy expanse of Ethan Pond, wind and ice conditions permitting. The openness and mountain views are exhilarating. Looking back, the steep looming face of Mt. Willey is an impressive, ice-draped sight. There's a wild, almost primeval feel to this place. It seems little changed from the days when Ethan Allen Crawford, the famed "giant of the hills," discovered the pond in 1829 and later guided fishing parties there in pursuit of its abundant trout.

Though for a time this was called Willey Pond, it later came to bear the name of its discoverer, who was renowned as a guide, innkeeper, hunter, trail-builder, raconteur and all-around woodsman. According to John H. Spaulding's *Historical Relics of the White Mountains*, published in 1855, Crawford happened upon the pond one day while setting a trapline. "The fresh signs of moose near, and trouts seen in its shining waters, was sufficient inducement to spend a night by its shady shore," wrote Spaulding. After snaring a string of trout, he spotted two large moose and dropped them with a pair of quick shots. "That night a doleful dirge rose in that wild gorge; but our hero slept soundly between two warm moose-skins. He cared not for the wild wolves that scented the taint of the fresh blood in the wind. That little mountain sheet is now, from the above circumstance, known as 'Ethan's Pond.'" Maybe not entirely accurate, but a great story!

On your return trip, once over the height-of-land, the Ethan Pond Trail is just the right grade for a delightful snowshoe descent.

ADDITIONAL OPTIONS

Shoal Pond *From trailhead: 11.2 miles round trip, 2250-ft. elevation gain, advanced* For a remote, full-day venture into the eastern Pemigewasset Wilderness, you can extend the Ethan Pond trip on to Shoal Pond, a picturesque oval secluded on a broad spruce plateau SW of the Willey Range. The route follows the Ethan Pond Trail and Shoal Pond Trail over gently sloping terrain. This territory is also popular with backcountry skiers, so please be courteous—don't snowshoe on an established ski track, and if the trail is unbroken, leave adequate room for a ski track alongside your snowshoe track.

From the side trail to Ethan Pond, the Ethan Pond Trail leads westward through spruce forest with a very gradual downgrade. Approaching a boggy area, the trail takes off on a recent relocation to the right through an open forest of fir, spruce, and birch, and after about 0.6 mile you swing back to the original route. Soon you pass a lovely spot on the trail beside an open, ledgy part of the North Fork. At 2.0 miles from Ethan Pond, the Shoal Pond Trail splits left on the old grade of J. E. Henry's Zealand valley logging railroad, which operated in the 1880s. Follow the easy, straight corridor through wild spruce woods for 0.7 mile to Shoal Pond, a bright, white expanse to the right of the trail. If the ice is solid, snowshoe out to the pond for majestic views south to the imposing bulk of Mt. Carrigain and its satellite, Vose Spur, and north to Zealand Ridge and Whitewall Mtn. framing Zealand Notch. From the west edge of the pond, you'll get a view back to the Willey Range. On a calm sunny day the beauty and isolation of Shoal Pond is almost heart-rending.

Other nearby snowshoe destinations include Thoreau Falls and Zealand Notch. The falls are topped by a broad snowy ledge with a wild view up to Mts. Bond and Guyot. To get there, snowshoe an easy 0.5 mile west on Ethan Pond Trail beyond Shoal Pond Trail, crossing a bridge over the North Fork, then turn left on Thoreau Falls Trail and descend 0.1 mile to the view ledge. If you continue another 0.7 mile on Ethan Pond Trail, following the railroad grade on a northward curve, you'll come out into an open area of rock slides in Zealand Notch—use caution if the snow is crusty. Here there are memorable views up the Notch to Mt. Hale, back to Mts. Carrigain and Hancock, and across to the high snowy crags of Zeacliff.

Note: Zealand Notch, Thoreau Falls, Shoal Pond, Ethan Pond, and Zea-cliff, with its spectacular views, can also be snowshoed from a base at the cozy and picturesque AMC Zealand Falls Hut, which remains open throughout the winter on a caretaker basis. The usual approach to the hut is from the Zealand winter parking area on the north side of US 302, 2.5 miles east of the junction with US 3 in Twin Mountain. Walk west up Rt. 302 for 0.3 mile, then turn left on Zealand Road (sometimes plowed for logging operations, but not open to auto traffic). There's a 3.5-mile slog up Zealand Road to its end, then you follow the Zealand Trail for 2.5 gentle miles up the pretty Zealand valley, passing numerous beaver ponds and meadows in the last mile, with views of Zealand Ridge and Mt. Tom. At the junction with the Twinway by Zealand Pond, turn right for a steep 0.2-mile climb to the hut. From the front of the hut there's a gorgeous vista through Zealand Notch to Mt. Carrigain. You must bring your own food and a winter-rated sleeping bag.

From the hut a stiff 1.3-mile, 1100-ft. snowshoe climb brings you to the airy perch atop Zeacliff, opening a stunning panorama across the eastern Pemigewasset Wilderness to Mts. Carrigain and Hancock on the horizon. The descent from here is fast under the right conditions. One March day with deep firm snow we whooped our way from Zeacliff down to the hut in less than twenty minutes.

13. Dry River Trail

LOCATION: Crawford Notch

DESCRIPTION: A short, easy ramble into the Presidential Range–Dry River Wilderness with secluded views of the Dry River; option to continue for a short but difficult climb to a unique view of Mt. Washington

TRAIL: Dry River Trail

DISTANCE: River View Option, 1.8 miles round trip; Mt. Washington View Option, 3.0 miles round trip

STARTING ELEVATION: 1205 ft.

HIGHEST ELEVATION: 1400 ft.; 1700 ft.

ELEVATION GAIN: 200 ft.; 500 ft.

RATING: Beginner; Intermediate / advanced

USGS MAP: Stairs Mtn.

TRAILHEAD: The Dry River Trail starts on the east side of US 302 in the lower end of Crawford Notch State Park, 2.6 miles south of the Willey House site and 0.3 mile north of the entrance to Dry River Campground. A parking area is usually plowed along the side of the road.

WMNF PARKING PASS: No

The valley of the Dry River extends ten miles from its remote headwaters in Oakes Gulf on the south side of Mt. Washington down to the Saco River in lower Crawford Notch. Bounded on the west by the Southern Presidentials and on the east by Montalban Ridge, this rough, wild country forms the secluded core of the 27,000-acre Presidential Range–Dry River Wilderness. The Dry River Trail traverses the length of the valley. It is lightly used even in summer, and in winter few hikers venture into its snowy enfoldments.

Beginning snowshoers can probe the lower edge of the valley with an easy trip that yields nice vistas of the boulder-choked Dry River and a surprising sense of isolation. Experienced 'shoers can continue a half mile upstream, tackling a short but challenging climb to a tree-framed vista of Mt. Washington at the head of the valley. In either case this is a fine trail for a leisurely afternoon of snowshoeing.

The Dry River Trail starts behind a wooden gate beside US 302. From here you can look back up at the side of brooding Frankenstein Cliff. You may hear the shouts of ice climbers clawing up one of the many frozen flows on this popular climbing spot. Beyond an information kiosk, the trail is wide and gentle as it follows an old woods road NE across a plateau of open hardwoods. Looking left through the trees there are glimpses of Mt. Willey and the southern spurs of Mt. Webster. After 0.5 mile of this pleasant snowshoeing you reach a junction with two trails. A spur path from Dry River Campground (closed in winter) comes in from the right, and to the left is the Saco River Trail, opened in 1999 and leading 2.8 miles north along the floor of the Notch to the Willey House site.

At this point the Dry River Trail joins the grade of a logging railroad that was pushed five miles up the valley in the 1890s. All the cutting was accomplished from 1892–1898. The conservative logging tactics employed by the Saco Valley Railroad shone in comparison to the clear-cutting of J. E. Henry in the Pemigewasset Wilderness to the west—the landowner restricted harvesting to trees eight inches or more in diameter at the stump. The area became part of the White Mountain National Forest in 1932 and was designated as Wilderness in 1975.

The going is easy as you rise gently along the old railroad grade. Soon the walls of the valley close in on either side, with the Dry River just a hundred feet off through the hemlock woods to your right. There are few walks in the White Mountains that can envelop you with a feeling of remoteness as quickly as the Dry River Trail. At 0.6 mile an open corridor to the right invites you to amble over to the bank and look down on the icebound river.

At 0.7 mile a signpost announces that you are entering the Wilderness.

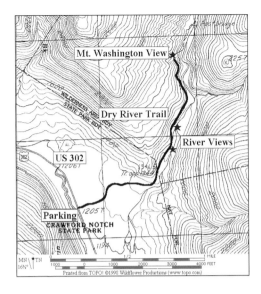

Now the unblazed trail makes a brief jog left around an auxiliary streambed, then angles back to the right and picks up the railroad grade again. Along the next 0.2 mile of this wide, level corridor there are several places where you can easily break off to the right through open woods for a look at the river. At this point it is strewn with huge snowcapped boulders. There's one flat sunny rock that you can snowshoe out onto for a view south down the wild stream to the high ridges of Mt. Bemis. Farther upstream is another vantage overlooking a large icebound pool in the river. (No matter how frozen it looks, this ice should be considered suspect. There is a swift and profoundly chilly current beneath.)

A short distance beyond, at 0.9 mile, the trail turns sharp left off the railroad grade at an arrow on a post. A short path on the right drops you down for one more look at the river. With caution, you can snowshoe out to an elevated snowy rock for a sunny perch and a better look in both directions. This is the turnaround point for the beginner's "River View Option."

Beyond here the Dry River Trail becomes more difficult. In accordance with Wilderness regulations, which mandate that trails provide a primitive recreation experience, there are no paint blaze markings. If there is no snowshoe track, following the trail as it meanders through the open hardwoods requires close attention to route-finding. Winter blowdowns can add to the confusion.

From this point the Dry River Trail also encounters rougher terrain. The lower valley is a sharp, almost canyonlike cut with little level ground. To keep a constant grade, the Saco Valley Railroad had to make numerous river crossings. After logging operations ended, the Dry River, a fast riser, washed out the trestles and parts of the railroad grade. In more recent times several up-and-down trail relocations have been made to bypass washouts and hazardous river crossings. This path is tougher than you would expect for a valley/railroad grade route. The next half mile to the Mt. Washington viewpoint is a case in point. Continue on only if you're sure you can find the way and handle some steep sidehill terrain. If the snow is glazed and "bulletproof," turn back here.

To proceed to the Mt. Washington view, bear left at the arrow, climb slightly, then swing right in front of several large boulders. The trail angles up across the slope on a mild sidehill until you gain a hardwood shelf a hundred feet above the river. You wander along the edge of this steep drop, with nice looks down at the snowy riverbed. The trail is obscure, but it mostly stays along the brink, passing a huge sawed trunk and crossing a tiny brook, then pulls slightly to the left to climb a knoll. It returns to the edge and soon angles down to the right back to river level, opposite a steep 2257-ft. knob on the far side.

Here, at 1.2 miles, you turn left onto the railroad grade for 0.1 mile. Again you cut left off the grade, this time to meander along the river's edge —a scenic 100-yard stretch. Then you veer left, up and away from the river, and begin an angled ascent up a steep hardwood slope—the most difficult stretch of the trip. The next 0.2 mile will challenge your sidehill technique. If you're lucky someone will have stamped out a platform ahead of you. After crossing a little streambed and nosing around a bulge, the trail continues on the level into a spruce grove. After one short steep pitch the going is easy as you swing around to the front of a wooded bluff that drops precipitously on the north side.

Around the corner, at 1.5 miles, you'll find the vista, a restricted but gorgeous one framed by spruce boughs. You look ten miles up the valley, beyond the snow-brushed river and waves of enclosing ridges, to the shining white cone of Mt. Washington. Below the great tower-topped peak is the rugged headwall of Oakes Gulf, the most remote of the glacial cirques in the Presidentials. The Dry River Trail eventually climbs up the left side of this bowl en route to the Lakes of the Clouds. The sharp peak of Mt. Monroe is to the left, the bare ridge of Boott Spur to the right. The view through this shady spruce window looks like a vision of Shangri-la. Here you can sense the sweep and solitude of this Dry River country.

Beyond, the trail becomes even trickier, making a steep descent to a suspension footbridge that can be seen on the river below. Only a few hardy snowshoers venture past here in winter. After enjoying the view, return to your car by the same route, using caution on the sidehill descent.

ADDITIONAL OPTIONS

Sam Willey Trail *1.0 mile round trip, minimal elevation gain, beginner* This pleasant path offers easy snowshoeing along the Saco River in the heart of

Crawford Notch. Park in the plowed area on the east side of US 302 at the Willey House site, with impressive views up to the snow-streaked Webster Cliffs. Cross the wooden dam over the Saco River and turn right at a T-junction in the woods. The Sam Willey Trail leads you southward along a wide corridor through hardwoods on the floor of the Notch. At 0.3 mile, the trail splits into a loop. Taking the left branch, you soon come to a junction where the new Saco River Trail continues downstream, leading 0.6 mile to the Webster Cliff Trail and 2.3 miles to the Dry River Trail. Bear right here on the west end of the Sam Willey Loop, passing through a clearing beside the frozen Saco and another with a view up to Webster Cliffs. The loop bears right along an alder swamp with partial views and leads back to the loop junction. Turn left to return to the Willey House site. You can extend the walk with a short jaunt around the Pond Loop Trail north of the junction by the dam. From the shore of "Willey Pond" (drained in winter) there are open views up to Mts. Willey, Avalon and Willard. Looking up at the imposing slope of Willey, you can picture the devastating landslide that tore down the mountainside in August, 1826, burying the seven members of the Willey family and two hired hands. To this day, it is the most compelling single event in the history of the White Mountains.

Mt. Crawford *5.0 miles round trip, 2100-ft. elevation gain, intermediate/advanced*   The open rock peak of Mt. Crawford (3119 ft.) is one of the best viewpoints in the Whites. It's well worth the grind-it-out climb up the Davis Path. The upper part of the route traverses many open ledges where wind gear and good snowshoe crampons or boot crampons may be needed, depending on conditions. The plowed trailhead parking area for Davis Path is on the east side of US 302 near the Notchland Inn, 5.6 miles south of the Willey House site in Crawford Notch.

The trail follows a road north along the Saco River, then turns right to cross on a large new bridge built in 2000. Follow the left edge of the field, turn left to a crossing over a small brook, then right on the far side. You meander through the woods at easy grades. After crossing a brookbed, you enter the Presidential Range–Dry River Wilderness and the climbing begins —easy at first, then steady and relentless, following the grade of the old bridle path laboriously built by innkeeper Nathaniel P. T. Davis in the 1840s. One sidehill section requires caution in crusty conditions. The hardest slogging comes after a left turn at 2600 ft.

Just when you're starting to despair of ever reaching the top, you swing left and scramble up to an open ledge at 1.9 miles, with a fine view SW towards Mt. Carrigain. From here, the Davis Path climbs easily through ledgy, scrubby terrain; deep snow may obscure the trail, which leads NE up the ridge. At 2.2 miles, you come to the base of a large, slanting ledge—turn left here on a spur trail to Mt. Crawford and snowshoe up the open face and continue up through ledge and scrub to the craggy summit at 2.5 miles. The wind may be fierce here, but the 360-degree view is sensational. To the north, you look into the great trough of Crawford Notch and along the chain of Southern Presidential peaks angling up to Mt. Washington. Close by to the NE are the remarkable cliff formation known as the Giant Stairs and the snow-splotched mass of Mt. Resolution. Kearsarge North is to the east, and to the south and SW are the Sandwich Range, Mt. Carrigain, and dozens of other peaks.

If time permits, you can continue an easy 0.7 mile NE on Davis Path beyond the Mt. Crawford spur junction, dipping slightly and rising to a wide, flat ledge on the shoulder of Crawford Dome, with a neat close-up view of the craggy summit of Mt. Crawford. In late winter, with much of the scrub buried in snow, this area has a real open ridge feel and is delightful to explore on snowshoes.

14. Diana's Baths

LOCATION: Near North Conway

DESCRIPTION: An easy woods ramble to frozen cascades and snowy brookbed ledges

TRAIL: Moat Mountain Trail (north end)

DISTANCE: 1.2 miles round trip

STARTING ELEVATION: 550 ft.

HIGHEST ELEVATION: 650 ft.

ELEVATION GAIN: 100 ft.

RATING: Beginner

USGS MAP: North Conway West

TRAILHEAD: From NH 16 in North Conway, turn onto River Rd. at the stoplight just north of Eastern Slope Inn. Keep straight at the intersection with West Side Rd. in 1.0 mile. Continue beyond the roads for Echo Lake and Cathedral Ledge. At 2.4 miles from NH 16 a hiker symbol on the left marks the recently relocated north trailhead for Moat Mountain Trail. Turn into the large, partially plowed parking lot.

WMNF PARKING PASS: Yes

The short trip into Diana's Baths on the Moat Mountain Trail is one of the easiest snowshoe jaunts in the White Mountains. In summer this series of cascades, potholes and pools is a popular destination for swimming and picnicking. It's less visited but no less beautiful in winter, when the cascades are muted and the broad ledges are cloaked in snow. If you or your companions are new to snowshoeing, this is a good one to start with.

The yellow-blazed trail enters the woods at the west side of the parking lot. You wind slightly downhill under tall red and white pines, making a sharp left turn and then a right. A pleasant meander through a deep forest of pine, spruce and hemlock leads to a horseshoe curve around to the left at 0.3 mile. The well-marked trail continues to weave through these attractive woods. At 0.5 mile you break out into young hardwoods and cross a nifty dogleg footbridge over a small brook. In another 200 feet this newly relocated section of trail joins the former route near the bank of Lucy Brook.

Turn right here at an arrow onto a wide old road. The clearing beside this corner marks the site of a former water-powered gristmill, the remains of which are evident beside the brook. Up ahead you can see the first cascade area of Diana's Baths. At a trail sign a few yards farther a short side path leads left to an old abutment above the lower cascade. Just beyond, at the base of a gigantic white pine, the Moat Mountain Trail forks to the right, while an unmarked side path leads left and up through hemlock woods alongside the cascades.

Follow this route to explore the tiers of snowy ledge along the brookbed. After one little easy ledge scramble in the woods you can cut left and out to a snowy mantel of rock for a view back down the cascades and out through the trees to Kearsarge North and Bartlett Mtn. across the valley. Continuing up the path beside the brook, past some boulders, you'll come to a wide, flat ledge area set back from the brink of the main cascades. A sign on a tree warns that no swimming is allowed beyond this point—not a concern for snowshoers! (Above here the brook is a public water supply.) This spacious shelf is a great lunch spot, with a view NE to the distant ridge of Walter Mtn. (surely one of the least-known summits of the region) and another

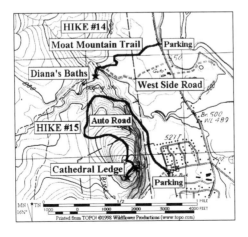

peek at Kearsarge North. It's possible to explore farther up the brook, but crossing over is not recommended for inexperienced snowshoers—it's hard to tell where the snow and ice bridges span potholes or flowing water.

In the winter much of the sculpted rock and cascading waters of Diana's Baths are masked by the snow. It's worth a return trip in summer for a very different experience. For a full description, see Bruce, Doreen and Daniel Bolnick's *Waterfalls of the White Mountains*. The Baths were named by a 19th-century visitor after the Roman nature goddess, Diana. They are also known as "Lucy's Baths," and were once called the "Home of the Water Fairies." According to legend, the local Native Americans thought these ledges were the abode of evil spirits. The Indians' prayers were answered when a mountain god unleashed a deluge that carried the spirits away.

15. Cathedral Ledge

LOCATION: Echo Lake State Park, North Conway

DESCRIPTION: A mild climb up an unplowed road to a clifftop with views over North Conway and surrounding mountains

TRAIL: Cathedral Ledge Auto Road

DISTANCE: 2.8 miles round trip

STARTING ELEVATION: 530 ft.

HIGHEST ELEVATION: 1150 ft.

ELEVATION GAIN: 650 ft.

RATING: Beginner/intermediate

USGS MAP: North Conway West

TRAILHEAD: This hike follows the unplowed auto road up Cathedral Ledge. From NH 16 in North Conway, turn onto River Rd. at the stoplight just north of Eastern Slope Inn. Keep straight at the intersection with West Side Rd. at 1.0 mile, and at 1.5 miles turn left on a road at a sign for Cathedral Ledge. (Don't take the road sharp left, which leads to Echo Lake.) Drive 0.3 mile to the end of the plowed road and park on the left side by an intersection where a road goes right into a residential area. Be careful not to block access.

WMNF PARKING PASS: No

Cathedral Ledge and White Horse Ledge are two impressive cliffs at the base of the Moat Range, facing east across the Saco valley in North Conway. They are best known as one of the East's prime rock and ice climbing venues, with hundreds of documented routes. Cathedral, the lower of the two, sports a paved auto road that brings thousands of visitors to the top each summer to gawk at the views.

In winter this road is not plowed and provides an excellent beginner's snowshoe route to the wide vistas at the top. The road is traveled by snow-mobiles, but it's wide enough to accommodate many users. If you go mid-week you'll likely encounter no snowmachines, and you'll find that the track they pack down makes for easy groomed snowshoeing. If there are snowmobiles around—and you'll hear them coming—it's your responsi-bility to yield the track, with a friendly wave.

Continue ahead on the unplowed road from your parking spot. In a cou-ple hundred feet it bends to the right to traverse northward along the base of the cliffs. At this corner you can look up at the impressive "Prow" of the ledge, where you'll come out at the top. The road runs level through a pine forest, passing a couple of marked climber's trails on the left.

At 0.4 mile swing left around a gate that blocks the road. Soon the wide road curves left and climbs steadily for 0.2 mile to another left turn; look back for views to the Green Hills. You continue upward with nice stands of hemlock fringing the road. The grade eases as you bend to the right and pass a red-blazed National Forest boundary.

At 0.9 mile a snowmobile trail departs right into the woods and the road again swings left and climbs steadily. Higher up white pine and oak mix in with the hemlocks. A sharp right at 1.2 miles brings a final easy-graded stretch leading 0.1 mile to the loop at the end of the road. Keep straight on the left side of the loop and bear left into the woods at a sign reading "Fenced Viewing Area." Various paths can be followed up to the chain link fence that zigzags along the top of the cliff.

Make your way out to the Prow that juts out from the main line of precipices. Here there's an open area of snowy ledge behind the fence, dot-ted with a few scrawny pines and spruces. Please heed the sign imploring you not to throw objects—including snowballs—over the cliff; there may be climbers below.

The wide view is an interesting blend of the civilized and the wild. Close by on your left you look down on the sheer rock walls named "Airation But-tress" (upper) and "Thin Air Face" (lower) by climbers. Beyond a piney hous-ing tract almost at the base of the cliff, you look north and east across the broad Saco valley, a patchwork of woods, white-carpeted fields and pockets of development. The windings of the Saco River can be traced for miles.

The horizon is ringed with mountains. On the far left, 14 miles north, are Wildcat, the U-shaped Carter Notch, and Carter Dome, with the dark face of nearby Humphrey Ledge beneath. Slightly east of north are Thorn Mtn., ski-trailed Black Mtn., and the long valley of the East Branch of the Saco. Among the peaks rimming this remote basin are Doublehead, Chandler, Sable, snowy South Baldface, Baldface Knob and Eastman. Looking NE the

Near the edge on Cathedral Ledge

great tower-topped dome of Kearsarge North looms right across the Saco valley, with its spur, Bartlett Mtn., jutting out on the left.

Moving over to the right (south) side of the Prow, there are views east and SE to the Green Hills—Hurricane, Cranmore with its ski trails, Black Cap (highest in the range), ledgy Peaked, Middle, and Rattlesnake. Just east of south you look down on little Echo Lake, frozen and ringed by pine woods. Southward there's a long view over West Side Rd. to distant lines of hills.

At the south end of the small summit ridge another, wilder view awaits. There's no marked trail; you generally make your way up towards the ridge-crest behind the cliffs, following any of several paths through the open woods. Continue a few hundred feet to the south, skirting to the left of the wooded outcrop that is the "summit" of Cathedral Ledge. You'll soon emerge on a sunny, open ledge area with an intimate view of the Moat Range and White Horse Ledge. North Moat, a high, graceful ridge with a tiny peak, is to the SW, looming 2000 feet above you. To its right is the darkly wooded backside of Attitash Mtn. To the left the bare snow-carpeted Red Ridge slants down towards the valley. Middle Moat peers over the back-side of White Horse Ledge. The side view of White Horse's great slabs is quite impressive, and provides a quick lesson in glacial geology.

The continental glacier flowed down over the White Mountains from NW to SE, moving smoothly up the backsides of knolls like White Horse and Cathedral, then plucking away rock as it rode down the lee side. This action created the great cliffs we see today. Geologists call this type of formation, with a gentle slope on one side and a steep face on the other, a *roche moutonnee*, or a "sheepback."

Echo Lake, which can be seen below here, is another legacy of the glacier—a "kettle pond" created when a chunk of ice was stranded at the end of the Ice Age. Sandy outwash filled in around the ice block, and when it melted the resulting depression filled with groundwater.

One other natural history note: come spring, the Cathedral cliffs often host a nesting pair of the endangered peregrine falcon. If you snowshoe here late in the season, you may spot one of these magnificent raptors winging around the area; they generally arrive in March. Hikers and climbers are urged to obey any posted access restrictions.

After making your way back to the top of the road, you'll enjoy a quick and easy snowshoe descent to the base of Cathedral Ledge. If you have time, you can stay awhile and watch climbers clawing their way up the various icefalls on the cliffs.

ADDITIONAL OPTION

Echo Lake *1.0-mile loop, minimal vertical rise, beginner*   To access this easy outing, take the other road that leaves West Side Rd. along with the road to Cathedral Ledge; this is called Old West Side Rd. Follow it for 0.7 mile to where it makes a sharp left by the entrance to the parking area for Echo Lake State Park, which is gated and unplowed in winter. Park beside the road here where a short spur continues ahead. Snowshoe down through the parking area and follow the easy loop trail around the shore, or shuffle across the frozen pond. Beautiful forests of red and white pine line the east shore, where there are great views across to the face of White Horse Ledge and to South and Middle Moat beyond. The west shore yields a vista of Kearsarge North, and from the south end you'll see Cathedral and Humphrey Ledges.

16. South Doublehead

LOCATION: Jackson

DESCRIPTION: A moderately steep climb to a 2939-ft. summit with excellent views; loop option over North Doublehead for more views.

TRAILS: Doublehead Ski Trail, Old Path, New Path

DISTANCE: 3.0 miles round trip (Loop option 3.9 miles)

STARTING ELEVATION: 1480 ft.

HIGHEST ELEVATION: 2939 ft. (Loop option 3053 ft.)

ELEVATION GAIN: 1500 ft. (Loop option 1850 ft.)

RATING: Intermediate

USGS MAP: Jackson

TRAILHEAD: This trip starts at a plowed parking area for Doublehead Ski Trail on Dundee Rd. in Jackson. From NH 16, drive through the covered bridge on NH 16A and into the village. In 0.5 mile, turn right on NH 16B by the Jackson post office. The road climbs steeply, with a view of Doublehead at 1.7 miles. At 2.2 miles, you bend right at Black Mountain Ski Area. Take the right fork onto Dundee Road at 2.4 miles and continue to the parking area on the left, 2.9 miles from NH 16.

WMNF PARKING PASS: No

The twin cones of Doublehead Mountain are an easily identifiable land-mark from many points in the Jackson area. Trails ascend to viewpoints atop both the North Peak (3053 ft.) and South Peak (2939 ft.). The most pop-ular winter route on the mountain, used by skiers and snowshoers, is the wide, sweeping Doublehead Ski Trail, which ends at a Forest Service cabin atop the North Peak.

However, the views on South Peak are better than those on North, so the featured route here will take you to South Doublehead via the lower por-tion of the Ski Trail, the Old Path and the New Path. This is a moderately challenging snowshoe climb, steady but never overly steep, and the summit vistas are ample reward for the effort. Snowshoers who want to double their pleasure can make an optional return loop over the North Peak and down the Ski Trail.

From the parking area, walk 100 yards up a private gravel road and bear right onto Doublehead Ski Trail at a sign. You soon cross the boundary into the National Forest and rise at easy to moderate grades up the wide trail

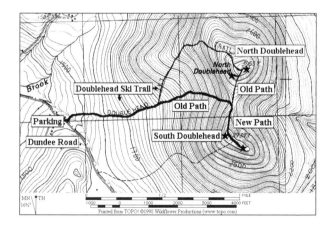

through open hardwoods. Remember that this first link of the hike is on a ski trail and be alert for descending skiers. As is generally the rule on ski trails, it is best to snowshoe along the edge. At 0.5 mile, you cross a small brook, and at 0.6 mile, you reach the signed junction with Old Path at a point where the ski trail makes a swing to the left.

Continue straight ahead up the slope on the Old Path, a much narrower trail that is not blazed and may require care to follow in its lower part through open mixed woods. It takes a generally direct course due east up the slope with a few minor deviations. Within 0.2 mile, the trail corridor becomes much more obvious as you climb steadily through an attractive open forest of spruce and fir. About 0.9 mile from your car, the trail twists left, right, then left again before tackling a fairly steep pitch. At 1.0 mile you swing left to traverse across the slope at a much easier angle through a spacious spruce grove. After 0.1 mile the trail loops to the right, climbs steadily again, then eases through a tunnel of young conifers to reach the 2700-ft. col between South and North Doublehead at 1.2 miles.

At the saddle you emerge into an open grove of ice-damaged hardwoods. Here the Old Path swings left to the North Peak, but your route follows the New Path to the right, winding gradually upward back into conifers. This area may be pockmarked with the tracks of snowshoe hares. After 0.2 mile of generally easy climbing along the ridgecrest you attain the summit of South Doublehead, where a side path drops a few yards right to an open ledge area with a sweeping westerly view—the finest vantage point on the mountain.

In the foreground are the fields and hills of Jackson, while across the horizon the high mountains spread in wave after wave of peaks and ridges, including the summits of twenty-six 4000-footers. To the SW you gaze out on the Sandwich Range, Osceola, and the jumble of peaks around the Pemigewasset Wilderness, with mighty Carrigain dominating the proceedings. Westward is the long Montalban Ridge, leading up to the great crags and ravines of Mt. Washington, the snowy centerpiece of the vista. There is an awesome look into the creased headwall of Huntington Ravine. To the right of Washington are the Wildcats, the deep gap of Carter Notch, and the wooded heights of Carter Dome. Closer to you in this direction is the long, wavy ridge of Black Mountain, with its ski area on the left (south) end.

If you can tear yourself away from these vistas—or if a cold wind drives you off—return to the New Path and turn right to visit two more summit knobs to the south, where other views await. The trail winds across the summit and dips slightly to a signed junction, where the New Path forks right and drops steeply to Dundee Road in 1.2 miles. Stay to the left on a spur trail that runs level a short distance then makes a quick climb to a semi-open knob marked by a large cairn. There are partial views here south to the Moats, Kearsarge North and the Saco valley, and north to North Doublehead and Mts. Chandler and Sable.

Mt. Washington from North Doublehead

Continue snowshoeing southward, following the path down the scrubby ridge. A slight upward pitch deposits you on the southernmost knob, 0.1 mile from the true summit of South Doublehead. From an open snowfield on the east side of a cairn there are excellent views east and north over a less-known area of the National Forest, including Mountain Pond, the valley of Slippery Brook, and the peaks of Chandler, Sable, South Baldface and Eastman. Close by is an interesting profile view of North Doublehead. Farther afield you can spot Carter Dome, Shelburne Moriah, parts of the Mahoosuc Range, Caribou Mountain, the Redrock ridge, and distant summits in western Maine. By poking around the sides of this knob you can find peeks at Kearsarge North, North Conway and the Moats.

This is the turn-around point for the trek to South Doublehead. To head home, follow your tracks back across the other summit knobs and down to the junction of the New Path and the Old Path in the col between South and North Doublehead. Turn left on Old Path for a fast and fun descent.

Loop Option Over North Doublehead

To extend your trip, follow the Old Path northward from the col. After an easy stretch of climbing, the trail commences a steep, winding surge up through the conifers that will test your snowshoe technique a bit. Nearing the top the grade slackens and you make a bend to the right. At this corner an unmarked side path diverges left, climbing slightly and then descending 100 yards to sloping ledges (use caution) with a good view west, though not quite up to the standard set by the south summit.

Beyond this side trail, Old Path reaches the junction with Doublehead Ski Trail and the summit of North Doublehead in another 100 yards of easy climbing. Just beyond you'll find a beautifully crafted cabin built in 1932 and available for overnight stays by reservation only. (For information, contact the Forest Service's Saco Ranger Station at 603–447–5448. The cabin is equipped with a wood stove and bunk space for eight.)

In front of the cabin there's a photogenic view of Mount Washington over the treetops. Behind the structure, a short side path leads to a beautiful eastern view over Mountain Pond, the Slippery Brook valley, Mounts Sable and Eastman, and far across the Maine lowlands beyond.

To return to the trailhead, go back in front of the cabin and turn right on the Doublehead Ski Trail. This wide route, cut by the Civilian Conservation Corps in 1934, descends the mountain's NW and western slopes at a moderately steep grade, with several sweeping turns. Please yield the way to descending backcountry skiers. Beautiful old conifer woods on the upper slopes give way to hardwoods below. A swing to the south brings you to the lower junction with Old Path, 1.2 miles from the north summit; from here it's an easy 0.6 mile back to your car.

ADDITIONAL OPTION

Perkins Notch *10.4 miles round trip, 1150-ft. elevation gain, advanced*   If you're looking to snowshoe into some truly remote country, the excursion from Jackson's Carter Notch Road along the Bog Brook Trail and Wild River Trail into the bog country of the upper Wild River Valley will provide plenty of solitude and adventure. It's best done during a spell of cold weather, when it's easier to negotiate the numerous brook crossings and explore the bogs around No-Ketchum Pond. The road to the parking area for Bog Brook Trail is not plowed, so the first adventure is finding a permissible parking space on Carter Notch Road. The Jackson Ski Touring Foundation plows a small parking area about one mile south of the Bog Brook trailhead. Backcountry snowshoers are permitted to use this space, but as a courtesy you should call JSTF (603–383–9355) to check current status, and upon arrival stop at their office in Jackson and buy a trail pass or make a donation. Otherwise, parking is extremely limited on Carter Notch Road. Please do not block driveways or the road. The distance and elevation figures for this trip are calculated from the JSTF parking place.

To get there, take Carter Notch Road north from NH 16A in the village of Jackson (the junction is by the Wentworth Hotel) and follow it about 4 miles to the JSTF parking spot on the right. Walk about 1 mile, with 350 ft. of elevation gain, up Carter Notch Road to the trail sign for Bog Brook Trail on the right. You descend to a trio of brook crossings, passing Wildcat River Trail on the left after the third crossing, 0.7 mile from the road. Snowshoe up the gently rising Bog Brook Trail for 2.1 miles through beautiful and varied forests, crossing the brook four times. Turn right on the rolling Wild

River Trail, soon breaking out into beautiful open birch glades. In 0.7 mile, you reach the junction with Rainbow Trail. Continue ahead on Wild River Trail through more birch forest for a traverse through Perkins Notch, the broad, flattish gap between Carter Dome and Black Mountain. In another 0.7 mile, you reach Perkins Notch Shelter and the bog complex around tiny No-Ketchum Pond. When the snow is deep and firm, you can explore the open bogs and gain impressive views up to Carter Dome and its bare-topped spurs, Rainbow Ridge (left) and Mt. Hight (right). The feeling here is one of true isolation. Be wary of weak ice covering boggy pools, and take care not to trample vegetation if snow cover is sparse.

17. Peaked Mountain

LOCATION: Green Hills Preserve, North Conway

DESCRIPTION: Moderate climb up a small mountain with good views and an unusual red pine forest

TRAIL: Peaked Mountain Trail

DISTANCE: 4.2 miles round trip

STARTING ELEVATION: 550 ft.

HIGHEST ELEVATION: 1739 ft.

ELEVATION GAIN: 1200 ft.

RATING: Intermediate

USGS MAP: North Conway East

TRAILHEAD: The hike up Peaked Mountain starts at the major trailhead for the Green Hills Preserve on Thompson Road in North Conway. From NH 16 just south of North Conway's village center, turn east on Artist's Falls Road. In 0.4 mile turn right on Thompson Road and drive 0.3 mile to the small trailhead parking area on the right, marked by a sign for Pudding Pond. The trailhead is just before the road crosses under a powerline.

WMNF PARKING PASS: No

Though only 1739 feet high, Peaked Mountain is perhaps the nicest snow-shoe trip in the Green Hills, the range of low mountains on the east side of North Conway. The 2822-acre Green Hills Preserve was created in 1990 with funding from the Anna B. Stearns Foundation and donations from a variety of businesses, individuals, and other foundations. The preserve is owned and managed by the non-profit Nature Conservancy. In recent years, the trail system has been expanded and reblazed, making the area more

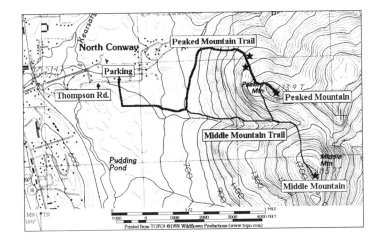

accessible and attractive for hikers and snowshoers. In addition to the fine
views provided by open summits such as Peaked, the preserve is home to a
variety of rare plants. The upper part of Peaked Mountain Trail passes
through unusual stands of red and pitch pine.

From the trailhead, follow the straight, level trail, jointly signed for
Peaked Mountain, Middle Mountain, and Pudding Pond, for 0.2 mile to a
kiosk at a T-junction. Here a map of the Green Hills Preserve is displayed
and free trail maps are often available in a box. Turn left here, following
signs for Peaked, Middle and Black Cap Mountains. You soon cross a powerline swath used by snowmobiles and squeeze through an opening in a snow
fence on the far side. Now you follow an old road, meandering gently upward through hemlocks, then open hardwoods, to a junction at 0.7 mile.
Here the Middle Mountain Trail splits right; bear left here on the Peaked
Mountain Trail and Black Cap Connector. You cross the boundary into the
Green Hills Preserve and climb up to a snow fence that blocks the trail, intended to keep snowmobiles out. Go around the fence and follow the trail
on a long northward traverse across the slope, rolling over a series of little
ridges and drainages amidst an open young hardwood forest. Looking left
through the trees you glimpse the Moat Range across the valley.

At 1.2 miles there's a short climb up to another kiosk. Here the Black Cap
Connector continues ahead; turn right on the Peaked Mountain Trail, now
blazed in blue, and begin a steadier climb, with peeks at the ski trails on Mt.
Cranmore on your left. You swing right to the base of snowy, scrubby
ledges, then veer left away from them at a trail sign. (Here the former route
of the trail up to the right has been closed to protect rare and endangered
flora.) The relocated trail circles around the north side of the mountain to a
sign and junction at 1.5 miles at the base of a snowy, sloping ledge. Here a

narrow spur drops steeply left to Black Cap Connector. The Peaked Mountain Trail makes a hard right and climbs up the snow-covered ledge, providing the first open views. Black Cap Mountain, the highest of the Green Hills, is seen to the NE. Looking north you can watch skiers schussing down Cranmore's trails. Stay to the right as you ascend this ledge.

From here to the summit, the trail passes through ledgy, scrubby terrain, with numerous views and interesting stands of red and pitch pines. If there is no snowshoe track the trail may be hard to follow in places, since many of the blazes are painted on the ledges and are hidden in the winter. Keep a sharp eye out for blazes on trees interspersed with the ledges.

A second ledge a short distance above the first offers a stunning view NE to the snowy peaks of Mt. Washington and the Presidentials, with the broad Saco Valley in the foreground. Look for a blue blaze on a tree at the upper left edge of this opening. The trail meanders up the ridge, soon passing a boulder with a plaque honoring Marland P. and Katherine F. Billings, noted White Mountains geologists and "Pioneers in the Establishment of the Green Hills Preserve." You wind upward past views of Montalban Ridge. A sign marks the upper end of the closed section of trail.

After ascending through more ledgy areas with occasional views, the trail swings left across the ridgecrest to a junction at 1.9 miles with the Middle Mtn. Connector. Stay left on Peaked Mountain Trail. Soon you make a short, steep scramble up to the right, then you climb steadily SE up the red pine ridge. A short traverse and final pitch lands you on the bare summit at 2.1 miles.

On a clear day, the sun exposure here can be downright toasty. The view is a 180-degree sweep to the south. The sharp little peak of Middle Mountain (1857 ft.) rises in front of you across a little col; to its left, you look out over the low hills of western Maine. On the right of Middle Mountain is Rattlesnake Mtn. (1590 ft.), the lowest of the Green Hills summits. Distant Green Mtn. in Effingham can be seen through the gap between Middle and Rattlesnake.

The long spread of the Ossipee Mountains dominates the horizon to the SW. To the right and closer in is the great rock-and-snow peak of Chocorua. In the foreground are the fields of the Saco Valley, the parking lots and buildings of the Settlers' Green complex on the North Conway strip, and the long, narrow Puddin' Pond.

In addition to Chocorua, you can spot the Sandwich Range peaks of Paugus, Whiteface, and Passaconaway. Facing more westward, the great wall of Moat Mountain rises across the wide valley, with North Moat the highest peak on the right. The snowy ledges of the Red Ridge slanting down towards the valley are especially prominent.

Unless you're going for the loop option (see below) return the way you came. With good snow conditions the descent back down the ledges is an enjoyable swoop with plenty of views to enjoy en route.

*Open ledges
abound on
Peaked Mountain*

ADDITIONAL OPTIONS

Loop Option   A slightly shorter option is to descend to the south via the Middle Mountain Connector and Middle Mountain Trail. Return 0.2 mile on the Peaked Mountain Trail, then turn left on Middle Mountain Connector, which descends 0.3 mile through ice-damaged hardwoods to the Middle Mountain Trail. Turn right here and descend steadily beside a hemlock-shaded ravine. You'll come back to the Peaked Mountain Trail in 0.7 mile; follow this 0.7 mile back to the trailhead. This descent option is 1.9 miles long, compared to 2.1 miles using the entire Peaked Mountain Trail.

Middle Mountain   This peak has several view ledges and is an attractive alternative to climbing Peaked Mountain, or both can be climbed in a single trip. To climb Middle Mountain alone, do the above loop option in reverse to the point where the Middle Mountain Connector breaks off to the left. Continue straight on Middle Mountain Trail, which soon bears right to cross a brook. Then ascend south up the ridge through fine woods of red pine. Around the summit area are ledges with views south and west. Middle Mountain only: 4.2 miles round trip; 1300-ft. elevation gain, intermediate. Peaked and Middle Mountains: 5.4-mile loop, 1750-ft. elevation gain, intermediate.

18. Kearsarge North

LOCATION: NE of North Conway

DESCRIPTION: A steady climb to an open summit with a firetower and one of the best views in the White Mountains

TRAIL: Mt. Kearsarge North Trail

DISTANCE: 6.2 miles round trip

STARTING ELEVATION: 680 ft.

HIGHEST ELEVATION: 3268 ft.

ELEVATION GAIN: 2600 ft.

RATING: Intermediate/advanced

USGS MAP: North Conway East

TRAILHEAD: From NH 16 just north of the rest area in Intervale, turn east on Hurricane Mtn. Road and drive 1.5 miles to the trailhead on the left, across from a residence. There is plowed roadside parking for several cars by the trail sign.

WMNF PARKING PASS: No

Set apart on the east from the main ranges of the White Mountains, Kearsarge North, also known as Mt. Pequawket, is a symmetrical dome with an expansive view over much of the high peaks region and western Maine. Its tower-topped peak dominates the horizon from many points around North Conway.

The climb to the 3268-ft. summit is a long, steady pull, never too steep, with an elevation gain that rivals many higher peaks. Varied forests and ledges with southern views partway up make for an interesting ascent. If the day is tolerably warm, the sweeping summit vistas—which include 36 of New Hampshire's 4000-foot peaks—will hold you for a while, especially when enjoyed from the comfort of the enclosed, historic tower.

From Hurricane Mountain Rd., the trail descends slightly through a brushy area, then rises gently past two houses up on the right and a summer cottage on the left. You pass through a deep forest with tall pines, then meander upward through young hardwoods and mixed woods.

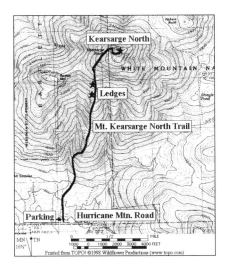

At 0.7 mile you enter a shady forest of hemlock, pine and spruce on the east side of a brook ravine. A sign welcomes you onto National Forest land. The trail angles up this slope high above the brook, climbing at a moderate grade. If snow cover is thin, this section of trail may be icy. At about 1.2 miles you start to climb more to the right, away from the ravine. Topping a rise, you swing right for a short traverse, then wrap around to the left, with views through the trees to the Green Hills.

Veer left again to resume the climb through an interesting forest of hemlock, red and white pine, spruce and oak. After crossing a level spot the trail winds up to the first semi-open ledges at about 2.0 miles (elevation 2000 ft.). You ascend open areas alternating with belts of woods. Look for yellow blazes on scrubby trees and cairns poking out of the snow. You soon gain partial views south down the Saco valley and SW to the Moat Range, with the rocky cone of Chocorua peering over the ridgeline. On a clear day the sun is bright on these piney, south-facing ledges.

Higher up you angle left to the uppermost ledges at 2500 ft. Here there's a clear view south to the Green Hills and the distant Ossipee Range. At 2.4 miles you attain the crest of the ridge that joins Kearsarge North with Bartlett Mtn. (2661 ft.), its lower western neighbor, and plunge into a deep spruce forest. The grades are easy as you cross two wooded ledges and pass a restricted view left towards the Twin and Franconia Ranges far to the west —a preview of the grand views above.

Now the trail drifts eastward around the NW side of the mountain. The climbing is moderate through the wild spruce forest that cloaks the upper slopes. You dip to cross a small gully, and after passing a couple of ledgy spots you make a sharp right up a steep pitch. A short climb lifts you into scrub. Layer up here, then follow a jog left for the final push up a series of

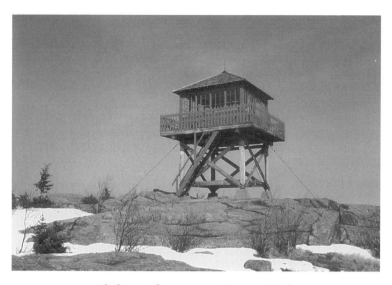

The historic fire tower atop Kearsarge North

open ledges to the bare summit and its little tower, with views exploding behind you.

Expansive open areas spread out on the south, west and east sides of the firetower. Views to the north and NW can be found by exploring open areas on that side of the summit, but are best obtained from the tower.

The first structure atop Kearsarge North was a small hotel built in 1845 by local entrepreneurs. Guests could arrive by horseback up a bridle path which forms part of today's hiking trail. The house was blown away by high winds in 1883. A second hostelry met the same fate in the early 1900s.

The first firetower was erected here in 1909, and a second tower served from 1918–1950. The present tower was built in 1951 and was staffed until 1969. In recent decades airplanes have been used for fire detection, leading to the closure of many firetowers around the state. This one is the last of its kind in the White Mountain National Forest. It was renovated in 1992 and is listed on the National Historic Lookout Register. It remains open for hikers to use for enjoying the 360-degree view. Take off your snowshoes before climbing the short, steep staircase to the deck that wraps around the tower cab. If it's windy you can retreat inside and look out through the windows. I'd recommend bringing a copy of the panorama from Brent Scudder's wonderful *White Mountain Viewing Guide*.

Looking south, you see the low Green Hills with frozen Conway Lake beyond. To the right is North Conway nestled in the broad Saco valley, with the Ossipee Range on the horizon. The Moat Range forms a mountain wall to the SW; the peaks of the Sandwich Range poke up behind. To the WSW is Attitash Ski Area, with the nearby spur of Bartlett Mtn., densely wooded with spruce, in front.

Westward you gaze up the valley of the Saco River and its tributary, Sawyer River, to an assemblage of peaks in the central Whites. Especially prominent are Mt. Osceola, Mt. Moosilauke framed by Hancock Notch, Mt. Carrigain, and the Bond-Twin Range with Lafayette peering over. To the NW is the spectacular spread of Mt. Washington and the Presidentials, including a look into the craggy maw of Huntington Ravine. To the right of the Presys are the Wildcats and Carters, separated by the deep gap of Carter Notch. The twin peaks of Doublehead are below the notch.

Northward there's an unusual view over a remote mountain country little known to hikers. Major peaks in this area include Mts. Chandler and Sable, the Baldfaces and Eastman Mtn. Old Speck and Goose Eye in the Mahoosucs can be seen beyond Eastman. Farther right, to the NE, are several low peaks in a trailless range extending north from Kearsarge: Rickers Knoll, the two Gemini (or Twins), Mt. Shaw and Walter Mtn. Beyond the latter are the mountains around Evans Notch, including the Royces, Caribou and Speckled. On clear days distant peaks such as Mt. Abraham and Mt. Blue can be seen far off in Maine.

The eastern horizon takes in a broad lowland sweep in western Maine, including Kezar Lake, Kezar Pond, Lovewell Pond and the long ridge of Pleasant Mtn. Closer in are the two Kimball Ponds, and you look right down on Kearsarge's own Shingle Pond, a tiny oval cradled on a spruce-wooded shoulder.

For those interested in such things, we've attached a list of the New Hampshire 4000-foot summits that can be seen from Kearsarge North.

As you depart the summit you snowshoe down into the western views. The long, steady downgrade makes for a fast and fun descent, especially along the lower ledges.

NEW HAMPSHIRE 4000-FOOTERS VISIBLE FROM KEARSARGE NORTH

Whiteface	Liberty	Pierce
Passaconaway	Lincoln	Eisenhower
Middle Tripyramid	Lafayette	Isolation
North Tripyramid	Bondcliff	Monroe
Tecumseh	Bond	Washington
Osceola	Zealand	Adams
East Osceola	South Twin	Madison
Moosilauke	North Twin	Wildcat D
South Hancock	Willey	Wildcat
North Hancock	Field	Carter Dome
Carrigain	Tom	Middle Carter
Flume	Jackson	Moriah

19. East of Chocorua

LOCATION: SW of Conway

DESCRIPTION: A mostly easy trip in a less-visited area on the east side of Mt. Chocorua, with attractive woods and two viewspots

TRAILS: Piper Trail, Nickerson Ledge Trail, Carter Ledge Trail

DISTANCE: 4.8 miles round trip

STARTING ELEVATION: 780 ft.

HIGHEST ELEVATION: 1900 ft.

ELEVATION GAIN: 1150 ft.

RATING: Intermediate

USGS MAP: Silver Lake

Trailhead: This trip starts on the Piper Trail, which leaves the west side of NH 16 behind the Davies General Store, 6.1 miles south of the junction with NH 112. The trailhead is on private land; there is a $2 parking fee per car (not covered by the WMNF parking pass). Purchase your pass in the store and drive around the north side of the building to a parking area in back on the left. (The large summer parking lot for Piper Trail is not plowed.)

WMNF PARKING PASS: No (private pass required)

The rocky peak of Mt. Chocorua is one of the most picturesque and popular destinations in the White Mountains. No fewer than ten trails wind their way up the various valleys and ridges of this sprawling mountain mass. Though a journey to the summit of Chocorua is a serious undertaking in winter, with much exposure to weather and a traverse of potentially hazardous ledges, some of the lower trails on the mountain provide excellent opportunities for beginning and intermediate snowshoers.

One such outing on the north side of Chocorua is described in the chapter on Champney Falls Trail. The trip outlined here takes you along scenic paths on the east side of the mountain: the Piper, Nickerson Ledge and Carter Ledge Trails. Attractions include a beautiful spruce-woods ridge stroll and two ledgy openings with limited but interesting views. This makes for a very enjoyable afternoon of snowshoeing. You may even find untracked snow on the little-used route above the Piper Trail. Much of this route is south-facing, so you'll find the best snow cover in midwinter.

From the parking lot, continue 100 feet up the plowed driveway and bear right at a fork in front of a home onto the unplowed road that leads to the summer parking area. Strap on your snowshoes and plod out to this spacious snowy opening, where you're greeted by a looming view of Mt. Chocorua and the Three Sisters Ridge. The Piper Trail leaves at a trail sign towards the far end on the left, 0.2 mile from your car.

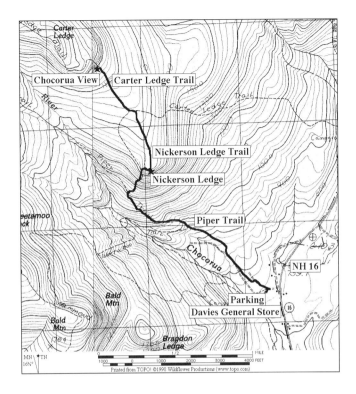

The yellow-blazed trail dips to cross a small brook on a log bridge and turns right to follow the stream at easy grades. At 0.5 mile bear left at an arrow, then soon make a right turn at another arrow, with a private road on the left, and recross the brook over a culvert. You snowshoe upward at a gentle slant through a nice open hemlock forest, passing the red-blazed National Forest boundary at 0.7 mile. The Weetamoo Trail leaves on the left at 0.8 mile.

Here you bend right and make a short, fairly stiff climb, then follow an old logging road along a bank through hardwoods and hemlocks. Along this traverse there are views left through the trees to Bald Mtn., the ledgy southern spur of Chocorua. The trail makes a right turn off the road and winds up to a higher shelf, then soon bends right again for a steady climb through open hardwoods, with log steps concealed under the snow. You swing left as the grade eases, then left again to attain a small plateau. A level stretch of snowshoeing leads to the junction with Nickerson Ledge Trail at 1.4 miles.

Bear right onto this lightly-used trail, faintly blazed in yellow. You quickly begin a fairly steep, winding climb that lasts for 0.2 mile. At the top you make a sharp right into spruces and pass a wooded ledge on the right (no view). The grade is now easier through snow-draped conifers.

The sun pours down on Nickerson Ledge

In about 0.1 mile from the turn the trail crosses a snowy, wooded ledge. As you enter this clearing you'll see an opening off to the right beyond some spruces. Follow a narrow side trail through a gap in the trees and you'll find Nickerson Ledge—an open sloping area with a clear view south to the distant Ossipee Range and a close-up vista of snow-splotched Bald Mtn. and part of the long southern ridge of Chocorua. Look closely and you may see Weetamoo Rock, an immense boulder jutting out of the forest. Nickerson Ledge is a nice sunny rest spot and could be the destination for a shorter trip (3.4 miles round trip, 900-ft. elevation gain).

Returning to the main trail, turn right, cross a viewless ledge, and re-enter the woods. The trail drifts left and levels out, beginning a half-mile traverse across a beautiful plateau of snow-laden spruces. On a sunny, 40-degree March day, when the snow was turning to glop on the south-facing slopes, we found dry powder and deep snowpack on this little 1700-ft. ridge. It has the look and feel of a much higher ridgecrest. The trail meanders through these conifers with little dips and rolls, then rises to meet the Carter Ledge Trail at 2.2 miles.

Make a left here and descend gently, bending right and down to a little brook. The steep, wooded south slope of Carter Ledge looms up to the right. Across the brook the trail angles left into open hardwoods, their tops mangled by the '98 ice storm. At 2.4 miles, after a moderately steep climb, you come beside a large, sloping ledge to the left of the trail. Oak branches frame a striking view of the stark, rocky cone of Chocorua. From here it looks forbidding and inaccessible, and indeed by this approach the top is still 2.8 often steep miles away. On a clear day the sun streams down through the bare branches on this south-facing slope. Photo buffs will want to capture this unique angle on Chocorua. You can carefully snowshoe out to the top of this ledge for a partial view south towards Ossipee Lake. This is the turn-around point for the East of Chocorua snowshoe trip; for a leisurely after-noon of snowshoeing, this outing is just right.

Note: The open summit of Carter Ledge, with a stunning vista of Mt. Chocorua and a distant view north, is just 0.3 mile farther, but above here the Carter Ledge Trail becomes very steep and rocky. It can be snowshoed only in deep snow winters, and then only by snowshoers comfortable and proficient in very steep terrain. Much of the time this section must be climbed in boots, and sometimes crampons are needed.

ADDITIONAL OPTION

White Ledge *3.6 miles round trip, 1300-ft. elevation gain, intermediate* White Ledge (2010 ft.) is a detached eastern spur of Chocorua with a steep east face. From various ledges near the summit there are views SW to Chocorua, east into Maine, and north to the Green Hills, Kearsarge North, the Moats and other mountains.

The west branch of the White Ledge Loop Trail, starting at White Ledge Campground, provides a moderately strenuous route to the top. The camp-ground is not open in winter and there is no sign. A small area is often, but not always plowed at the entrance on the west side of NH 16, 5.0 miles south of the junction with NH 112, across from a red house. From the en-trance, snowshoe 100 yards up the main road across the campground to the trailhead (sign) at the north end. The trail meanders through a low-lying area of hemlocks; bear left at the loop junction at 0.3 mile. Soon the trail be-gins climbing a southerly ridge cloaked in small, open hardwoods. The snow melts early on this section. At about 1.1 mile the ascent steepens and you pass a side trail right to a ledge perch with a good view east.

The climb is fairly steep to the crest of the ridge, where it runs along ledges near the east edge. If there are no tracks, the trail may be hard to fol-low. After passing a view left to Chocorua you reach the flat ledgy summit at 1.7 miles. For the best eastward views, continue 100 yards north along the trail, then descend to the right to an open perch. (Use caution if crusty or icy.) Good views to the north are found from a scrubby, ledgy area 0.1 mile farther north on the main trail. Descend by the same route; the eastern branch of the loop is a mile longer.

20. Boulder Loop Trail

LOCATION: Kancamagus Highway, by Albany Covered Bridge

DESCRIPTION: A nice afternoon snowshoe climb to a clifftop vantage with views of the Swift River valley and the Sandwich Range

TRAIL: Boulder Loop Trail

DISTANCE: 3.0 miles round trip

STARTING ELEVATION: 860 ft.

HIGHEST ELEVATION: 1750 ft.

ELEVATION GAIN: 900 ft.

RATING: Intermediate

USGS MAP: North Conway West

TRAILHEAD: Take the Kancamagus Highway (NH 112) to the junction with Dugway (Passaconaway) Road, 6.3 miles west of NH 16 and 5.9 miles east of Bear Notch Road. Turn onto Dugway Road and then quickly into a large plowed parking area on the right, with toilet facilities provided. The road is blocked by a snowbank just before it enters the Albany Covered Bridge over the Swift River.

WMNF PARKING PASS: Yes

This trail up a low, ledgy spur of the Moat Range is one of the best half-day snowshoe hikes along the Kancamagus Highway. For a modest climb of 900 feet, accomplished at relatively painless grades, you are rewarded with a spectacular clifftop view of the valley and peaks to the south and SW. Parts of this south-facing trail lose snow cover during major thaws and late in the winter.

From the parking area, climb over the snowbank blocking Dugway Road and walk "bareboot" through the covered bridge, where there's a good view

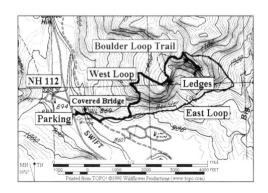

upstream to ledgy Table Mtn. Once through the bridge, you can strap on your snowshoes and follow the road 100 yards right (east) to the sign for Boulder Loop Trail on the left. Please stay out of the ski tracks along the road.

The yellow-blazed trail angles right a short way in from the road, climbing gently past some large boulders, and reaches the loop junction in 0.2 mile. A sign, LEDGES, 1.3 MILES, points to the west, or left-hand loop. Most people go up and back on this side in winter. Turning left onto the west loop, you zigzag upward at moderate grades through ice-damaged hardwood forest, passing along the base of a rock face. Soon the trail swings left to wind upward through mixed woods. You climb NE to the first viewpoint (1450 ft.) at about 0.8 mile. A few steps right there's a ledgy perch with a vista SE over the Swift River valley to the spruce-clad knob of White Ledge. The horn of Mt. Chocorua and the Three Sisters ridge peer over on the right.

The trail runs along the edge of the ridge, passing another outlook ledge up to the right which offers a close-up of the impressive cliffs you're heading for, along with a distant view eastward. The trail dips into hemlock and spruce, then slabs upward through sunny open hardwoods. At a sharp right you climb into a shady hemlock grove. After looping briefly out to the front of the ridge, you scrabble up a short steep pitch and come to the junction with the spur trail to the clifftop at 1.3 miles. A sign, VIEW 0.2 MILE, directs you to the right.

A quick scramble up a rocky step immediately lifts you to the first view ledge. To the right is a beautiful view SW to the Sandwich Range, and NW through the trees you can spot Bear Mtn., fire-scarred Table Mtn. and distant Mt. Carrigain between them. A few yards to the left is a vista towards Middle and South Moat Mtns.

The spur trail runs eastward across the snowy ledges. Though the blazes are covered, the route is obvious along this little open rocky ridge, and with good cover it's a wonderful place to snowshoe. Red oaks and scrubby white pines eke out a living in this dry, sunny habitat. You pass two more outlooks on the right, climb over a ledge and drop carefully down through a miniature flume, and emerge on the main clifftop perch 0.2 mile from the junction. The elevation here is 1750 ft. The flat, south-facing ledges are ideal for a lunch and viewing stop. Use caution near the edge—the dropoff is sheer!

The view from here is impressive, one of the best along the Kancamagus Highway. Nearly a thousand feet below you the highway and the Swift River wind through the valley, with a panorama of mountains beyond. On the left, due south, is darkly wooded White Ledge, with distant Green Mtn. in Effingham on its left and Mt. Shaw in the Ossipee Range on its right. Directly across the valley the sharp snowy peak of Mt. Chocorua and the ledgy Three Sisters ridge rise beyond the many lower spurs of these mountains. To the right (SW), beyond a nearby cliff and the windings of the Swift River valley, a striking panorama of the Sandwich Range unfolds. Left to right, you see the humpy ridge of Mt. Paugus; the steep-sided ridge of Mt.

Whiteface; the graceful dome of Mt. Passaconaway, scarred by a white slide on its face; the rounded ridge of The Sleepers; and the three peaks of Mt. Tripyramid plus its sharp outlier, Scaur Peak. The lower, ledgy summits of Mt. Hedgehog (left) and Mt. Potash (right) can be seen in front of the Tri-pyramids. Farther right the main and east peaks of Mt. Osceola poke their heads above distant Mt. Kancamagus. Farthest right and much closer is a long ridge leading up to the rolling crest of Bear Mtn.

By probing a short distance eastward along the north edge of this spine of ledge, you'll find a wild view across the valley of Big Brook to nearby Middle and South Moat Mts. and a southerly spur known as Haystack.

To make the descent, return along the spur path to the junction and turn left to retrace your tracks down the west side of the loop.

ADDITIONAL OPTION

Loop Option   If you wish to complete the loop by descending the east half, turn right where the clifftop spur comes back to the main trail. This part of the loop is less traveled in winter and may present unbroken snow. After passing through a saddle, the trail quickly begins to drop down a shallow ravine through a hardwood forest badly damaged by the 1998 ice storm. As it descends the trail begins to swing more to the right (south). After skirting an area of saplings from an old clearcut on the left, you make a sharp right turn at the base of the cliffs.

Now the trail makes a long, gently descending traverse to the SW through more hardwoods, with the cliffs looming up on your right. At 1.0 mile from the spur trail junction you cross a small brook at the base of a second cliff west of the main crags. Just beyond is a large overhanging boulder. Many other big rocks dot the woods as you hike this section. Another 0.3 mile of easy walking brings you to the lower loop junction, 0.2 mile from Dugway Road. The distance for the entire loop, including the spur trail to the ledges, is 3.3 miles with 900 feet of climbing.

21. Champney Falls Trail

LOCATION: North side of Mt. Chocorua

DESCRIPTION: An excellent snowshoeing trail with objectives for both beginning snowshoers (frozen waterfalls and a trailside vista) and inter-mediate/advanced snowshoers (ridgetop ledge vantages with wide views)

TRAILS: Champney Falls Trail; Middle Sister Cut-Off (for intermediate/ad-vanced option)

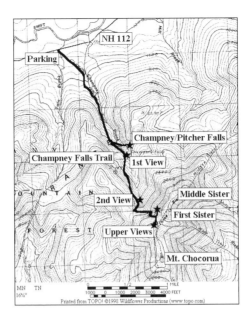

DISTANCE: 3.6 miles round trip (beginners option); 7.0 miles round trip (intermediate / advanced option)

STARTING ELEVATION: 1260 ft.

HIGHEST ELEVATION: 1850 ft.; 3200 ft.

ELEVATION GAIN: 650 ft.; 2000 ft.

RATING: Beginner; Intermediate / advanced

USGS MAP: Mt. Chocorua

TRAILHEAD: The large plowed parking lot for the Champney Falls Trail is located on the south side of the Kancamagus Highway (NH 112), 10.6 miles west of NH 16 and 1.6 miles east of Bear Notch Road

WMNF PARKING PASS: Yes

The Champney Falls Trail on the north slope of picturesque Mt. Chocorua is a great snowshoeing trail, with something to offer all levels of experience and ambition. Novice snowshoers can enjoy the modest two or three hour jaunt to Champney and Pitcher Falls and a trailside vista just beyond. Experienced snowshoers seeking an all-day trek can continue up to trail's end at the top of the ridge between the Three Sisters and Mt. Chocorua, enjoying several good views without tackling the exposed and potentially dangerous final leg to the rocky summit. (Only veteran winter mountaineers equipped with crampons and clothing suitable for above-treeline travel should attempt to reach the peak.)

The Champney Falls Trail is sheltered by the trees all the way up, and its

Ice sculptures
at Pitcher Falls

northern exposure ensures reliable snow cover through most of the winter. It's a popular trail throughout the year and will often be packed out with a solid track. Snowshoeing is most enjoyable here after the trail has been freshened up with some new snow.

The trail begins by a kiosk at the east end of the parking lot. It enters the woods and quickly crosses a footbridge over Twin Brook. (If the brook is well-frozen, it may be easier to cross the streambed rather than tight-rope across the sometimes icy bridge.) You head gently uphill to the south, soon picking up the track of an old logging road. At 0.1 mile the Bolles Trail splits off to the right, heading for the pass between Mt. Chocorua and Mt. Paugus. Continue ahead on Champney Falls Trail and enjoy easy snowshoeing through open hardwoods.

At 0.4 mile the woods darken with hemlocks as you approach Champney Brook on the left. The yellow-blazed trail makes a sharp right turn, then veers left to scramble up to a hemlock-clad bank above the brook. You climb steadily through this attractive grove, where the cover can be thin or icy in lean snow times. At 0.6 mile you drop left off the bank (may be tricky if icy) and back down to brook level. Here you turn right to pick up the old road along the brook, with occasional views of the snowbound streambed. Soon you see the first broken treetops from the January 1998 ice storm, which devastated the hardwood and birch forest in this valley at middle elevations. This basin suffered an earlier catastrophe in 1915, when fire laid waste to what timber remained after intensive logging operations.

There's a steadier pitch for about 0.1 mile, lifting you higher above the brook, then the grade eases again. A northerly knob of the Three Sisters ridge rises across the valley on the left. You pass a limited vista up to Middle Sister's rounded, snowy crown and reach the junction with the loop trail to Champney Falls at 1.4 miles.

Going left towards the falls, you descend easily and swing to the right. You cross a streambed and contour above Champney Brook through ice-damaged birches. For a short distance you're right beside the stream, then you climb slightly to the base of Champney Falls. Go left across the brook-bed for the best view of the frozen, tiered cascade. A couple hundred feet farther east the mountainside opens in the cut of a rock flume. If you make your way across to the floor of this small chasm, you'll see the picturesque ice flows of Pitcher Falls adorning the right (south) wall. There may be climbers clawing their way up the blue and brown-tinted pillars of ice—a feat suited only to those with proper equipment and training.

Returning to the side loop trail, it's best to turn right and retrace your tracks for 0.2 mile to get back to the main trail. The upper section of the loop is very steep and difficult to snowshoe as it climbs alongside Champney Falls—not recommended.

Back at the lower junction of the side trail with Champney Falls Trail, turn left to access the first viewpoint along the main trail. You climb at a moderate grade with one sidehill spot that can be a bit tricky if icy. In 0.2 mile, at 1850 ft. elevation, you'll find a framed vista of mountains to the north. From left to right are pointed Mt. Tremont, Mt. Nancy, Mt. Bemis, Bartlett Haystack, and the broad mass of Bear Mountain. This view is the turnaround point for the beginner's snowshoe trip—it's an easy 1.6-mile downhill shuffle back to the parking lot.

Experienced snowshoers can forge on up Champney Falls Trail to great ridgetop views 1.6 miles ahead with 1350 ft. of elevation gain. The upper junction with the falls loop trail is 0.1 mile above the vista. You snowshoe gradually upward on the main trail through a shattered hardwood forest, where countless treetops were snapped off by the '98 ice storm. As the trail lifts you high up on the west side of the valley there are occasional peeks up through openings to the Middle (left) and First (right) Sisters.

About 0.7 mile above the upper loop junction (2.4 miles above the trail-head), a startling view, enhanced by the ice storm, opens out to the left over the valley to distant Mt. Washington. In addition to the peaks visible at the lower viewpoint described below, you can see Mts. Willey and Webster by Crawford Notch, Mts. Franklin and Monroe and Boott Spur on either side of Washington, the gap of Pinkham Notch, and Wildcat Mtn. on the far right with fire-scarred Table Mtn. in front. Your elevation here is 2500 ft.

A few yards beyond this excellent view the Champney Falls Trail makes a sharp right turn and commences a series of switchbacks that ease you up to the top of the ridge. The first two switchbacks are the longest, taking you up through white birches to 2850 ft. At the end of the third switchback, where the trail goes sharp left, there's a northern vista out over the Champney Brook valley to Mt. Washington and many other mountains.

The fourth switchback leads you up with a bit of sidehilling to the junction with Middle Sister Cutoff (elevation 3000 ft.), 3.0 miles from the trailhead. Here the Champney Falls Trail swings right again. For a highly rewarding diversion, continue ahead on Middle Sister Cutoff, climbing gradually for 0.1 mile to a sloping ledge area (use caution if icy) with a choice view west and north. On the left (west) are the sprawling peaks of the Sandwich Range: Sandwich, Whiteface, Passaconaway, the Tripyramids and Paugus. To the NW and north the view sweeps over Mts. Carrigain and Hancock, the distant Franconias, Mt. Washington & the Presidentials and around to Wildcat Mtn.

Return to Champney Falls Trail and continue ahead up the last three short switchbacks. Along the final switchback a "VIEW" sign on the right points you up to a gently sloping open ledge area with a magnificent view to the north. Both this vantage and the one on Middle Sister Cutoff can be swept by cold NW winds, but it's worth bundling up and enjoying the panorama for at least a few minutes.

Close by on your right is the barren, rocky First Sister, coated in snow and ice. The distant view starts on the left (west) with Passaconaway, Tripyramid, the lower Hedgehog and Potash, the Osceolas, Mt. Kancamagus and the cliff-shod north arm of Paugus. To the NW there's a broad view across the Albany Intervale to the Hancocks, Franconias, Carrigain, Carrigain Notch and much more. Northward you see Crawford Notch, nearby Bear Mtn., an impressive spread of the snowy Presidentials, Pinkham Notch, Wildcat, Carter Notch and Carter Dome.

After absorbing these views, you can continue a short distance up the trail to the top of the ridge and the intersection with the Piper Trail. Flat ledges in this area give you glimpses of the stark, wintry cone of Chocorua, ice glinting in the sun, looming close by to the south. Unless you're prepared and equipped to tackle the exposed, icy ledges of the main summit, 0.6 mile away, or the nearby First Sister, you should turn around here for an enjoyable 3.2-mile snowshoe back down Champney Falls Trail to your car.

22. East Ledges— Hedgehog Mountain

LOCATION: Kancamagus Highway

DESCRIPTION: A moderate climb to open south-facing ledges with intimate views of the Sandwich Range.

TRAIL: UNH Trail

DISTANCE: 4.0 miles round trip

STARTING ELEVATION: 1250 ft.

HIGHEST ELEVATION: 2300 ft.

ELEVATION GAIN: 1100 ft.

RATING: Intermediate

USGS MAP: Mount Chocorua

TRAILHEAD: This trip follows the UNH Trail from a plowed parking area at the end of a short side road off the south side of the Kancamagus Highway, marked by a cross-country skier symbol and a sign for "UNH, Downes Brook and Mt. Potash Trails." This is directly opposite the Passaconaway Campground (closed in winter), 2 miles west of Bear Notch Road.

WMNF PARKING PASS: Yes

The East Ledges of Hedgehog Mountain are an ideal objective if you're looking for a half-day snowshoe trip with a modest amount of climbing. South-facing and sunny, these secluded clifftop perches command wide views of Mounts Chocorua, Paugus, and Passaconaway in the eastern Sandwich Range.

From the parking lot and information kiosk, walk south a short distance on a wide trail and turn left up a bank at a sign for UNH Trail. The yellow-blazed way leads straight and level through woods of spruce and pine, following the bed of the old Swift River logging railroad. This portion of the trail is shared with skiers. In 0.2 mile the west branch of the loop departs at the right, leading to Allen's Ledge at 1.1 mile and the 2532-ft. summit of Hedgehog at 1.9 miles (see "Additional Options" below). Continue ahead on the east branch of the loop, which follows the old railroad grade another 0.2 mile.

At a sign for "UNH Trail" bear right off the grade as a X-C ski trail continues ahead. You climb at easy to moderate grades through hemlocks and hardwoods. The snowy face of Allen's Ledge can be seen up through the trees to the right. After a steeper pitch you swing right around a spruce-covered knoll at 1.3 miles, then dip left to cross White Brook near its headwaters.

Now you rise through a sunny hardwood grove with evidence of ice

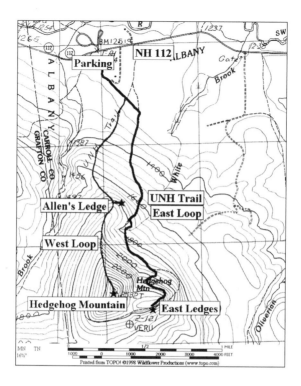

storm damage. You traverse a bouldery area, then ascend into a quiet spruce forest, with a line of wooded ledges on your right. Work your way left, right, then left again up through switchbacks across this shady northerly slope. You drop over a little ledge and come to a right turn at 1.9 miles. Here you can spot your first views of the day just left of the trail, NE across Albany Intervale to the broad spread of Bear Mountain, fire-scarred Table Mountain, and the long snowy ridge of the Moats.

The trail now swings south and makes a steady climb of 0.2 mile up to the East Ledges, which are located on an eastern spur of this bristling little mountain. As you emerge on the lower ledges, you can find eastward views to the Moats just off to the left. The trail bears right (west) and leads you on a scramble up snow-covered ledges to the flat perches atop the cliffs. Your snowshoe crampons will come in handy here. Exercise caution if it's icy. There's plenty of room to enjoy the sun and views back from the edge of the precipice.

And a fine view it is—an intimate look into the heart of the eastern Sandwich Range. The dominant sight is Mt. Passaconaway, a huge wild-looking bulk rising 1500 feet above you to the SW. Its subpeaks "Nanamocomuck" (marked by a slide), "Wonalancet Hedgehog," and Square Ledge (showing its wooded backside), drop off in steps to the left. Southeast you look over the broad, remote upper valley of Oliverian Brook to Paugus Pass, the sprawling, darkly wooded mass of Mt. Paugus (several old clearcuts can be seen on its slopes) and the trademark rocky cone of Mt. Chocorua, attended by its rounded spurs, The Three Sisters. The Moats can be seen off to the NE. Because of its southern exposure, out of the prevailing wind, this is a great lunch spot.

Adventurous snowshoers can continue a bit farther west on the trail for additional views. The trail drops briefly into the woods and crosses the top of a little gully. A side path leads a hundred feet to the right to a nice open area with partial views north to Mt. Carrigain. The main trail then edges along a clifftop—this bit of tightroping may not appeal to some snowshoers —be careful! You quickly emerge onto broad ledges that reveal views west to the Sleepers and the South Peak of Tripyramid, and up to the summit cliffs on Hedgehog looming right above you. The UNH Trail continues to the summit in another 0.8 mile, but parts of that final ascent are steep and tricky in winter. I recommend instead that you retrace your steps from the East Ledges, and perhaps return another day to scale the higher summit via the west branch of the UNH Trail (see below.)

ADDITIONAL OPTIONS

Allen's Ledge *2.2 miles round trip, 600-ft. elevation gain, beginner/intermediate* Follow the west branch of the UNH Trail on a steady climb to a right turn at 1.1 miles, where the side trail to Allen's Ledge climbs steeply up to the left. The best views are obtained by proceeding east and carefully down the sloping rock face to a level perch at its lip. (Don't attempt this in icy conditions.) There's a broad vista north and east over Albany Intervale to Bear Mountain, the Moats, Mt. Chocorua, and Mt. Paugus. The top of Mt. Washington can also be seen.

Summit of Hedgehog Mountain *3.8 miles round trip, 1300-ft. elevation gain, intermediate* Beyond Allen's Ledge, the west branch of the UNH Trail ascends steadily through a deep spruce forest, with a few steep pitches. As you near the 2532-ft. summit of Hedgehog you pass through scrubby areas with views north to Mt. Washington and the Presidentials and west to the Tripyramids. The summit ledge, 0.8 mile above Allen's Ledge, has a good view north and west to Carrigain Notch, Mt. Carrigain, Mt. Hancock, Mt. Osceola, and more distant peaks. On the SE side of the summit another ledge looks toward Mounts Passaconaway, Paugus, and Chocorua.

Potash Mountain *4.4 miles round trip, 1450-ft. vertical rise, intermediate* This ledgy western neighbor of Hedgehog is another excellent half-day snowshoeing objective off the Kancamagus Highway. There is some sidehilling and ledgy climbing along the summit approach, but nothing an intermediate 'shoer couldn't handle in ordinary conditions. The trailhead is the same

Passaconaway's dome towers over Hedgehog Mtn.

as for UNH Trail. Go straight (south) 200 feet then turn right on Downes Brook Trail, then left in another 0.1 mile. A short distance further the Mt. Potash Trail branches to the right and soon crosses Downes Brook (difficult in open/high water.) Traverse to a logging road, which provides an alternate access to avoid the brook crossing. (It leaves the Kancamagus Highway 0.6 mile west of the trailhead; park so that you don't block the gate.) Cross the road, angle across a hardwood slope, then make a winding climb through hemlock and spruce to a level shoulder at 1.6 miles, where a sunny ledge provides a view of slide-scarred Mt. Passaconaway and the Downes Brook Valley. After traversing through lovely spruce forest, the trail steepens again and cuts across the rocky south face of the mountain, with some side-hilling. You emerge atop snowy slabs with fine views south and east. Turn right for a steep climb up ledges to the scrubby 2700-ft. summit, where you'll enjoy excellent views to south, west, and north. The close-in views of Passaconaway, Whiteface, the Sleepers, the Tripyramids and the intervening valleys are outstanding. Out over the Swift River valley you see the Osceolas, Kancamagus, Huntington, Hancock, and Carrigain. By poking around on the north side, you can find views of Church Ponds, the Presidentials, and other distant ranges.

Easy Snowshoe Trails Along the Eastern Kancamagus Highway

East of the Kancamagus Pass, the Kancamagus Highway descends into the Albany Intervale, a broad basin ringed by high mountains. Several trips described in this book lead to objectives around the Intervale, including

Hedgehog Mtn., Potash Mtn., Champney Falls Trail, Boulder Loop Trail, and Livermore Pass. In addition to these, there are a number of easy trails, or portions of trails, in the floor of the valley that can be used for leisurely woods rambles. Some of these suggestions have no particular destinations; they are merely pleasant paths for travel on snowshoes. In general, I have avoided including WMNF cross-country ski trails in these descriptions. In a few instances, there may be a short section along a ski trail. On these, and anywhere you encounter skier use, please do your best to stay off the ski tracks and make a separate snowshoe track.

Trails are covered from west to east.

Sawyer River Trail   There is a plowed parking area for several cars here, 0.6 mile east of Lily Pond. A nice short objective is to descend 0.2 mile to a frozen cascade and pool. The trail makes a crossing of Swift River at 0.3 mile. In this rocky, upper section of the Swift, there's often a good snow-bridge for crossing. For the next 2.3 miles the trail follows a logging railroad grade; it is sometimes used by snowmobiles. After crossing Meadow Brook on a bridge at 1.3 miles, it runs through an interesting area of beaver ponds and meadows with some limited views. Ambitious snowshoers could continue all the way to beautiful Sawyer Pond via the Sawyer River and Sawyer Pond Trails—a 10.6-mile round trip with an elevation gain of 850 ft.

Sabbaday Brook Trail   The parking lot at the trailhead, 3.3 miles west of Bear Notch Road, is plowed. A quick round trip of 0.6 mile can be made to Sabbaday Falls, a picturesque ice and snow sculpture. The tourists' side path may actually be treacherous to negotiate in winter due to ice and snow build-up—be careful! The trail is often well-packed up to the falls. Whether you can snowshoe much beyond the falls depends on the condition of the brook crossings—there are three in the first mile. If there are good snow-bridges, you can access a beautiful section of this trail that follows the easy grades of an old logging road high above the brook, from about 1.0 mile to 2.8 miles, where there's a fourth crossing. Views of The Fool Killer, and later the Tripyramids, can be seen through the bare trees. The trail continues up this secluded, curving valley, with two more brook crossings, to the last crossing at 4.1 miles (elevation 3000 ft., 1700 ft. above the trailhead). Above here, it becomes more difficult and the upper half mile to the ridge of Mt. Tripyramid is exceedingly steep.

Downes Brook Trail   From the plowed trailhead parking area (shared with the UNH and Mt. Potash Trails, across from Passaconaway Campground), the first 0.7 mile is an easy, pleasant snowshoe. Here you confront the first of ten crossings of Downes Brook made by this trail in the next 4.5 miles. Four of them are in the next half mile, so if this first crossing is difficult, there's not much point in going further. If the crossings are easily negotiable, this can be a nice, long, gently graded snowshoe up an isolated valley.

The head of the valley is 5.2 miles and 2150 ft. up from the trailhead. For hardcore snowshoers, it's another 0.9 mile/600 ft. to the ledgy south summit of Mt. Whiteface and great views.

Oliverian Brook Trail   The parking area at the trailhead, on a short side road off the Kanc 1.0 mile west of Bear Notch Road, is plowed. The Oliverian Brook Trail is an easy lowland ramble up a broad basin between Hedgehog Mtn., Mt. Passaconaway, and Mt. Paugus. It makes a left and right turn in the first 0.2 mile—follow signs carefully, as it coincides with a ski trail for a short distance. Then, it runs south along a logging road and then an old logging railroad bed, soon coming close to Oliverian Brook. There are nice winter brook vignettes as you climb easily to the junction with Passaconaway Cutoff at 1.9 miles, a 250-ft. elevation gain from the trailhead. This is a good turnaround point for an easy half-day outing. The trail receives some winter use to this point—it's part of the northern route to Mt. Passaconaway. Beyond here, Oliverian Brook Trail is less often broken out, so if you're looking for some real back-country 'shoeing, with several brook crossings, plod on. Paugus Pass (2220 ft.)—the col between Passaconaway and Paugus—is 2.5 miles further and 700 ft. higher up the valley.

For a short trip to a good view from this trailhead, continue straight on a logging road where the Oliverian Brook Trail turns left, just south of the parking area. This road leads to the "East Loop" X-C Trail (stay off any ski tracks). In 0.1 mile bear right at a Y-junction, and 0.1 mile farther stay straight where the main road goes left and uphill; follow the sign "To West Loop." In another 0.1 mile you'll emerge in a large snowy field with excellent views of the surrounding mountains. By wandering around you can see Hedgehog, Potash, Middle Tripyramid, Kancamagus, Huntington, Hancock, Green's Cliff, the tip of Carrigain, Lowell, Anderson, Owl Cliff, Tremont, Paugus and Chocorua. Not bad for a 0.6-mile round trip with no climbing!

Lovequist Loop   Accessed from the plowed parking area for Rocky Gorge Scenic Area, 3.2 miles east of Bear Notch Road, this short loop trail provides a nice circuit around Falls Pond. From the parking area follow the walkway north to the snowy ledges near Rocky Gorge (use caution if icy). Cross the bridge over the scenic, ice-choked chasm and ascend a sometimes icy staircase to the junction with Lovequist Loop. A short spur leads down to the shore of the pond and a view up to a shoulder of Bear Mtn. The loop makes several ups and downs through spruce forest as it circles the pond; I prefer the counterclockwise circuit. At the beginning and end of the loop the trail coincides with a ski trail—please snowshoe along the edge and stay off ski tracks. If Falls Pond is well-frozen, you can also snowshoe out to the middle for a view north to bare-faced Table Mtn. and a nearer cliff on a spur of Bear Mtn. The trip across Rocky Gorge and around the pond is 1.0 mile long with about 100 feet of elevation gain.

23. Hancock Notch

LOCATION: Kancamagus Highway

DESCRIPTION: An attractive sprucewoods ramble to a remote backcountry notch with limited views

TRAIL: Hancock Notch Trail

RATING: Beginner/intermediate

DISTANCE: 5.2 miles round trip

STARTING ELEVATION: 2129 ft.

HIGHEST ELEVATION: 2800 ft.

ELEVATION GAIN: 800 ft.

USGS MAPS: Mt. Osceola, Mt. Carrigain

TRAILHEAD: The Hancock Notch Trail starts on the north side of the hairpin turn on the Kancamagus Highway, 4.7 miles east of the parking area at Lincoln Woods. Parking at the trail entrance is strictly prohibited; drive 0.1 mile farther east and park at the plowed Hancock Overlook parking area.

WMNF PARKING PASS: Yes

Hancock Notch is a spruce-clad pass hidden between two high, wooded mountains—Mt. Hancock (4420 ft.) on the north and Mt. Huntington (3700 ft.) on the south. The snowshoe in to the notch follows easy to moderate grades along an old logging railroad bed and tote roads, through miles of remote spruce forests. It's especially pretty when fresh snow drapes the evergreens. The notch itself is a wild, secluded place where the snow piles deep and where few visitors venture. A couple of small open boggy spots offer limited views up to the rocky slope of Mt. Huntington. This sheltered trek is a fine choice on one of those bitter midwinter days when the winds rule up on the ridges, or on a cloudy day when summit views are obscured.

From the west end of the parking area at Hancock Overlook, a path descends a bank down to the hairpin turn; you may have to climb over a high snowbank to exit the overlook. With caution, cross the highway at the curve to the start of the Hancock Notch Trail, marked by a sign. The snowshoeing is easy along the grade of one of the earliest logging railroads built in this region by J. E. Henry, the notorious Lincoln-based timber baron. This area along the North Fork of the Hancock Branch was logged in the 1890s.

The smooth northbound 'shoeing is interrupted only by an occasional washout dip. White and yellow birches line the trail, mixed with small spruce and fir. You're quickly enveloped by a sense of seclusion as you draw away from the highway.

At 0.4 mile you pass a large peaked boulder on the right, and at 0.6 mile

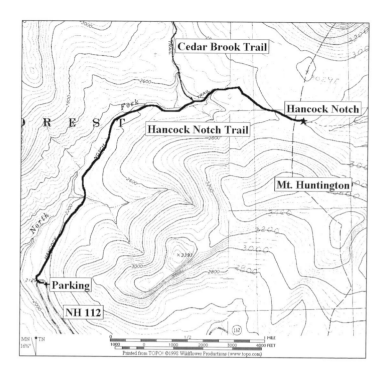

Cedar Brook Trail

Hancock Notch

Hancock Notch Trail

Mt. Huntington

Parking

NH 112

Printed from TOPO! ©1998 Wildflower Productions (www.topo.com)

you descend to cross a small nameless brook and scramble up the bank on the far side. The snowshoeing alternates between wide-open corridors and stretches where snow-draped evergreens crowd the yellow-blazed trail. About a mile in you start passing through some stately stands of spruce, where hundreds of scaly gray trunks poke up from the snowpack.

You soon approach the North Fork, and at 1.2 miles there's a small vista from a bank five feet left of the trail, looking downstream to a spur of Mt. Hitchcock. At 1.4 miles the trail hops up to the right, leaving the railroad grade, and follows the North Fork on an eastward bearing; look for a yellow blaze and blue diamond marker at the turn. (The old railroad grade continued ahead across the brook here.) After 0.1 mile along a high bank, look off to the left, over the trees, for a glimpse of the high, sharp, rime-frosted peak of South Hancock and its wild southern spur, which forms the north side of Hancock Notch. Beyond, the trail dips and jogs left to cross three small brooks, then swerves right along a wide straightaway to a junction with the Cedar Brook Trail at 1.7 miles. Often the trail will be broken out to this point by trampers intent on "bagging" the two 4000-foot peaks of Mt. Hancock.

Stay straight on the less-used Hancock Notch Trail. You may be plowing through unbroken snow up towards the notch. The trail angles moderately up the north side of a ravine, with peeks up at the wooded ridge of Mt. Huntington on the south side of the valley. At 1.9 miles a new relocation takes the trail left off its former route and ascends up a widely cut corridor through the spruces. In 0.1 mile you crest a rise amidst heart-leaved birches. The new section now bends right and makes a weaving descent to the SE. It then rises gently, crossing several small brooks, and rejoins the old route at 2.3 miles.

Snowshoeing gradually uphill to the east, you encounter a narrow, over-grown section of trail where you may need to knock snow off hanging spruce branches with your ski pole. The trail levels as you crest the west end of the broad, flat notch at 2.5 miles (elevation 2800 ft.). The entire pass is carpeted with snow-laden conifers. It's a wild, isolated setting. On one March visit here, the snow measured four to five feet deep.

The trail soon comes near a small, open bog on the right. If you venture a hundred feet off the trail through open woods, curling out to the bog edge beside a split boulder, you'll find a nifty view up to the steep north face of Mt. Huntington. Much of the mountainside consists of snow-covered rock slides and conifer scrub.

The trail continues on a gentle meander across the floor of the spruce-shaded notch. At 2.6 miles a small opening on the trail provides another look up at the snowy north slope of Huntington. Soon thereafter the trail begins its descent into the Sawyer River valley. Unless you want to explore further, and make the climb back up over the pass on the return trip, this is a logical turnaround point. Return to your car by the same pleasant route, with about a hundred feet of climbing on the relocated section.

ADDITIONAL OPTIONS

Mt. Hancock *9.8 miles round trip, 2650-ft. elevation gain, advanced*   The loop over the wooded peaks of North Hancock (4420 ft.) and South Hancock (4319 ft.) is a difficult but rewarding trip. The first 1.7 miles are the same as for Hancock Notch. The route then follows the Cedar Brook Trail for a gentle 0.7 mile to Hancock Loop Trail, making five crossings of the North Fork (some of these can be bypassed). Climb moderately for 1.1 miles on Hancock Loop Trail, including a sixth brook crossing near the start, to the loop junction. The loop can be done in either direction. Both ascents are very steep, requiring aggressive snowshoeing; the climb to South Peak is 0.5 mile, to North Peak is 0.7 mile after an initial short descent. There's a fine south view to Mt. Osceola and the Sandwich Range and down the North Fork valley from an outlook on a short spur trail off North Peak. At various points around South Peak there are vistas north, east, and west, much improved by the deep snows of winter. Likewise, the winding, wild 1.4-mile Ridge Link between the peaks offers several interesting winter-only views into various nooks and crannies of the Pemigewasset Wilderness. In good snow conditions the descent down either end of the loop can be very rapid!

*A hard-earned view
of Osceola from
North Hancock*

Cedar Brook Trail   Beyond the Hancock Loop Trail junction, Cedar Brook Trail offers fine snowshoeing in a remote, little-visited area. Climbing moderately, in 0.7 mile it enters the Pemigewasset Wilderness on a high, boggy plateau that forms the 3100-ft. height of land between Mts. Hitchcock and Hancock. At the north edge of this flat, there's a glimpse through the scrubby conifers to Mt. Lafayette in the distance. As an alternative to Hancock Notch, a round trip to this point from the Hancock overlook on the Kancamagus Highway is 6.2 miles with a 1000-ft. elevation gain.

Beyond the saddle, the Cedar Brook Trail—often with untracked snow —makes a long, easy descent down the isolated valley of Cedar Brook into the drainage of the East Branch of the Pemigewasset. Along the way, you'll pass the clearing of Camp 24 of the East Branch & Lincoln logging railroad. It's 4.1 miles from the saddle to the Pemi East Side Trail and another 0.6 mile to the Wilderness Trail at the "Swinging Bridge" over the river. Either of these trails can be followed out 5+ miles to the Lincoln Woods parking area. This makes a 13-mile loop possible with a car spot. It's a long day through remote country and is for experienced snowshoers only.

Livermore Pass *4.2 miles round trip, 850-ft. elevation gain, intermediate* From a plowed roadside parking area beside Lily Pond on the Kancamagus Highway, the Livermore Trail leads up to Livermore Pass, a high, flat saddle between Mt. Kancamagus on the NW and Mt. Tripyramid's Scaur Peak on the SE. In the first section you cross logging clearings with views back to the north. Look for a left turn at 0.6 mile and a right turn at 1.0 mile. The climb becomes fairly steep as the trail slices up the side of a beautiful hardwood gorge; if crusty, the sidehilling can be tough. The pass, a neat, wild plateau of spruce woods with a few little boggy meadows, is reached at 2.1 miles.

You can extend the trip through the pass to the Flume Brook Camp clearing at 2.8 miles. From here, the primitive Kancamagus Ski Touring Trail (which eventually connects with Greeley Ponds Trail 1.3 miles from its south end) can be followed through boggy terrain about 0.3 mile to two frozen beaver ponds with views of Mt. Tripyramid. Back at the trailhead, a jaunt out onto frozen Lily Pond will give you another perspective on Tripyramid, along with vistas of Mt. Kancamagus and mighty Mt. Carrigain.

24. Greeley Ponds

LOCATION: Off Kancamagus Highway

DESCRIPTION: An easy half-day trip to a pair of ponds nestled in a deep backcountry notch.

TRAIL: Greeley Ponds Trail

DISTANCE: 4.4 miles round trip

STARTING ELEVATION: 1940 ft.

HIGHEST ELEVATION: 2300 ft.

ELEVATION GAIN: 450 ft.

RATING: Beginner

USGS MAP: Mt. Osceola

TRAILHEAD: This hike begins at the north end of Greeley Ponds Trail, accessed via the Kancamagus Highway (NH 112), 9.8 miles east of the stoplight at Exit 32 off I-93. It's 4.7 miles east of the Lincoln Woods trailhead. Approaching from this direction, you'll first come to a marked pulloff for the Greeley Ponds X-C Trail. Continue ahead another 0.3 mile, over a bridge and around a curve, to the sign for the Greeley Ponds hiking trail on the right. A small plowed parking area is provided here. Coming in the other direction on "the Kanc" you'll find the trailhead on the left 0.8 mile beyond the hairpin turn by Hancock Overlook.

WMNF PARKING PASS: Yes

Beginning snowshoers can rejoice that a scenic backcountry spot such as Greeley Ponds is so easily accessible. With a relatively short and gently graded snowshoe ramble you can seclude yourself in the inner sanctum of glacier-carved Mad River Notch. The two small frozen ponds provide amazing vistas up to the enclosing cliff-studded walls of Mt. Kancamagus and the East Peak of Mt. Osceola.

From the parking area the yellow-blazed Greeley Ponds Trail leads into a deep mixed forest of evergreens and hardwoods. This is a popular trail throughout the year, so you'll often have a nice firm snowshoe track to ease you along. In fact, this trail is easier in winter with its often rocky, rooty, and muddy footing masked by deep snow cover.

After a rolling 0.3 mile, you dip to cross two adjacent branches of the South Fork of the Hancock Branch. The former bridge at this spot was washed out a few years ago, but these crossings normally present little difficulty. Soon you pass a large boulder on the left and twist gradually upward along the east side of the shallow valley drained by the South Fork. In a few places there are bog bridges buried under the snow.

At 0.9 mile the trail makes a left turn onto an old logging road that climbs gently southward toward Mad River Notch, whose steep slopes can

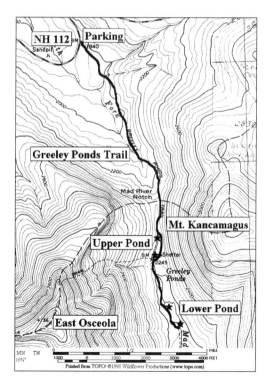

*Snowshoeing across
Upper Greeley Pond*

be glimpsed ahead to the left and right. At 1.2 miles you swing right, then left and up to the 2300-ft. height of land in the notch, where the Mt. Osceola Trail splits right at 1.3 miles. Just beyond this junction, the Greeley Ponds X-C Ski Trail joins the hiking trail, having followed a course on the west side of the South Fork valley. Note this junction for the return trip. The hiking trail is blazed in yellow while the X-C route is marked with blue diamonds.

The Greeley Ponds Trail now descends gently towards the Upper Pond, passing an interesting boulder on the right. At 1.5 miles, the X-C trail diverges left while the hiking trail angles right. Either can be followed to the north end of the Upper Pond. In midwinter, when the pond is well-frozen, the X-C route is more interesting. After a short, steep drop, it emerges at the NE corner of the pond, where there's a view across the snowy opening to the steep SE spur of East Osceola. From here you can traverse southward across the pond. Keep to the middle or the east edge, avoiding the inlet at the NW corner and the outlet at the SW corner. This small pond is generally well-frozen through most of the winter. From the center, you can look up at the steep, ledgy slopes on either side—Mt. Kancamagus on the east and East Osceola on the west. It's a magnificent winter scene. Shuffle over to the SE corner for the best view up to the great mountain wall of East Osceola, scored with snowy slides. A northern spur is armored with a long line of cliffs. The clearing at the shore here was the site of a lean-to until it was removed in 1969 to protect the area from overuse. Camping is prohibited year-round within the 810-acre Greeley Ponds Scenic Area that surrounds the ponds.

If you're unsure about ice conditions, this scenic spot can also be reached by following the hiking trail along a bank above the west shore. At the SW corner of the pond, an unmarked side path leads left across the outlet brook and through the woods to the clearing with the view up to East Osceola.

To continue southward to the Lower Pond, follow the side path back to the hiking trail and turn left. You descend over easy ground and snowshoe through a nice hardwood stand. Stay right on the hiking trail where the X-C trail angles off to the left. At 0.3 mile from the Upper Pond, you drift past a bog on the left and come to the NW corner of the larger, more open Lower Pond. A short jog to the left brings you out to a shoreline opening with a view across the pond to the south ridge of Mt. Kancamagus.

Lower Pond is shallow and boggy, with less reliable ice than the deep Upper Pond. Beware of weak ice and air pockets at the boggy north end. In midwinter it's usually fine to traverse southward along the west edge from the viewpoint—look for recent snowshoe or ski tracks. If you cut across the windswept ice to the SE corner of the pond, you'll find perhaps the most dramatic view in the notch, where the eastern front of East Osceola spreads for nearly a mile stem to stern. This is a great lunch and photo spot.

If a traverse of the ice on Lower Pond seems uncertain—you should always err on the side of caution—you can continue snowshoeing southward on the hiking trail behind the west shore. At the pond's SW corner, 2.2 miles from the trailhead, the trail swerves left to a clearing in the woods. Here a short jaunt left will bring you to a shoreline vista looking north up Lower Pond to the profile of Mad River Notch.

If you wish to reach the fine viewpoint at the SE corner of Lower Pond without crossing the pond, you must proceed about 0.2 mile farther south on the hiking trail to where it crosses the Mad River (here a small brook), then turn left on the east bank and follow a X-C trail back to the north for 0.2 mile to the vista. It's worth the extra 0.8-mile round trip added to the listed distance.

No matter which option you choose at Lower Pond, the return trip involves about 100 feet of gentle climbing back to the height-of-land in Mad River Notch before the easy descent to the trailhead.

ADDITIONAL OPTION

East Pond *7.4 miles round trip, 1900-ft. elevation gain, intermediate/advanced*
For a remote snowshoeing adventure off the Kancamagus Highway, con-

sider the East Pond Trail, which leads up over a gap in the Mt. Osceola/Scar Ridge range and down to scenic East Pond. This route sees little use beyond the first mile or so, and its moderate grades are ideal for snowshoeing. The parking area for the East Pond Trail is usually plowed. You'll find it on the south side of the highway 3.8 miles east of the Lincoln Woods trailhead and 0.9 mile west of the Greeley Ponds hiking trailhead.

For the first 0.8 mile the East Pond Trail follows a curving old logging railroad spur from the J. E. Henry days in the 1890s. It leaves the grade to cross Pine Brook, then climbs at easy to moderate grades to a crossing of Cheney Brook at 2.0 miles. Next you undertake a long, steady climb up an old logging road on the west side of the Cheney Brook basin, through dense conifer and birch forest. At 2.6 miles you hook left around the head of the ravine and reach the wild, windswept wooded col (elevation 3100 ft.) at 2.9 miles. From here you descend 0.8 mile and 500 feet to six-acre East Pond (elevation 2600 ft.). The trail tracks through the woods on the west side of the pond—if it's well-frozen you can pop out for a traverse across the ice. At the south end of the pond, a short side path leads left to an opening at the shore with a view up to the gap you came through on the ridge. Snowmobilers occasionally come up to East Pond from the south end of East Pond Trail off the unplowed Tripoli Road; otherwise you're likely to have the pond to yourself.

If you crave an even more remote spot, you can snowshoe the East Pond Loop, which leaves East Pond Trail by the south end of the pond. This narrow, wild trail rolls across a couple of low ridges and in 1.5 miles drops you at Little East Pond, a tiny tarn huddled in the shadow of Scar Ridge. To visit both ponds entails a 10.4-mile round trip with 2300-ft. elevation gain. In either case, remember that you have a 500-ft. climb over the ridge to return to your car.

25. Lincoln Woods Trails

The trail system at Lincoln Woods, near the western end of the Kancamagus Highway, is one of the most popular winter playgrounds in the White Mountains for snowshoers, cross country skiers and winter hikers. Trails on either side of the East Branch of the Pemigewasset River—the region's premier wilderness watercourse—offer a variety of options, all at easy grades. Although there are no easily accessible mountaintop vistas at Lincoln Woods, you can snowshoe to such attractive destinations as Black Pond, Franconia Falls, and a number of scenic spots along the wide, rocky East Branch itself. Lincoln Woods is also the gateway to the 45,000-acre

Pemigewasset Wilderness, where adventurous snowshoers can launch off on longer treks with a better chance for solitude than during the busy months of summer and fall. There's a fine winter adventure here for every level of snowshoer.

The Lincoln Woods trailhead is located on the north side of the Kancamagus Highway (NH 112), 5.6 miles east of the stoplight at the I-93 exit ramp in Lincoln and 5.5 miles west of the hairpin turn by the Hancock Overlook. It's just east of the bridge over the East Branch of the Pemigewasset River. There's a large, plowed parking lot that can accommodate over 100 cars. A WMNF Parking Pass is required. The Forest Service staffs a visitor center here in a beautiful log building heated by a wood stove. Free literature and trail advice are available here, and refreshments such as hot chocolate may be purchased. There are toilet facilities in the center of the parking area. From the walkway in front of the cabin there are views south to Black Mtn. and Scar Ridge, the latter scored by snowy slides.

There are two main "trunk trails" at Lincoln Woods. The **Lincoln Woods Trail** follows the west side of the river along the wide, level grade of the East Branch & Lincoln logging railroad. After 2.9 miles, this becomes the Wilderness Trail, bending east and extending another 6 miles deep

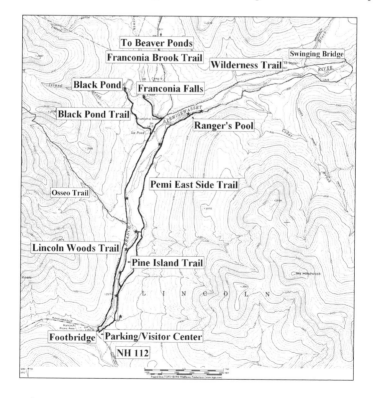

into the Pemigewasset Wilderness. The **Pemi East Side Trail**, also known as the East Branch Truck Road, shadows the east side of the river along an unplowed road for 2.8 miles to the Franconia Brook Campsite and a gate marking the Wilderness boundary. Here it, too, swings to the east, running another 2.3 miles to end at the Cedar Brook Trail, 0.5 mile above the "Swinging Bridge" over the East Branch. Side trails branch off both of the main routes, offering a variety of easy, interesting trips. In general, the west side sees much more use than the east. This entire area is covered by the USGS Mt. Osceola quadrangle. Trailhead elevation is 1160 ft.

The Forest Service often grooms both of these trails up to the Wilderness boundary. To accommodate all users in this heavily trafficked area, both the Lincoln Woods Trail and Pemi East Side Trail have designated "lanes" for winter travel. Snowshoers should use the middle of the trail, between the inbound and outbound ski tracks. Be a courteous winter trekker and don't trample the ski tracks. Except at the Franconia Brook Campsite, camping is not allowed within ¼ mile of these trails until you're about four miles in. Also, note that crossing the East Branch is not recommended in winter; if exploring along the shore, keep to the snow and ice by the edges and away from the main current.

There is little elevation gain on these trails, so unlike many snowshoe hikes, your return will not be significantly faster than your inbound time. You'll have basically the same plodding lowland pace the whole way. Some snowshoers will find this monotonous after a few miles, while others may relish the relative ease of penetrating deep into remote country.

To access the trails on either side of the river, follow the well-packed walkway that leads north past the front of the visitor center and curves left down to a T-junction with the Pemi East Side Trail. Turn right here to head up the east side of the river. For Lincoln Woods Trail, turn left, then in 200 feet swing right past a kiosk and cross the East Branch on a 160-foot suspension bridge. On the far side, turn right on the wide railroad bed.

Lincoln Woods Trail

TRIP OPTIONS

- **East Branch/Bonds Viewpoint** *3.2 miles round trip, 150-ft. elevation gain, beginner*
- **Black Pond via Black Pond Trail** *6.8 miles round trip, 450-ft. elevation gain, beginner/intermediate*
- **Franconia Falls via side trail** *6.6 miles round trip, 350-ft. elevation gain, beginner/intermediate*
- **Franconia Brook Beaver Ponds via Franconia Brook Trail** *10.4 miles round trip, 600-ft. elevation gain, intermediate/advanced*
- **Swinging Bridge Loop** *11.0-mile loop, 600-ft. elevation gain, intermediate/advanced*

Camp 8 clearing along Lincoln Woods Trail

The Lincoln Woods Trail provides a painless introduction to snowshoeing on a trail that is nearly always packed out. The grade is smooth and level, and there are scenic spots to visit along the way. It's a good place for "never-ever" snowshoers to start. This is one of the most heavily used trails in the White Mountains, winter and summer, so expect plenty of company on weekends, especially in the first couple of miles. In times of snow drought the wide trail becomes hard-packed and sometimes icy.

From the end of the suspension bridge, turn right onto the railroad grade and snowshoe northward under a canopy of hemlock and pine. The short section at the start is the first to ice up in lean snow times. After 0.2 mile you emerge into an open hardwood forest. At 0.4 mile there's a nice section along a high bank above the East Branch—a west spur of Mt. Hitchcock, slashed by a whitened rock slide, can be seen across the river. You cross a culvert over Osseo Brook at 0.8 mile, and at 1.0 mile you swing into a long straightaway that leads to a birch glade and the junction with the **Osseo Trail** on the left at 1.4 miles. (The Osseo Trail provides good snowshoeing up the valley of Osseo Brook, following old logging roads at easy upgrades for about two miles with one stretch of sidehill maneuvering a short way in. There are no views in this section, but it is a nice, quiet place to snowshoe. Beyond the two-mile mark, the Osseo Trail becomes much steeper and is suitable for advanced snowshoers.)

Just beyond the junction with the Osseo Trail, the Lincoln Woods Trail passes a clearing on the left that marks the site of Camp 8, one of over two dozen logging camps operated across the East Branch drainage by the East

Branch & Lincoln Railroad. The Lincoln Woods Trail follows the main rail line, from which spur lines were spun off into various valleys. This railroad sprang into existence when J. E. Henry, the most infamous of the White Mountain lumber barons, brought his entourage to the sleepy village of Lincoln in 1892. Rails were first laid up the lower East Branch and the Hancock Branch, and by the turn of the century the line was being pushed farther up the East Branch valley along the section you're snowshoeing now.

Eventually, over fifty miles of railroad laced the East Branch country, accessing over 60,000 acres of prime timber, mostly spruce. At its height the J. E. Henry Co. employed over 500 men. Massive clear-cutting was the order of the day, and photos from the early 1900s depict a landscape ravaged by lumbering and subsequent fires. The Parker–Young Co. took over the operation in 1917 and ran the East Branch & Lincoln railroad until 1948, picking over the remaining timber stands. In its five decades of operation, the EB&L hauled over one billion board feet of lumber out to the mills in Lincoln a few miles downstream. (For a full recounting of the fascinating history of the East Branch & Lincoln Railroad, see *J. E. Henry's Logging Railroads*, by Bill Gove, published by Bondcliff Books.)

Camp 8 beside the Lincoln Woods Trail was first established in 1902 and remained intermittently in use until 1945. Here, the EB&L loggers lived, swore, ate, and snored in between dawn-to-dusk workdays in the woods. Winter, when it was easiest to skid logs, was the prime working season. Though the camp buildings are long gone, the soil in the area was so compacted that trees have yet to gain a foothold.

Continuing on the trail beyond the camp, the grade is slightly downhill, then at 1.6 miles you come close by the edge of the river. If you snowshoe out among the rocks along the shore, you'll gain a gorgeous vista up the wide, snowbound river to the high and remote ridge of Bondcliff. This treeless peak rises in the heart of the Pemigewasset Wilderness, a 45,000-acre logging-free preserve established by Congress in 1984. Downstream you can see the rugged ridge of Mt. Osceola. This scenic spot is a nice objective for snowshoers out for a short and very easy trek.

The Lincoln Woods Trail continues up the grade, crossing Birch Island Brook on a bridge, and enters a straightaway where you can see a half mile or more ahead. At 2.6 miles, the **Black Pond Trail** (see below) diverges left, and after passing the former Franconia Brook Campsite area (closed to all camping), you come to the junction with the trail to **Franconia Falls** at 2.9 miles (see below). On the right, a wide path leads down 200 feet to a rocky area at the confluence of Franconia Brook and the East Branch—a scenic spot worth the short detour.

Just beyond, the Lincoln Woods Trail crosses Franconia Brook on a footbridge at the site of a former railroad trestle. Look upstream for a view of Mt. Flume. On the north side of the bridge, the trail enters the Pemigewasset Wilderness and becomes the Wilderness Trail.

Here the **Franconia Brook Trail** climbs left up a bank and embarks on a 5-mile journey to the scenic 13 Falls area. Most of this trail is on another railroad grade. The first mile is a plod through the woods, with two crossings of Camp 9 Brook. At 1.0 mile from Lincoln Woods Trail, there's a bypass to the right, 0.2 mile long, where beavers have flooded the location of J. E. Henry's Camp 9. To the left, this bypass offers interesting vistas across the swamps to the wild cliffs and ridges of Owl's Head Mtn. At the north end of the bypass, the trail crosses Camp 9 Brook again and climbs back to the left, soon rejoining the railroad grade. Other beaver ponds at 1.8 miles (just past the Lincoln Brook Trail junction) and 2.3 miles (0.3 mile south of Hellgate Brook) open views up to the lower ridges of the Bond range to the east. Be wary of venturing too far out on the ice. Snowshoeing out into this remote valley gives you a nice taste of the interior of the Pemigewasset Wilderness with relatively little effort. Round-trip from the parking lot to the northernmost beaver pond is 10.4 miles with just 600 feet of elevation gain.

Beyond the junction with Franconia Brook Trail, the **Wilderness Trail** heads eastward, parallel to but mostly away from the East Branch. An interesting historic objective, at least temporarily, is the last remaining logging trestle in the valley, located by the trail bridge at the crossing of Black Brook at 4.7 miles. This is just beyond the old Camp 16 location and the junction with Bondcliff Trail. This timbered bridge is slated for removal and is unsafe to walk on, but is fascinating to inspect from below. At 0.7 mile beyond the trestle, the Wilderness Trail crosses the East Branch on the "Swinging Bridge" and meets the Cedar Brook Trail (elevation 1640 ft.) From here it's 5.4 miles to return the way you came, or 5.6 miles back via the Cedar Brook Trail and Pemi East Side Trail, creating an 11-mile lowland loop.

Black Pond Trail This narrow, less-used trail leaves the Lincoln Woods Trail 2.6 miles from the parking lot and leads 0.8 mile to sheltered, secluded Black Pond, where there are views of Owl's Head and the Bond Range. At first, the trail follows a short railroad spur, with an open, snowy meadow to the left. This was known as Ice Pond, an impoundment created by J. E. Henry's crews to make ice for refrigeration in the logging camps. The yellow-blazed trail winds along the edge of a beaver-flooded area, then joins an old logging road that leads through a clearing at the site of the loggers' Camp 7.

Now you snowshoe gently along a bank above Birch Island Brook, winding through a pretty hardwood glen. At 0.5 mile you dip to cross the tiny outlet brook from Black Pond, then follow it upstream, crossing twice more. As you approach the outlet, a view opens to the sharp pyramid of the south peak of Owl's Head. The trail tracks through conifers and ends at 0.8 mile by a spruce-shaded boulder on the SW shore of the pond. The picturesque view across the snowy opening takes in the distant ridges of Bondcliff and West Bond rising over the treetops. If the ice is solid—and this small, protected pond usually freezes early in the winter—you can find additional views around the pond looking up to Owl's Head, Mt. Flume and Whaleback Mtn. Avoid the ice by the outlet.

Franconia Falls Trail   Franconia Falls is a beautiful and popular area of ledges, potholes, and cascades along a wide, sloping section of Franconia Brook. In winter, when the surging water is muted by ice and snow, the beauty is more subtle here.

The spur trail departs left from the Lincoln Woods Trail 2.9 miles from the trailhead, just before the footbridge over Franconia Brook. You meander easily upward under tall pines beside the wide, snowbound brook. After pulling briefly away, the trail returns close to the stream and reaches the falls at 0.3 mile. A side path right brings you out to snowy ledges at the top, where there is a view of the north peaks of Mt. Hitchcock and Mt. Hancock to the SE. It's fun to explore this open area on snowshoes, but be careful in places where there may be water running underneath.

Pemi East Side Trail

TRIP OPTIONS

- **Scar Ridge View** *1.0 mile round trip, minimal elevation gain, beginner*
- **Pine Island Loop** *2.8 miles round trip, 100-ft. elevation gain, beginner*
- **Riverbank View and Ranger's Pool** *6.8 miles round trip, 350-ft. elevation gain, beginner/intermediate*

The Pemi East Side Trail (East Branch Truck Road) follows the bed of a road built in the 1940s, during the twilight of the East Branch & Lincoln Railroad logging operation. From 1941–1948, it was used to haul timber out of the Mt. Hitchcock and Camp 16 areas. The road later served as a snowmobile route into the East Branch country, but that use ended with the establishment of the Pemigewasset Wilderness in 1984. It provides easy snowshoeing with several good riverside vistas, and can be used with the Pine Island Trail to make a nifty beginner's loop.

Turn right at the bottom of the path by the visitor center and follow the roadbed northward through mixed woods. At 0.2 mile a narrow spur road veers off to the right, leading 0.1 mile to an open field recently used as a logging yard. From various points around the opening there are views north to West Bond and Bondcliff and south to Scar Ridge and Black Mtn.

The main trail winds through tall pine, spruce, and hemlock. At 0.5 mile, just past a dip in the road, a short spur leads left to the river's edge. Dip down to the snowy rocks here for a view downstream to the dark, massive bulk of Scar Ridge, wearing a necklace of snowy slides. This is a nice objective for a very short, easy outing.

The Pemi East Side Trail now runs alongside the river through a hardwood stand, and in 0.1 mile comes to the base of a short, steep hill—watch for descending skiers. Here the Pine Island Trail splits left (see below). If not doing the Pine Island loop, bear right and climb the hill, then ascend more gradually along a high bank. At 1.0 mile, a short descent leads to a crossing of Pine Island Brook over a culvert.

You snowshoe up the winding road through birch stands, passing a series of small beaver meadows on the right. At 1.4 miles the north end of Pine Island Trail comes in on the left. The Pemi East Side Trail passes more beaver openings and wanders through birch glades. You climb a couple of minor hills, cross over a knoll at 2.1 miles, and emerge in a clearing on a high bank overlooking the East Branch at 2.5 miles. Across the wide river is a procession of high ridges. To the west are ledgy Whaleback Mtn and Mt. Flume, with a prominent white patch to the right of its summit. Looking to the NW you see the sharp south peak of Owl's Head and the high, snowy crest of Franconia Ridge.

Beyond the outlook the road passes the relocated Franconia Brook campground area (24 sites) and its attendant port-a-potties. At 2.8 miles you reach a gate and the Pemigewasset Wilderness boundary. A spur on the left descends to the river's edge across from its merge with Franconia Brook. *Crossing the East Branch in winter is not recommended.*

Up to this point the road is improved and is used in summer by Forest Service vehicles for administration. Beyond the gate the Pemi East Side Trail bends eastward with the river. Usage is lighter here, and the trail assumes a wilder persona. After 0.3 mile of pleasant snowshoeing, look for a side path descending left to a large frozen pool in the river, known locally as the "Ranger's Pool." You can snowshoe down to a small snowy beach area and adjacent ledges. Along the bank are several white cedar trees—a rarity in the White Mountains. Look left for a wintry view downstream to the steep-sided ridge of Whaleback Mtn. (Even if the pool looks frozen, I would not venture out on the ice—there's still a current running underneath.)

Beyond the Ranger's Pool, the Pemi East Side Trail continues to shadow the river for another 0.3 mile, passing more old white cedar trees and providing attractive river views. At 3.4 miles, beyond the east end of a wooded island, the trail touches the river's edge beside gentle, snow-covered slabs and a pool fringed by large boulders. This scenic spot is a good turnaround point for a leisurely day of snowshoeing with very little climbing.

The Pemi East Side Trail continues eastward for another 1.7 miles to the Cedar Brook Trail, winding through fine forest, mostly away from the river. There's a crossing of Cedar Brook at 3.9 miles. In its last 0.2 mile it climbs moderately. A left turn on Cedar Brook Trail leads you gently down an old railroad grade to meet the Wilderness Trail by the "Swinging Bridge." It's 5.6 miles to return the way you came, or 5.4 miles to complete the loop via the Wilderness and Lincoln Woods Trails.

The Ranger's Pool on the East Branch

Pine Island Trail   This narrow riverside trail, 0.8 mile long, offers some of the most scenic no-stress snowshoeing in the mountains. There are several points where you can scoot out to the fringe of the East Branch for wide views of the river and encircling mountains. Combined with the Pemi East Side Trail it makes a terrific 3-mile beginner's loop. The only fly in the ointment is the crossing of Pine Island Brook near the start of the trail, which can be tricky if the stream is not well-frozen.

The Pine Island Trail splits left from the Pemi East Side Trail at a sign, 0.6 mile from the parking lot. Well-blazed in yellow, it follows an old roadbed a short distance, then angles left to the crossing of Pine Island Brook. In another 100 feet you cross a second stream bed which usually doesn't freeze well and requires a bit of maneuvering on snow-covered rocks. After a slight rise, the trail bends north (right) and at 0.2 mile the broad East Branch comes into sight on the left.

If you immediately cut to the left through open woods, you'll come out past a low-spreading oak tree to a rocky fringe of the river that is dry in summer and buried in snow in the winter. Looking upstream from this outlook you'll see the triple humps of South Twin Mtn. and the blade-like ridge of West Bond, striped with slides.

The Pine Island Trail tracks northward along the river through open woods—follow the yellow blazes carefully. At 0.4 mile you enter an area of small, open groves of red pine, and at 0.5 mile you bend left, then right into a scrubby area of birch and alder. Here the trail angles across a rocky brookbed that is dry most of the year—this forms the north end of "Pine

Island." Snowshoe a few yards left to an open outwash area alongside the East Branch for a photogenic view upstream to West Bond (left) and Bond-cliff (right).

After crossing the dry brookbed, Pine Island Trail plunges into a dark conifer forest and continues northward along the river, with glimpses left to Whaleback Mtn. and ahead to Owl's Head. At 0.8 mile the trail makes a 90-degree right turn. Here a short spur bears left and drops down an overgrown bank to an extensive streambed area that is nearly dry most of the year. A snowshoe exploration up and down this open swath rewards with views south to Scar Ridge and pyramidal Black Mtn. and NW to Mt. Flume and the ledgy spurs of Whaleback Mtn.

At the right turn the Pine Island Trail runs 200 feet east to its northern terminus on the Pemi East Side Trail, 1.4 miles from the trailhead. Turn right to complete the Pine Island loop.

26. Flume–Pool Loop

LOCATION: Franconia Notch

DESCRIPTION: A woodland loop that includes two covered bridges, frozen waterfalls and scenic gorges at The Flume and The Pool.

TRAILS: Flume Path, Rim Path, Ridge Path, Wildwood Path

DISTANCE: 2.2 miles

STARTING ELEVATION: 1400 ft.

HIGHEST ELEVATION: 1560 ft.

ELEVATION GAIN: 400 ft.

RATING: Beginner (but see cautionary notes)

USGS MAP: Lincoln

TRAILHEAD: This ramble starts at the northernmost parking area at the Flume Visitor Center in Franconia Notch State Park. Take Exit 34A off the Franconia Notch Parkway (I-93). If going north, continue up US 3 from the exit ramp for 0.3 mile to the second entrance to the Flume on the right and loop around to the farthest parking area to the left (north). Heading off the southbound exit, drive down US 3 0.4 mile to the first Flume entrance on the left and loop around to the northern parking area. There's plenty of plowed parking space at this popular jumping-off place for walkers, snowshoers, skiers, and snowmobilers.

WMNF PARKING PASS: No

In summer and fall, The Flume Gorge is one of the most popular attractions in the White Mountains. Throngs of tourists parade through this narrow, 800-foot long chasm to gawk at its mossy rock walls and the tumbling waterfall at its head. In winter, The Flume is transformed into a wonderland of deep snow and gleaming icefalls. Although you can't walk *through* the gorge in winter—the boardwalk is taken up at the end of the season—you can still enjoy a short snowshoe trek to views from below and above. From the top of the Flume, you can continue on a loop along woodland paths to view Liberty Gorge and Cascade, The Pool, the Sentinel Pine Bridge, and a vista of Mts. Liberty and Flume. There are enough attractions here to fashion a leisurely, enjoyable several hours of snowshoeing. It's an easy trip with only a few hundred feet of climbing, but you should exercise caution near the steep drop-offs above the Flume, Liberty Gorge, and The Pool. With deep snow, the fences enclosing some of the viewing platforms could be buried! In that case, or if conditions are crusty or icy, it's safest to avoid the side paths down to several of the viewing platforms. Unlike the summer, there is no admission charge to The Flume in winter. The Flume Visitors' Center and all other facilities here are closed from late October through mid-May.

From the northernmost parking area for the Flume, walk north on the Franconia Notch State Park Recreation Trail (a.k.a. "the bike path"), which is packed down by snowmobiles. Climb gradually for about 150 yards, passing the Mt. Pemigewasset Trail on the left, to a stop sign. Turn right on an unplowed road that descends, then levels and comes to a closed wooden gate. Snowshoe around the gate and reach a T-junction. Turn right here, then left where a road, and usually a beaten track, joins from behind the Visitor Center. From here to the Flume the trail is often hard-packed. You descend rather steeply to the 1871-vintage Flume Covered Bridge at 0.3 mile. The red bridge is often bedecked with a wreath; as you approach you can see Mt. Liberty looming overhead.

You'll want to take your snowshoes off to walk through the bridge, which spans the Pemigewasset River. Beyond, follow the walkway (the "Flume Path") to the left of the gray Boulder Cabin. Bear right at a fence and climb easily alongside the snowy ledges of Flume Brook. You soon enter a hemlock grove where the footing can be icy in lean snow times. Continue past a footbridge on the left and in another 100 feet, angle left across a second bridge and up to a third bridge at 0.6 mile, where further access is barred in winter. Here you'll enjoy a neat view up into The Flume, whose walls are 70 to 90 feet high and 12 to 20 feet apart. The right hand wall is draped with fantastic flows of blue, gray and brown ice. You may see ice climbers kicking and clawing their way up the steep pillars.

The Flume was formed by the erosion of a dike of basalt that intruded long ago into a vertical fracture in the granite bedrock. Over time, water

The Flume has a different look in winter

eroded the relatively soft basalt, leaving the narrow gap between steep walls of erosion-resistant granite.

To continue the loop trip, return across the upper two bridges and turn right on the lowest bridge, crossing the brook and emerging into an open hardwood forest. You soon come to a T-junction at a signpost—turn right and climb for about 0.1 mile on the "Rim Path," passing a viewpoint on the right looking over the lower gorge.

Turn right at a fork, and in 75 feet right again and make a short, steep climb, then dip and curve left to an open-front resting shelter at 0.8 mile, near the top of The Flume. Down a few yards to the right you'll find fenced platforms for viewing the ice formations of Avalanche Falls and the upper gorge. Use caution as there are steep drop-offs in front.

Retrace your steps down to the last junction and proceed straight ahead on the Ridge Path, quickly passing another junction on the left. This is a very pleasant meander through an open hardwood forest, slightly uphill at first, then gently downhill. Mt. Pemigewasset can be glimpsed out to the left through the trees. The wide trail weaves downward to a bridge across a brook at 1.4 miles.

Beyond a shelter you swing left to a fenced side path that drops steeply left to a high, fenced-in viewing platform looking across Liberty Gorge to frozen Liberty Cascade. (Use caution.) From this junction, the Ridge Path jogs right and descends to a high bluff overlooking The Pool, a huge pothole in the riverbed rock far below. Stay back from the edge here as the rock wall embracing The Pool has a sheer 100-foot drop. In the 1800s, an eccentric character named "Professor" John Merrill, also known as "The Old Philosopher," gave visitors a tour around The Pool in his rowboat while enriching them with his homespun philosophy.

The trail now zigzags down to the Sentinel Pine Bridge, a span built in 1939 high above the river at the north side of The Pool. The bridge rests on the trunk of a giant white pine felled by the 1938 hurricane. If there's not enough snow drifted inside, you may need to take your snowshoes off to cross through. From the bridge, there's a nice view down to The Pool and the snowbound river beyond.

Exit the bridge with a sharp left turn and climb 100 feet to a right turn in the main trail, now called the "Wildwood Path." Here, a side trail leads ahead, then left and steeply down to a viewing platform (again, use caution). There's an impressive view of the cliffs on the other side of The Pool, and the Sentinel Pine Bridge up to the left.

Beyond this side trail, the Wildwood Path switchbacks upward to the "Westside Shelter," then continues another 100 feet to a beautiful cleared vista up to the craggy, snow-clad crest of Mt Liberty, buttressed by broad ridges, with the scarred face of Mt. Flume peering over on the right. These summits rise 3000 feet above your lowly viewing spot.

The Wildwood Path now rolls, weaves, and dips through an area of large boulders, brushes close by the bike path on the right, then veers left and descends. At the bottom swing right, pass a huge boulder on the right, and at 2.0 miles reach a junction with the unplowed road you came in on to start the loop. Turn right here and climb up past the wooden gate to the bike path, then turn left for the short descent to the parking lot.

ADDITIONAL OPTION

Pemi Trail   This valley trail runs 5.6 miles up the length of Franconia Notch from the Liberty Spring parking area to the Old Man parking area north of Profile Lake. It roughly parallels the parkway and the bike path, which is a major snowmobile corridor route. The Pemi Trail offers easy snowshoeing through attractive woods from various locations in the Notch. Plowed access points include parking areas at the Liberty Spring trailhead, the Basin, Lafayette Place, and the Cannon Mountain Tramway (via the un-plowed access road leading south to the northern terminus of the trail.) One drawback of the trail is that parkway traffic noise is never far away.

From the Liberty Spring trailhead, the Pemi Trail coincides with the Whitehouse Trail for 0.6 mile and the bike path for 0.2 mile. It then splits left under the parkway with the Cascade Brook Trail and in another 0.2 mile peels right to follow the west side of the Pemigewasset River north up the notch. There are several nice sections along the river, including some cascades and the "Baby Flume" gorge just south of the great rock pothole known as The Basin, which is reached at 1.7 miles.

A side excursion west partway up the **Basin-Cascades Trail** is highly rewarding—in about 0.2 mile you come beside an open ledgy stretch of Cascade Brook where you can snowshoe right up the brookbed with views back to Mt. Liberty, and rejoin the trail farther up along the bank. Beyond the brook crossing above Kinsman Falls at 0.5 mile, the trail becomes quite rough and makes for difficult snowshoeing.

Beyond the Basin, the Pemi Trail continues gently up through the woods and along the river to Lafayette Place at 3.6 miles. It meanders through the quiet campground, soon crosses the river on a footbridge, and about 0.2 mile beyond passes by an interesting area of beaver meadows and ponds on the left. By snowshoeing out to the edge of the open area you can find a neat view north to Cannon Cliff and Eagle Cliff framing the notch.

Easy grades are the rule all the way up to the south end of Profile Lake at 5.1 miles; partway along a bridge takes you back to the west side of the river. Here the trail edges along the west shore of the lake with views across to the ice-draped face of Eagle Cliff and the steep west buttress of Mt. Lafayette. If the pond is safely frozen, you can snowshoe across to the NE corner for views up to the Old Man of the Mountain, 1200 feet above on the side of Cannon Mountain. (Avoid the inlet at the NW corner and the outlet at the south end.) From the NW side of the lake, the Pemi Trail climbs to its northern terminus at 5.6 miles; this point can be reached from the Old Man viewing area by following the walkway used by tourists in summer. From trail's end, the Cannon Tram parking lot is 0.2 mile ahead via the unplowed access road.

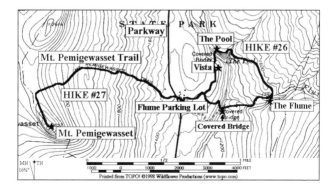

27. Mount Pemigewasset

LOCATION: Franconia Notch

DESCRIPTION: A moderate half-day climb to the clifftop viewpoint on the "Indian Head."

TRAIL: Mt. Pemigewasset Trail

DISTANCE: 3.6 miles round trip

STARTING ELEVATION: 1400 ft.

HIGHEST ELEVATION: 2557 ft.

ELEVATION GAIN: 1150 ft.

RATING: Intermediate

USGS MAP: Lincoln

TRAILHEAD: This trip starts on the Franconia Notch State Park Recreational Trail at the northernmost parking area for the Flume. Take Exit 34A off the Franconia Notch Parkway (I-93). From the northbound exit, continue north on US 3 and turn into the second of two Flume entrances on the right, and loop around to the north end of the parking complex, which is plowed. From the southbound exit, drive south on US 3 and turn into the first Flume entrance on the left, 0.1 mile south of the trailhead parking for Liberty Spring Trail.

WMNF PARKING PASS: No

The mildly strenuous climb of Mt. Pemigewassset has been a Franconia Notch favorite for many years. The moderate grades of the Mt. Pemigewasset Trail are ideal for snowshoeing and the broad ledges of the summit—where you're perched stop the cliffs that form the famous Indian Head profile—open sweeping views to the west, south and east.

From the Flume parking lot—a busy launching point for snowmobilers, snowshoers, and cross-country skiers—snowshoe north and uphill for 100 yards on the recreation path, which is well-packed by snowmobiles. Here the Mt. Pemigewasset Trail turns left to descend to an underpass beneath US 3. The trail sign may not be present in winter. From this turn-off you can see the wooded east side of Mt. Pemigewasset looming high above to the west.

Follow the blue-blazed trail through the underpass and then left as it descends to a bridge over a small brook. You hump over a knoll and then head upward through the underpasses for the northbound and southbound lanes of the parkway. If snow hasn't drifted in, you may have to take your snowshoes off to traverse the underpasses. After the last tunnel you climb up into the woods at 0.4 mile.

The trail angles upward across the slope to the right, crossing several small streams on log bridges. Farther along you swing left and mush up the slope at a moderate grade through an expansive northern hardwood forest, with an open feeling not found in the leafy tunnels of summer. At 1.3 miles the trail wiggles around a big boulder and swings left for a somewhat steeper climb. Spruce and fir darken the forest as you reach the ridgecrest and turn to the left (south). The Indian Head Trail comes in on the right at 1.7 miles. You continue a short way along the conifer-clad ridge, then veer left for a short scramble up to a ledge swath that leads along the cliff edge to the open summit ledges. *There's a major drop-off on the right here, so focus carefully on your footing.*

The broad fan of ledge atop the south cliff has plenty of flat perches, but use caution if crust or ice coat the rock, and stay back from the edge. From this main outlook ledge there's a sweeping vista south down the Pemigewasset River valley, with the twin ribbons of I-93 winding off into the distance amidst numerous hills and ridges. At your feet a hardwood plateau stretches out to a swampy area known as Bog Eddy. To the SW (right), beyond a powerline swath, is the long sloping crest of Mt. Wolf. The great snow-capped mass of Mt. Moosilauke hovers ghost-like behind and to the left through a notch in the ridgeline. Farther around to the right is a high wooded spur of South Kinsman Mountain.

An entirely different view awaits around the corner at the east ledges of Mt. Pemigewassset. Snowshoe left across the gently sloping slabs to find a terrific panorama of the Franconia Ridge. The bright spires of Mts. Lafayette, Lincoln, and Little Haystack line up to the NE, while eastward across the valley there's a broadside view of Mt. Liberty on the left, showing a notched rock summit, and Mt. Flume set back on the right, its face clawed by massive snowy slides. Due north there's a glimpse of Eagle Cliff and Cannon Mountain at the head of Franconia Notch.

Looking to the right (SE), you see the double-humped summit of Big Coolidge at the south end of the Franconia Range. Behind and to the right are Mt. Osceola, the lumpy mass of Scar Ridge, Loon Mountain and its ski trails, and the sharp cone of Mt. Tecumseh.

The Mt. Pemigewasset Trail is conducive to a quick snowshoe descent. Be sure to bear right behind the summit where the Indian Head Trail breaks off to the left.

ADDITIONAL OPTION

Lower Georgiana Falls *1.6 miles round trip, 300-ft. elevation gain, intermediate*
This is a nice, easy brookside trip with a short scramble at the end to the bottom of the falls. From Exit 33 off I-93, drive 0.2 mile north on US 3 and turn left on Hanson Farm Road. In 0.2 mile, where the main road bends right, continue straight to a plowed parking area. Watch out for snowmobiles, which use this short stretch of road to get across Rte. 3. Snowshoe the edge of the snowmobile trail west and under the northbound lanes of I-93, then

The east view from Mt. Pemigewasset

turn right (sign: Georgiana Falls) off the main snowmobile trail and follow a yellow-blazed roadway, which soon curves left up under southbound I-93. The road climbs gradually through the woods to a wider clearing at 0.5 mile; snowmobiles often pack the trail to this point. Just beyond, the unofficial trail to the falls veers left off the old road into the woods—look for a yellow blaze. Follow the trail up alongside Harvard Brook through pretty hemlock woods. The stream is picturesque in winter, with many large snow-draped boulders. Red blazes replace yellow and become more sparse, but the trail doesn't stray far from the brook. At 0.7 mile cross a rocky side stream and scramble up a steep pitch beyond. You can then snowshoe up the ledges on the right edge of the brook, or follow an easier path through the woods, emerging at 0.8 mile on open ledges beside the pool at the base of Lower Georgiana Falls—a steep, snowy face in winter. Beyond, the trail continues 0.5 mile to Upper Georgiana (Harvard) Falls. You could continue up through the woods to the right of the brook less than 0.1 mile and then cut left out to the snowy streambed for a framed view southeast over the Pemigewasset Valley. Past this point, the trail is too steep and rough for good snowshoeing.

28. Mt. Liberty

LOCATION: Franconia Notch

DESCRIPTION: A long, steady climb to a 4000-footer with panoramic views of Franconia Notch and the Pemigewasset Wilderness

TRAILS: Whitehouse Trail, Liberty Spring Trail, Franconia Ridge Trail

DISTANCE: 8.0 miles round trip

STARTING ELEVATION: 1400 ft.

HIGHEST ELEVATION: 4459 ft.

ELEVATION GAIN: 3250 ft.

RATING: Advanced

USGS MAP: Lincoln

TRAILHEAD: This hike begins at a plowed trailhead parking area for Liberty Spring Trail/Appalachian Trail on US 3, 0.1 mile north of the parking area for The Flume. Take Exit 34A off the Franconia Notch Parkway. Going north, the parking area will be 0.5 mile north of the exit ramp, on the right. Going south, it will be 0.2 mile south of the exit ramp, on the left. If the trailhead parking area is not plowed, you can park at The Flume lot and use the Franconia Notch Recreation Path in lieu of the Whitehouse Trail.

WMNF PARKING PASS: No

Spectacular views await the experienced and determined snowshoer who slogs up the long climb to the rock-crowned 4459-ft. summit of Mt. Liberty. This open peak reveals an astonishing wintry panorama of jumbled mountains in every direction. The trip is an all-day endeavor and calls for an early start. Although not really above treeline, Liberty's peak is fully exposed to winter's blasts and may be sheathed in crust and ice. Bring plenty of outerwear and perhaps a pair of instep crampons for the final scramble to the top.

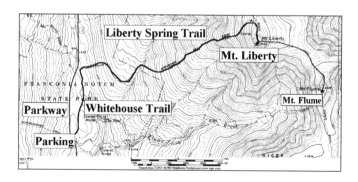

The summit of Mt. Liberty rises like a rock fortress from the snow

The first link in the hike follows the Whitehouse Trail. From trailhead parking this path climbs into the woods and winds along a hardwood plateau with several rolls and dips. At 0.6 mile it descends to the Franconia Notch Recreation Path (the bike path). Turn left on the bike path and follow it north on a snowmobile-packed surface. (Watch out for passing snowmobiles.) After brushing close by the parkway the path swings right across a bridge over a minor brook and follows a scenic course alongside the Pemigewasset River. At 0.8 mile you cross an arched bridge over the river, passing the junction with Cascade Brook Trail / Pemi Trail on the left. About 100 feet beyond the bridge, turn right on the white-blazed Liberty Spring Trail, a link in the Appalachian Trail.

The Liberty Spring Trail starts off with a traverse northward, rising moderately across a slope of open hardwoods. At 1.2 miles you make a sharp right and climb to the junction with Flume Slide Trail on the right at 1.4 miles. Continue ahead on Liberty Spring Trail. The grade is very easy for a while—you'll make up for it farther along. At 1.9 miles you cross a nameless brook and ascend moderately through hardwoods.

A sharp left at 2.3 miles marks a traverse up the slope to the start of a long, grinding climb to the ridge. The next mile is all business, pushing relentlessly upward through a forest of white birches and conifers. If you're breaking trail, plan on an hour or more for this section. Even with a packed trail the ascent seems to spin out endlessly—never too steep, but never letting up.

A grove of open firs signifies the approach to Liberty Spring Campsite at 3.4 miles / 3870 ft. On a side path right there's a partial view west to the Kinsmans and Moosilauke—a welcome excuse to take a break. The campsite area is to the left of the trail.

Above the campsite another 0.3 mile of steady slogging lifts you to the ridgecrest and the junction with Franconia Ridge Trail. Turn right here and wend your way up through the evergreens until you level on a little open ledgy ridge, with the castle-like wall of the summit crags looming close ahead. The views west and north are exhilarating after hours of mushing up through the woods. Look back to see the sharp snowy pinnacle of Mt. Lincoln a couple of miles up the ridge.

Use care as you scramble across this narrow crest, then around to the left and up to the right over snow-crusted ledges to the flat top of the rock peak, 4.0 miles from your car. If you're lucky enough to enjoy a calm, clear winter day, the 360-degree view from this lofty granite perch will hold your attention for a while. One glorious February day I spent three hours surveying the vast panorama, which includes 32 White Mountain 4000-footers.

Perhaps the finest vista is east into the Pemigewasset Wilderness. Mt. Liberty is positioned for a long look up the remote valley of the East Branch of the Pemigewasset River, hemmed in by Mts. Hancock and Carrigain on the south. Look NE for a broadside sweep of the Twin-Bond Range, where bright snow clings to the ragged face of Bondcliff and the massive rock slides in the wild glacial cirques on Mt. Guyot. Mt. Washington and the Presidentials gleam regally above and behind the Bonds.

Northward you gaze up the secluded drainage of Lincoln Brook, with the crouching ridge of Owl's Head on the right, the soaring Franconias on the left, and shapely Mt. Garfield floating at the head of the valley.

To the south, snowy slides gash the steep face of nearby Mt. Flume. Numerous peaks of the Osceola and Sandwich groups cluster beyond to the SE. The I-93 corridor and parts of the towns of Lincoln and Woodstock are seen in the Pemigewasset valley just west of south, with an untold number of hills and low mountains beyond.

The ghostly dome of Moosilauke hovers to the SW, and westward across lower Franconia Notch are the rolling twin summits of the Kinsmans. On clear winter days a long chain of Green Mountain peaks spans the horizon, including the distinctive tilt of Camel's Hump between the Kinsmans. To the NW the great cliff of Cannon Mtn. and its attendant talus slope are unmistakable landmarks.

After carefully negotiating the summit ledges and the rocky ridge beyond, you can enjoy a whooping, breathless slide down the long grade off the ridge. If the snow conditions are right it's feasible to snowshoe the three miles back to the bike path in an hour!

ADDITIONAL OPTION

Mt. Flume Strong snowshoers with plenty of stamina and daylight can scoot over to the summit of Mt. Flume and back on the Franconia Ridge

Trail. Because of the fairly deep col between the peaks, this 2.2-mile round trip involves an additional 1000 feet of elevation gain, bringing the day's total to 10.2 miles and 4250 ft. of elevation gain. The descent off Liberty is fairly steep. Down towards the col the trail is easy to lose; it heads generally SE towards Mt. Flume, then swings due south higher up.

The final approach to Flume's dramatic, knife-edged summit leads you up through snow-packed scrub. The high point (4328 ft.) is at the north end. Use care as there is a precipitous drop on the west side. The views are similar to those from Liberty, though from a different perspective, with the added pleasure of looking almost straight down the slides on the west face.

A loop descent via Flume Slide Trail may look tempting on the map, but this route is treacherous and difficult and is emphatically not recommended for most snowshoers. Better to huff up the 600-ft. ascent back over Liberty and descend the safer Liberty Spring Trail.

29. Lonesome Lake

LOCATION: Franconia Notch

DESCRIPTION: A short, steady climb to a high mountain pond with gorgeous mountain views.

TRAILS: Lonesome Lake Trail, Cascade Brook Trail, Fishin' Jimmy Trail

DISTANCE: 3.0 miles round trip

STARTING ELEVATION: 1770 ft.

HIGHEST ELEVATION: 2760 ft.

ELEVATION GAIN: 1000 ft.

RATING: Intermediate

USGS MAP: Franconia

TRAILHEAD: This trip begins on the west (southbound) side of the Franconia Notch Parkway at Lafayette Place. (The campground is open on a limited basis in winter.) Follow the exit ramp as it curves around to the right to a plowed parking area. The parking area off to the left (south), at the actual start of Lonesome Lake Trail, is not plowed in winter. If you're approaching from the south, you can either park in the plowed lot on the east (northbound) side at Lafayette Place, or drive north to exit 2 to reverse direction and park on the west side.

WMNF PARKING PASS: No

Lonesome Lake is a picture-perfect mountain pond snuggled on a high plateau beneath the south ridge of Cannon Mountain and the twin

A bright winter day on Lonesome Lake

peaks of Kinsman Mountain. On a clear day its shores and frozen surface offer gorgeous vistas of the Kinsmans and snow-crusted Franconia Ridge. The moderate, steady grade of Lonesome Lake Trail—largely along the route of an old bridle path—makes this a choice destination for the intermediate snowshoer. It's a very popular winter route and is usually well-packed; snowshoes may be superfluous except for the traction. With a fresh fall of snow it is a pure joy to snowshoe here.

From the parking area on the west side of the highway, walk south back down the entrance road to the unplowed southern parking lot, yielding the track to passing snowmobiles. Look for the Lonesome Lake Trail sign at the far end of this parking lot on the right. You immediately cross a bridge over the Pemigewasset River—a small stream here—and follow a yellow-blazed path gently upward through the quiet Lafayette Campground. After crossing a couple of campground roads, the trail enters the forest for good and ascends easily through a forest of large northern hardwoods.

You soon swing left and cross two small wooden bridges. At 0.4 mile the Hi-Cannon Trail splits off to the right. Lonesome Lake Trail continues ahead, cutting up across the steep mountainside at a pleasant grade. At about 0.7 mile, there's a steep, sometimes icy pitch, at the corner where the trail turns sharp right to begin a long switchback to the NW. White birches and evergreens join the forest procession as you angle up the slope. Looking to the right through the trees, you have frequent glimpses of the snowy ramparts of Franconia Ridge—views denied to the hiker in summer when the trees are in leaf.

At 1.0 mile the trail makes a fairly steep turn up to the left near the edge of a small ravine. You climb steadily for about 0.1 mile, then the grade eases as you gain the high plateau that holds Lonesome Lake. The sounds of parkway traffic fade away as you snowshoe through a wonderful forest of snowclad evergreens and glistening birches. After cresting a small rise, the Lonesome Lake Trail dips to a major trail junction near the east shore of the pond, 1.2 miles from the trailhead.

Trails radiate in several directions from here. On your right, the Dodge Cutoff heads NE and the upper section of Lonesome Lake Trail heads NW past the north end of the pond. On your left, the Cascade Brook Trail wanders SW towards the south shore. Ahead, a short spur path leads a few yards to an opening on the east shore. By all means, shuffle out here to catch the pretty view across to the rolling summits of Kinsman Mountain (South Kinsman on the left, North Kinsman on the right). Snow-speckled evergreens line the shore, completing a picturesque winter scene.

In the late 1800s this pond, formerly known as Tamarack Pond and Moran Lake, was the private preserve of William C. Prime and William Bridges. They built a cabin on the east shore and entertained favored guests, among them General George B. McClellan of Civil War fame. Prime was famous for authoring the angling classic, *I Go A-Fishing.*

An even more dramatic view awaits on the far side of the pond, below the AMC's Lonesome Lake Hut (closed in winter.) Through most of the winter the pond is solidly frozen, and most likely there will be a set of tracks leading directly across the wind-rippled expanse of snow from the Kinsman viewpoint. On a sunny day with light wind it's an exhilarating traverse. There are views to the Kinsmans ahead and the lumpy ridges of Cannon and the Northeast Cannonball off to the right, the latter pair separated by the deep scoop of Coppermine Col. If poking around the pond, avoid the areas around the outlet at the south (left) end and the inlet coming in from the beaver ponds on the NW side. As you approach the open area by the SW shore—a swimming dock in summer—the stunning view of Franconia Ridge opens behind you.

If you're unsure about crossing the ice early or late in the season, or after a thaw, or if the NW wind is barreling across the pond, you can easily reach the SW shore by trail. From the junction by the eastern shore, follow the Cascade Brook Trail SW for 0.3 mile to a junction with the Fishin' Jimmy Trail. Bear right on the latter trail, cross the outlet brook on a bridge, and in another 0.1 mile you'll come to the opening by the shore down on the right.

Looking east here, the arching crest of Franconia Ridge, draped in snow and ice, rises dramatically across Lonesome Lake. Mt. Lafayette is on the left, Mt. Lincoln in the center, and Little Haystack to the right. On a sunny, calm winter day the clarity is almost surreal. You may be tempted to fashion a seat from your pack and bask in the sun for a while.

For further easy exploration, you can follow Fishin' Jimmy Trail a short distance up to the hut, roam around other parts of the pond, or follow the

Around-Lonesome Lake Trail and the Lonesome Lake Trail to make a circuit around the north end of the pond, ending back up at the east shore junction in 0.5 mile. The loop passes through interesting bogs by the NW corner of the pond, with a view of Mt. Liberty. There are numerous bog bridges along the circuit that can make for awkward snowshoeing in some snow conditions.

However you decide to return to the trail junction by the east shore, the trip back down Lonesome Lake Trail provides a fast and easy exit to the trailhead—a half-hour or less in good conditions.

ADDITIONAL OPTIONS

Hi-Cannon Trail Outlook *3.2 miles round trip, 1600-ft. elevation gain, intermediate/advanced* A trek partway up the rugged Hi-Cannon Trail on the south ridge of Cannon Mountain makes an interesting and fairly challenging snowshoe excursion with a fine viewpoint across Franconia Notch as the turn-around point. The trail is rocky near the vista, so wait for good snow cover to tackle this one. Follow the Lonesome Lake Trail for 0.4 mile from parking at Lafayette Place, then veer off to the right on Hi-Cannon Trail. It's a wiggly trail, quite unlike the long, straight switchbacks of Lonesome Lake Trail. Follow the blue blazes carefully as dozens of little zigs and zags lift you up the steep slope. At 1.2 miles from your car (elevation 2960 ft.) the Dodge Cut-off enters on the left. (This lightly-used trail descends 0.3 mile to the junction at the east shore of Lonesome Lake, offering a loop possibility for that snowshoe trip.) Beyond, the Hi-Cannon Trail makes a strenuous ascent of 0.4 mile to the east-facing outlook (3300 ft.), with a dramatic base-to-summit broadside view of the brilliant-white Franconia Ridge seen across Franconia Notch. In good snow conditions, the zig-zag descent of Hi-Cannon Trail below Dodge Cut-off is great fun on snowshoes. *Note:* Above the outlook the Hi-Cannon Trail gets steep, rough, and bouldery and is suitable for expert snowshoers only.

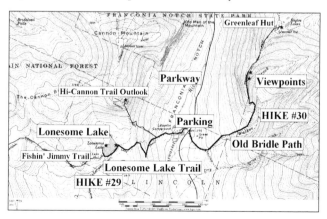

Kinsman Pond *7.2 miles round trip, 2200-ft. elevation gain, advanced* If you want to extend your snowshoe hike beyond Lonesome Lake, and are ready for some bursts of steep, rugged climbing, you can tackle the Fishin' Jimmy Trail up to frozen Kinsman Pond, nestled below the cliff-shod face of North Kinsman Mountain. Beyond Lonesome Lake Hut, the trail traverses a wild basin with several ups and downs. After a mile, the climb gets more serious, rising steeply in fits and starts. Several pitches may require vigorous use of your snowshoe crampons. At 1.9 miles above Lonesome Lake Hut, you come to four-way Kinsman Junction. Turn left and follow Kinsman Pond Trail 0.1 mile to the long, narrow pond with the frosted cliffs of North Kinsman looming close by on the west—a spectacular scene in winter. (*Note:* The 4293-ft. summit of North Kinsman, with a magnificent outlook east to the Franconia Ridge, is a rugged 0.6 mile and 550 ft. above Kinsman Junction via the southbound Kinsman Ridge Trail.)

30. Old Bridle Path

LOCATION: Franconia Notch

DESCRIPTION: A moderate, half-day climb up a well-traveled trail to ledges with spectacular views of Franconia Ridge

TRAIL: Old Bridle Path

DISTANCE: 4.0 miles round trip

STARTING ELEVATION: 1780 ft.

HIGHEST ELEVATION: 3400 ft.

ELEVATION GAIN: 1620 ft.

RATING: Intermediate

USGS MAP: Franconia

TRAILHEAD: This hike starts at the major trailhead parking area, plowed in winter, on the east (northbound) side of the Franconia Notch Parkway (I-93) at Lafayette Place, between Exits 34A and 34B. If you're coming from the north you can park on the west (southbound) side of the Parkway and walk through a pedestrian underpass, or drive 2½ miles south to Exit 34A to reverse direction and drive north to the east-side trailhead.

WMNF PARKING PASS: No

At any time of year, the Old Bridle Path up the SW shoulder of Mt. Lafayette is one of the most popular trails in the White Mountains. Most hikers who set forth on this trail are bound for the barren summit of Lafayette. In winter this is a serious undertaking with much exposure to weather and some icy footing requiring the use of boot crampons.

Less ambitious snowshoers can aim for a more modest but still highly rewarding objective: a series of ledges hanging on the edge of the deep ravine of Walker Brook, with impressive views up to the snowy crest of Franconia Ridge. As often as not this trail is a packed-out sidewalk of snow, rendering snowshoes unnecessary. In a fresh snow it's an excellent trail for 'shoeing, with a few mildly challenging spots. Even when the treadway is firm your snowshoe crampons may come in handy for extra traction.

This is one of the older trail routes in the White Mountains. According to Laura and Guy Waterman's *Forest and Crag*, the trail was originally built about 1850 and improved for horseback travel in 1852. Guests from nearby hotels would ride to the summit, where a crude stone structure provided shelter from the elements. The trail fell into disuse for several decades but was restored by AMC trail workers in 1929.

From the parking area the Old Bridle Path climbs easily up through a clearing and enters the woods. At 0.2 mile the Falling Waters Trail splits right, crossing Walker Brook on a bridge. Continue straight on Old Bridle Path, snowshoeing briefly alongside the frozen stream. Soon the trail turns sharp left and makes an easy northward traverse through open hardwood forest.

At about 0.6 mile you swing right and climb up the slope at a moderate grade. You bear right again at 1.0 mile and angle upward through white birches, entering the WMNF at a sign at 1.1 mile (elevation 2400 ft.). In another 0.1 mile the trail bends left and climbs steadily up the ridge along the edge of Walker Ravine. The woods here are a pleasant open mix of conifer and birch.

At 1.6 miles the trail makes a sharp left at the edge of the ravine. Look right for a framed view up to the frosty crags of Mt. Lincoln rising above the ravine of Walker Brook's south branch. Above this steep corner the trail makes a brief traverse through small birches, then winds up through some ledgy terrain with a steep pitch or two. At about 1.8 miles the grade eases. The trees diminish to rime-whitened scrub and views up to Franconia Ridge begin to pop out.

At 1.9 miles you emerge on the first of two spectacular open ledge perches on the brink of Walker Ravine. The second outlook is just a couple of hundred feet farther and has a slightly wider view. The elevation here is about 3400 feet. You gaze across the yawning ravine to the slide-slashed buttresses and snowy ramparts of Franconia Ridge, towering over 1600 feet above you. It's a stunning, majestic view, with Mt. Lafayette on the left and Mt. Lincoln on the right. With fresh snow and bright sun the scene is dazzling. Up to the left the ridge you're on crests with a series of scrubby knobs known as "The Agonies"—so named by AMC hut crew members humping loads up to Greenleaf Hut. There's also a distant view SW to the ridges in

Snow-crusted Franconia Ridge from Old Bridle Path

the Carr Mtn.–Mt. Kineo area, but the Franconia Ridge close-up will hold your attention for as long as you care to linger.

The snowshoe descent from the outlooks can easily be managed in less than an hour with good snow conditions.

ADDITIONAL OPTIONS

Greenleaf Hut *5.8 miles round trip, 2450-ft. elevation gain, advanced*   Experienced snowshoers looking for a longer outing can continue up Old Bridle Path to the AMC's Greenleaf Hut (closed in winter), climbing an additional 800 feet in 0.9 mile above the outlooks. There are more good views up to Franconia Ridge en route, and another to the west towards Cannon, Kinsman and Moosilauke. You'll have to claw up some steep sections as you ascend "The Agonies"—one rocky dike in particular can be difficult if icy.

As you emerge in the open area by the hut (elevation 4220 ft.), you're presented with an impressive close-up of the long, snowy crest of Lafayette. Frozen Eagle Lake nestles in a hollow below the hostelry. An outlook to the west can be found a short distance down the Greenleaf Trail, which comes in on the left.

Only veteran winter hikers equipped with crampons and other necessities for above-treeline travel should attempt to climb the last exposed mile on the Greenleaf Trail to the barren 5260-ft. peak of Lafayette and only in clear weather. In recent winters several parties have lost their way on the summit cone in snowstorms, triggering expensive and dangerous search missions. One steep section just below the summit tends to have particularly tricky footing where crampons are essential. Lafayette summiteers savor ethereal views down the snowy ridgeline and across the Pemigewasset Wilderness.

Mt. Garfield *12.4 miles round trip, 3100-ft. elevation gain, advanced* The long, gradual climb to the bare 4500-ft. summit of Mt. Garfield, with a short steep pitch near the top, rewards hardy snowshoers with an awesome view south over the remote interior of the western Pemigewasset Wilderness. The road to the summer trailhead is not open for vehicles; park in a plowed area by the entrance to the west end of the Gale River Loop Road on the south side of US 3 between Franconia Notch and Twin Mountain, 0.3 mile west of the junction with Trudeau Road. Do not block the gate.

Snowshoe 1.2 easy miles up the Gale River Loop Road, which may be packed by snowmobiles. Just after the road bends left and crosses a bridge, look for the sign for Garfield Trail on the right. The trail rolls along a little hemlock-clad ridge for 0.7 mile, then drops down to follow the grade of an old tractor road that served a former fire lookout on the summit. Grades are gentle as you snowshoe through hardwood forest and over three brook crossings. After a long upgrade, you crest a low rise 4.0 miles from your car and traverse a section of white birch forest, beautiful in the snow.

Now you plow through snow-plastered firs up a series of easygoing switchbacks on the NW side of Mt. Garfield. This is one of the deeper snow areas of the Whites. At 5.3 miles, you swing left for a long eastward traverse, curving south to meet the Garfield Ridge Trail at 6.0 miles. The grade has been unfailingly mellow to this point, but when you turn right here you soon encounter a startlingly steep pitch that forces you to claw your way up a winding ledgy chute. In 0.2 mile you gain over 300 feet in elevation.

At the top you break into the open on the often cold and windy north side of the small rocky cone. Scrabble up to the left and around to the front of the old fire lookout foundation—use caution as the dropoff is steep on the south side. The view into the Pemi Wilderness is a favorite of many a hiker. The Twin-Bond range is on the left, with the snowy rock slides on Mt. Guyot especially prominent. The mighty Franconia Range, crowned by the white serration of Mt. Lafayette, is on the right. Sprawling between the two great ranges are the isolated valleys of Franconia and Lincoln Brooks, ringing the crouching wooded mass of Owl's Head. If you're lucky enough to have a calm, sunny winter day, there's no better place to be than the south side of Garfield's summit. There's also a wide prospect over lower country on the north side, but the Pemi view is the attention-getter here. Just be sure to allow enough time for the trip out—the upper switchbacks go quickly, but the gradual descent through the hardwoods and the final road walk can be a trudge if you're tired.

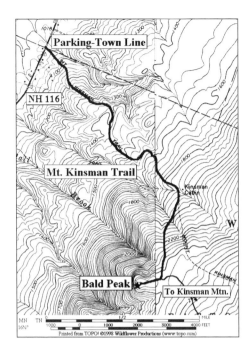

31. Bald Peak

LOCATION: Easton

DESCRIPTION: A moderate climb to a rocky 2470-foot spur of Kinsman Mountain with wide western views.

TRAILS: Mt. Kinsman Trail, Bald Peak Spur

DISTANCE: 4.6 miles round trip

STARTING ELEVATION: 1030 ft.

HIGHEST ELEVATION: 2470 ft.

ELEVATION GAIN: 1450 feet

RATING: Intermediate

USGS MAPS: Sugar Hill, Franconia

TRAILHEAD: This hike follows the Mount Kinsman Trail, beginning on the east side of NH 116 in Easton. From I-93, take Exit 38 and drive west into the village of Franconia. Go straight across the intersection with NH 18 and proceed south on NH 116 for 4.4 miles. The trail begins on the left beside a green sign marking the Easton/Franconia town line. (Coming from the south, it's 7 miles north on NH 116 from NH 112.) There is no trail sign; the trail starts as a road with two stone pillars and a chain at the entrance, a few steps south of the town line sign. There is no designated parking area; take care not to block the entrance to the road. You should be able to find room to park on the shoulder a short distance north of the trailhead. On occasion you may have to shovel out a space—or choose an alternative hike nearby such as Bridal Veil Falls or one of several in Franconia Notch

WMNF PARKING PASS: No

Bald Peak, a landmark of the pastoral Easton valley, presents a wonderful expanse of open ledge jutting out of the side of massive Kinsman Mountain. After warm spells or in late winter, you're liable to find some bare rock from which to enjoy the expansive views of the valley, Mt. Moosilauke, and distant peaks in Vermont. The trip up takes you through a variety of attractive forests. It's a perfect trip for a sunny March day.

The Mount Kinsman Trail begins on the road beyond the stone pillars. The first mile of the trail is on private land, and there may be skidder tracks in the snow and other evidence of logging activity down near the highway. The road rises steadily under pines and hemlocks. You soon bear right where a short spur road loops up to the left past a deserted house. Bear right again at an arrow where the spur rejoins on the left. The grade eases as you cross a logging yard.

At 0.6 mile the road swings left and passes an old sugarhouse on the left, then curves right. You rise gently through an open hardwood forest that was once operated as a sugarbush. At 1.1 mile the trail enters National Forest land, and you turn 90 degrees right off the old road; this junction is marked by cairns which may be buried in snow. In another 100 feet you bear left onto another old road and climb moderately across a beautiful hardwood slope.

At the top of this grade you swing right again into dark conifers and climb along the edge of a brook ravine. Up to here the trail has been sparsely marked; now blue blazes begin to appear. At 1.5 miles a clearing on the left marks the location of the former Kinsman Cabin. The trail turns right to make an easy crossing of the brook; there's a steep pitch beyond. The snow is deeper here above 2000 feet. You traverse southward across the slope, climbing at easy grades. Massive yellow birches dot the forest.

At the 1.8 mile mark you cross a snowbound little brook with a frozen cascade up to the left. In another 0.3 mile you snowshoe over the buried Flume Brook. A sign points right to Kinsman Flume slightly downstream, but in winter this side excursion to the edge of the steep-walled cut in the mountainside can be tricky and is best avoided.

After climbing slightly through a tunnel of conifers you'll come to the junction with the spur trail to Bald Peak (Bald Knob on the sign) branching off to the right. (Here the Mount Kinsman Trail bangs a left and climbs steadily for 1.6 miles to the Kinsman Ridge Trail 0.4 mile below the 4293-foot summit of North Kinsman.)

Turn your snowshoes right and follow the Bald Peak spur on a meander through dense, wild conifers. The snow drifts deep in here. In 0.15 mile you make a short, steep descent to a col, then veer up and left to the flat, open top of Bald Peak. Though you're just shy of 2500 feet, the place has a decidedly alpine feel to it, and the wind can be biting. The local name for the fierce winds that often blow up the Easton valley is the "Bungay Jar." Supposedly this wind from the south is a sure sign of an impending storm. The origin of this curious name dates back to the days of the early settlers (Asa Kinsman and his wife first settled the Easton valley in the 1780s). When farmers discouraged by the rocky soils departed for more productive climes, they were said to have "bunged out."

The main ledgy area of Bald Peak faces south, offering good sun exposure and a chance to hunker down out of the wind. The view sweeps over nearby peaks and lowlands and distant horizons. Looming close by on the left (SE) is the great wooded swell of North Kinsman. Rime ice often frosts the upper ridge, which runs northward to the Cannon Balls and the ledgy backside of Cannon Mtn. Soaring ravens may croak overhead.

Southward you see massive, snow-capped Mt. Moosilauke, with the dark dome of Mt. Clough on its right, marked by snowy slides. To the SW is the long expanse of the lower Benton Range: Jeffers Mtn., The Hogsback, Sugarloaf and Black Mtn. Westward you gaze across the broad Easton valley—spotted with fields and a few roads and houses—to the nearby wooded ridges of Cooley Hill and Cole Hill. On clear days various distant peaks can be seen in Vermont, including Killington Peak and Lincoln Mtn., both striped with ski trails.

By walking to the north edge of the ledges, you can enjoy (wind permitting) views in that direction over the scrub: Burke and other mountains in northern Vermont; and the Percy Peaks, Pilot Mountains, Mt. Cabot, Mts. Starr King and Waumbek, and Cherry Mtn. in New Hampshire's North Country.

After enjoying these vistas, follow your tracks back to the Mount Kinsman Trail and down the same route. The grade is just right for a quick and delightful snowshoe descent.

ADDITIONAL OPTIONS

Kinsman Mountain *Advanced* Experienced snowshoers can extend this into a full-day outing by following the Mt. Kinsman Trail 1.6 miles up to the ridgecrest, at moderate and occasionally steep grades. A right turn and some steep, ledgy climbing will lead to the 4293-ft. peak of North Kinsman in 0.4 mile. A flat ledge on the east side of the summit opens a spectacular broadside view of Franconia Ridge rising from the depths of Franconia Notch. Totals for Bald Peak and North Kinsman are 8.6 miles round trip

Approaching Bridal Veil Falls

with 3400 ft. of elevation gain. For South Kinsman (4358 ft.), an open peak with expansive views, add 1.8 miles round trip with 650 ft. elevation gain.

Bridal Veil Falls *5.0 miles round trip, 1100-ft. elevation gain, beginner/intermediate* Another nice trip in the Easton–Franconia area follows the gently-graded Coppermine Trail to frozen Bridal Veil Falls in a deep ravine on the west side of Cannon Mountain. Park off NH 116 at the start of Coppermine Road, 3.4 miles south of NH 18 in Franconia. Walk up the road and bear left off it in 0.4 mile at a hiker symbol, snowshoeing up an older road. At about 1 mile you approach Coppermine Brook on the right. The grades are easy, with an occasional moderate pitch, all the way to the falls, and the woods and brook scenery are pretty in this secluded valley. At 2.3 miles the trail crosses the brook on a bridge, passes a lean-to, and ends at the base of the falls. The tiered cascades of ice are a spectacular sight and sometimes provide sport for technical ice climbers.

Kinsman Ridge/Gordon Pond *7.2 miles round trip, 2250-ft. vertical rise (1500 in, 750 out), advanced* If you're looking for a challenging snowshoe trek across a trail less-traveled in winter, the route across Kinsman Ridge Trail to Gordon Pond should fit the bill. There's a steep climb at the start and plenty of additional ups-and-downs along the ridge. Rewards include a nice easterly view and a remote mountain pond.

The trailhead is on the east side of NH 112 at the top of Kinsman Notch, 0.4 mile north of Lost River and just south of Beaver Pond. Park in the plowed lot for Beaver Brook Trail on the west side of the road. The Kinsman Ridge Trail (part of the Appalachian Trail) starts at a sign a few yards to the north up and across the highway. The trail begins with a steep angling ascent for 0.4 mile that will test your climbing technique. The grades eases to the Dilly Trail Junction at 0.6 mile. Then you climb over a knob and drop steeply to a hardwood col. The trail follows a roller coaster route along the ridge through a long procession of snow-plastered conifers, with an occasional glimpse of a distant ridge. At 2.4 miles there's a fine outlook to the east, improved by the lift of winter snows. The view includes Mts. Liberty, Flume, Whaleback, Carrigain, Hancock, Osceola, Tecumseh, Tripyramid, Whiteface, and Sandwich Dome.

Past the outlook, you hump over a 3000-ft. knob and descend to Gordon Pond Trail at 3.3 miles. Turn right and descend easily for 0.3 mile towards Gordon Pond (2567 ft.). A side trail leads to the shore of this high, remote pond, huddled at the base of Mt. Wolf, which rises balefully to the north. A forest of stark snags pokes up at the far end of the pond. Unless a stray snowmobile ventures here up Gordon Pond Trail or across an unmaintained route from Bog Pond, you're likely to have this wild place to yourself.

Save enough energy for several stiff climbs on the return trip, including a 450-ft. grunt up from the Gordon Pond Trail junction.

32. Dickey Mtn. Ledge

LOCATION: South of Waterville Valley

DESCRIPTION: A moderate climb partway up Dickey Mountain to an impressive ledge with views near and far; a bit of scrambling at the end

TRAIL: Welch–Dickey Loop Trail (west side)

DISTANCE: 2.4 miles round trip

STARTING ELEVATION: 1060 ft.

HIGHEST ELEVATION: 2200 ft.

ELEVATION GAIN: 1150 ft.

RATING: Intermediate

USGS MAP: Waterville Valley

TRAILHEAD: Take Exit 28 off I-93 and drive north on NH 49. At about one mile there's a stoplight at the junction with NH 175; from this point proceed another 4.4 miles north on NH 49 and turn left on Upper Mad River Rd. at a hiker symbol. This road climbs steeply, then levels off. In 0.7 mile turn right on Orris Road and drive another 0.6 mile to a corner where it bears sharp left; continue straight here to a plowed loop parking area for the Welch–Dickey Loop Trail.

WMNF PARKING PASS: Yes

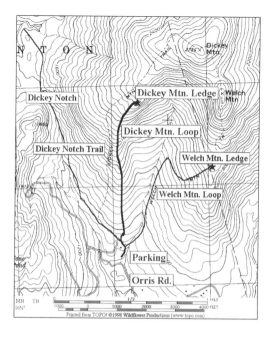

During the winter months the snowy ledges of Welch and Dickey Mountains are white beacons in the distance as you drive up I-93 north of Plymouth. These two low peaks (2605 ft. and 2734 ft.), perched at the end of the long south ridge of Mt. Tecumseh, were burned over many years ago, leaving their upper slopes largely devoid of vegetation. The 4.4-mile Welch–Dickey Loop Trail offers nearly two miles of open ledge walking at an unusually low elevation. In summer and fall it's one of the most popular half-day hikes in the White Mountains.

Doing the entire loop in winter is a more difficult proposition. Some of the steeper slabs, especially on the south ridge of Welch, can be dangerous in icy conditions, and in places the trail can be hard to follow with blazes covered by snow. Thus the full loop is for expert snowshoers only. But less ambitious trekkers can still enjoy this terrific trail on snowshoes with a shorter trip up either end of the loop to the first view ledges. The route described here takes you up to the first outlook on the SW ridge of Dickey, an impressive rock slab with local and distant views. The trail climbs steadily but not steeply, with two lightly challenging scrambles at the end. For these and the ledge itself you'll want good snowshoe crampons, or you could bring along regular boot crampons.

From the trailhead, the Welch Mountain end of the loop leaves immediately on the R. Continue straight ahead up an old road, and at 0.1 mile turn R at a sign where the Dickey Notch mountain bike trail goes left. You climb easily, crossing an old logging road, and follow yellow blazes up through open hardwoods and an occasional dark patch of hemlock and spruce.

At about 0.6 mile you wander up through an oak forest as the ridge becomes more defined. Peering through the bare trees you glimpse the white ledges of Welch off to the right and the great slab you're aiming for up ahead. You cross an open ledge in the forest and slip upward through woods that are wonderfully bright on a sunny winter day. (Because of its southern exposure this stretch of trail loses snow early in the spring.)

At about 1.0 mile the trail bears left and zigzags up a steeper pitch. At the top you angle R into dark conifers, an abrupt forest transition from the cheery hardwoods. Soon you're traversing along the base of a long, low rock wall draped with huge glistening icicles. Watch for icy patches underfoot here. At the end of this ramp the trail makes a sharp right up a rock step to access a snowy, viewless ledge—your first little challenge.

Snowshoe across this ledge, then make a short climb through woods to the bottom of the big open slab. Here you can scramble up another rock step to the right, or take a longer, less steep route around to the left. In either case be prepared to dig your snowshoe crampons into the crusty snow.

You emerge atop the lower end of the long granite slab, which drops precipitously into the valley between Dickey and Welch. The bottom of the slab is a spacious level perch; if you explore higher up, stay along the top, up on the left, the route the trail follows. Keep back from the rounded edge, and take care not to trample any exposed vegetation.

Looking up the ledges you see the broad summit of Dickey, marked by whitened cliffs on its south face. The view east across the little valley to the snowy pile of Welch is quite dramatic. Beyond Welch to the right is the spreading bulk of Sandwich Mountain and its long spur ridges. Due south is the long, low line of the Campton Range. A bit west of south you look far down I-93 and the Pemigewasset River valley to distant Mt. Kearsarge. Farther right the bald dome of Mt. Cardigan can also be seen on the horizon. Closer in to the SW are the long wooded ridges of Stinson Mtn. and Carr Mtn., on either side of nearby Cone Mtn. Farther right, almost due west, is Mt. Kineo, another long wooded ridge, topped by a small pointy peak. From the bottom of the slab you have a glimpse of massive Mt. Moosilauke to the NW.

With good snow conditions, the trip back down to your car can be very quick—a half hour or less.

ADDITIONAL OPTIONS

Welch Mtn. Ledge *2.6 miles round trip, 850-ft. elevation gain, intermediate* This trip to the first view ledges on the Welch side of the loop is a bit easier than the climb to the first Dickey ledge. Turn right at the loop junction near the trailhead. In 100 yards you cross the brook that drains the bowl between Welch and Dickey. The trail swings left to follow the brook through hard-

Snow-plastered ledges on Dickey (left) and Welch (right)

woods and hemlocks at mostly easy grades. At 0.7 mile you start to climb away from the brook and soon the trail makes a sharp right turn and slabs southeast across the side of the ridge. At 1.2 miles you swing to the left up moderately inclined ledges and soon reach the edge of a spacious open ledge area on the flat south shoulder of Welch Mtn. The trail stays on the south edge of the open area as it runs across to the east side—take care not to trample any of the fragile low-lying vegetation.

The best views are from the flat perches at the tip of the eastern cliffs. It's an expansive, exhilarating open area. The Mad River and NH 49 wind through the valley below. Across to the east is the great bulk of Sandwich Dome and its subsidiary peaks and ridges. The low gap of Sandwich Notch can be seen to the SE between Black Mountain and the Campton Range. Northeast up the valley is a great view of Mt. Tripyramid's three summits with Scaur Peak on the left and the flattened domes of the Sleepers on the right. Close by to the left (north) the cone of Welch rises steeply. If you turn around and look west, you'll gain an impressive view of the great snowy cliffs of Dickey, including the ledge described in the trip above.

From here, follow your tracks back down to your car.

Dickey Notch *3.6 miles round trip, 500-foot vertical rise, beginner* This easy trip follows a little-used mountain bike route past snow-draped beaver ponds into a roadless notch between Dickey Mountain and Cone Mountain. Trailhead parking is the same as for the Dickey Mountain and Welch Mountain ledge hikes. Follow the Dickey (west) branch of the Welch–Dickey loop trail for 0.1 mile, then bear left onto the Dickey Notch mountain bike trail as the Welch–Dickey Trail turns to the right. The trail rises gently on an old road, passing a series of small, terraced beaver ponds on the left at 0.8 mile. Ledges on a spur of Cone Mtn. loom above the ponds. The yellow-blazed trail soon narrows and climbs through nice hardwood forest along the east side of Dickey Notch. This pleasant woods meander continues through a gentle downhill section to a small stream crossing and a left turn leading into an open logging yard at the end of Forest Service Road 23A. From here, you follow your tracks back to your car.

Smarts Brook Trail   This trail leads 5.1 miles up the remote, attractive valley of Smarts Brook to the high ridgecrest of Sandwich Mtn. Its easy to moderate grades are good for snowshoeing. A nice objective for an easy trip is an open beaver meadow on the right side of the trail (*3.0 miles round trip, 300-ft. elevation gain, beginner*). If you snowshoe across to the SW corner of the meadow, you'll find an interesting view to the ridge of Black Mtn. leading up to Sandwich Dome. Along the way, at 1.1 miles, you'll pass a nice frozen cascade in Smarts Brook. This lower portion of the trail is a wide old logging road popular with skiers and hikers. (There's also a network of WMNF ski trails in the area; snowshoers should stay off these. The Smarts Brook Trail is blazed in yellow.) The upper valley is seldom visited in winter —expect to break trail. The plowed trailhead parking is on the east side of NH 49 a short distance S of Upper Mad River Road. Follow the signs for Smarts Brook Trail back across the bridge over the brook and then left into the woods.

33. Jennings Peak

LOCATION: Waterville Valley

DESCRIPTION: A steady climb, steep at the very top, to a rocky spur of Sandwich Dome with wide views south, east and north

TRAILS: Drakes Brook Trail, Sandwich Mountain Trail, Jennings Peak Spur

DISTANCE: 7.0 miles round trip

STARTING ELEVATION: 1400 ft.

HIGHEST ELEVATION: 3460 ft.

ELEVATION GAIN: 2100 ft.

RATING: Advanced

USGS MAPS: Waterville Valley, Mount Tripyramid

TRAILHEAD: Take Exit 28 off I-93 and follow NH 49 north towards Water-ville Valley. At 10.2 miles from I-93 a hiker symbol on the right marks the plowed parking area for Drakes Brook Trail and Sandwich Mountain Trail. Drive up a short entrance road to the parking spaces. If the entrance is un-plowed or looks too icy, you can probably find a place to park off Tripoli Road (the access road for Mt. Tecumseh ski area), which leaves Rt. 49 0.4 mile farther north on the left.

WMNF PARKING PASS: Yes

Though it's 500 feet lower than the summit, the rock nubble of Jennings Peak is the most dramatic viewpoint found anywhere on the broad bulk of 3980-ft. Sandwich Dome (also known as Sandwich Mountain). Some consider it the best vantage in the entire Waterville Valley region. Located midway along a curving NW ridge of the mountain, Jennings commands dazzling vistas of the Smarts Brook valley, the summit and south ridges of Sandwich, the other peaks of the Sandwich Range, and distant horizons. The climb up the Drakes Brook Trail is steady but never too steep, with one major brook crossing to negotiate at the start. For a final challenge there's a short, steep scramble at the top of the spur path leading to the peak.

The Drakes Brook Trail leaves from the left (NE) corner of the parking lot. You start out snowshoeing gradually upward along a smooth, groomed track that is part of the Waterville Valley cross-country network. No trail fee is required, but please snowshoe on the skate-groomed lane in the cen-

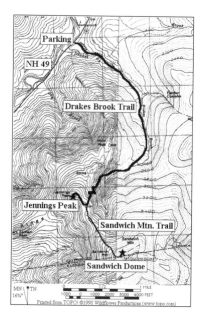

The great bulk of Sandwich Dome, with Jennings Peak on the left

ter or along the outer edges. Don't snowshoe on the set ski tracks, and be alert for passing or oncoming skiers.

You quickly pass the Jennings Peak ski trail on the left. At 0.4 mile the groomed trail splits left and you bear right on the Drakes Brook hiking trail to cross the brook. It's a good-sized stream that may present a challenge early in the season, before a good snow bridge forms, or after a major thaw.

The brook was named after the Drake family, a hard-working, taciturn clan who were among the early settlers of Waterville Valley in the mid-1800s. For some years they operated a mill on the Mad River north of the Drakes Brook trailhead.

The trail climbs easily up old logging roads alongside the brook, with an occasional steeper pitch. This valley was first logged in the 1880s, and a short-lived sawmill was built near the brook crossing. Today the forest cover here is open hardwoods dotted with many yellow birches. You gradually curve right (south) into the deep ravine between the summit of Sandwich and its northern spur, Noon Peak.

A steadier half-mile pull gets you up to an elevation of 2400 ft., about 2.2 miles and 1000 ft. above the trailhead. There's a brief easy stretch, then you climb more steeply again. At 2.6 miles the trail leaves the brookside logging road and begins a series of switchbacks up the head of the ravine through a forest of conifer and birch, with some mild sidehill stretches. Higher up you enter the beautiful fir forest typical of the upper ridges of Sandwich Dome, a snow-crusted wonderland in winter. At 3.2 miles the Drakes Brook Trail reaches the ridgecrest and a junction with the Sandwich Mountain Trail (elevation 3240 ft.).

Turn left here on the Sandwich Mountain Trail. The snow piles deep on this high, wooded ridge. You snowshoe moderately uphill for 0.1 mile to the junction on the right with the side trail to Jennings Peak. This narrow spur winds about at easy grades for 0.15 mile, then tackles a short, very steep pitch that will require some step-kicking or crampon-clawing, depending on snow conditions. Above this tough little spot the grade abruptly eases again and you pass two outlooks on short side paths left that open views to the NE. (See view description below.) The trail leads a short distance beyond through snow-packed scrub conifers to an open south-facing clifftop perch close by the summit of Jennings Peak. Don't venture too close to the edge — the view is just as fine from the safer ledges at the top.

This sunny, exhilarating spot gives you a striking look south over the wild, wooded upper valley of Smarts Brook, closed in on the left by the massive dark ridge of Black Mountain and on the right by ledgy Acteon Ridge, crowned by the bald Sachem Peak. Southwest beyond Black Mtn. is the low Campton Range, with Mt. Kearsarge and other blue ridges far off on the horizon. Mt. Cardigan can be seen in the distance to the left of Sachem Peak, and Stinson Mtn. and part of the broad Pemigewasset River valley are prominent to the right. Turning to the left and facing SE you look up the ridge to the broad fir-clad summit of Sandwich Dome, looming 500 feet above you.

The NE viewpoints a few yards back of the summit cliff offer a completely different perspective, featuring a wild view across the upper Drakes Brook basin to the Sandwich Range. The lumpy mass of Flat Mountain sprawls just across the valley. Behind Flat is the hunch-shouldered Mt. Whiteface, with the cone of Mt. Passaconaway peering over on the left. Farther left the twin rounded domes of The Sleepers lead across to the three peaks of Mt. Tripyramid, with the snowy South Slide marking the South Peak. Between North Tripyramid and its spur, Scaur Peak, Carter Dome and Wildcat Mtn. can be spotted in the distance. A bit more to the left your eye is drawn to the great white beacon of Mt. Washington, flanked by Boott Spur on the right and Mt. Jefferson on the left. On the far left the great dark bulk of Mt. Carrigain sweeps upward beyond the rolling crest of Mt. Kancamagus. In the foreground is the scrubby ridge leading out from Jennings Peak to Noon Peak.

After absorbing these stellar panoramas, retrace your steps down the way you ascended. Work your way carefully down that steep spot just below the viewpoints. The moderate grades of the Drakes Brook Trail are conducive to a rapid, swooping snowshoe descent.

ADDITIONAL OPTION

Sandwich Dome Summit   Ambitious snowshoers can opt to continue along the Sandwich Mountain Trail from the Jennings Peak side trail up to the summit of Sandwich Dome. This will add 2.2 miles round trip and 650 ft. of elevation gain to the trip. The first 0.5 mile is nearly level along a beautiful ridge clad in snow-draped firs. After the junction with Smarts Brook Trail you ascend steadily to the wooded 3980-ft. summit.

There's an excellent view to the north, improved by the deep snows of late winter. In addition to the peaks visible in this direction from Jennings Peak, you see Mt. Osceola rising on the far side of the Waterville Valley, with the Franconia Range on its left and Mad River Notch, the Twin-Bond ridge and Mt. Hancock on its right. Farther left are Mt. Tecumseh and the Waterville ski slopes. Mt. Moosilauke hovers on the horizon out to the left of the snowy, craggy knob of Jennings Peak. On days when a face-numbing wind blows in from the north, you can retreat into the scrub behind the opening. Standing atop the snowpack here you can peer out and see Mt. Chocorua to the east and Squam Lake, Lake Winnipesukee and surrounding ridges to the south.

34. The Kettles and The Scaur

LOCATION: Waterville Valley

DESCRIPTION: An easy to moderate hike past glacial kettle holes, ending with a steep climb to a south-facing viewpoint

TRAILS: Livermore Trail, Kettles Path, Scaur Trail

DISTANCE: 4.0 miles round trip

STARTING ELEVATION: 1580 ft.

HIGHEST ELEVATION: 2230 ft.

ELEVATION GAIN: 700 ft.

RATING: Intermediate

USGS MAPS: Waterville Valley, Mount Tripyramid

TRAILHEAD: This trip starts at the Depot Camp trailhead parking area outside Waterville Valley. Take Exit 28 off I-93 and follow NH 49 for 10.3 miles, then turn left onto Tripoli Road (also the access road to the Mt. Tecumseh slopes of Waterville Valley Ski Area). At 1.2 miles from NH 49 turn right off the ski area road, following the plowed lower portion of Tripoli Road. In another 0.6 mile, where Tripoli Road is gated ahead, turn right onto West Branch Road, cross a bridge, and immediately turn left into the Depot Camp parking area. This is the starting point for the Livermore Trail, actually a wide road groomed for cross-country skiing in its first couple of miles. Numerous trails diverge off this central artery. You don't have to pay a Water-

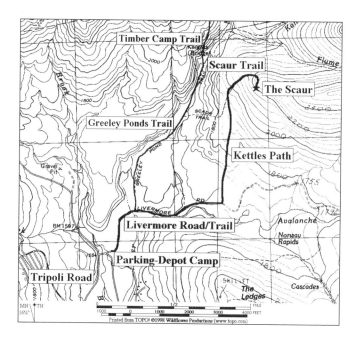

ville Valley trail fee to use Livermore Trail for accessing ungroomed back-country trails.

WMNF PARKING PASS: Yes

This moderately difficult half-day snowshoe trek from Waterville Valley leads past The Kettles—a series of small glacial hollows in the woods—and up to a sunny, ledgy outcrop known as "The Scaur." Grades are easy except for an occasional steeper pitch and the last rugged surge up to the viewpoint.

From the Depot Camp parking area, set off on the Livermore Trail—a wide, groomed cross-country trail. Snowshoers should stay in the wide central lane or along the edges, and should not tread on the set ski tracks. Be prepared to yield to skating skiers. In 0.2 mile, as you approach the large clearing at the site of Depot Camp (a base of operations for loggers in earlier days), your objective, The Scaur, looms ahead as a spruce-topped, snow-dappled knob at the left end of a long level ridge. Behind it is the dark mass of Mt. Kancamagus, with wooded Flume Peak to the right. As you cross the opening you get a glimpse of Mt. Tripyramid to the east and Mt. Osceola to the north.

Beyond the clearing you cross a brook on a bridge and pass the junction with Greeley Ponds Trail on the left at 0.3 mile. Continuing ahead you cross the Mad River on a bridge, then snowshoe past the Boulder Path on the right at 0.5 mile (leading 200 feet to a view of a huge rock in the middle of Avalanche Brook; use caution if venturing onto the ice) and the Big Pines Path on the left at 0.7 mile (a 0.2-mile side trip with two short, steep drops to a stand of massive white pines). These short trails are part of an extensive local network of footpaths maintained by the Waterville Valley Athletic & Improvement Association (WVAIA.)

At 0.9 mile turn left off Livermore Trail onto the yellow-blazed Kettles Path. This narrower, ungroomed trail meanders northward at a gentle grade for about 0.3 mile, with several twists and turns, then scoots up a couple of short, steep pitches. At 1.3 miles you come to The Kettles—a grouping of bowl-shaped depressions in the forest. These hollows were created at the end of the last glacial era, when large chunks of ice were stranded in the wake of the retreating glacier. Meltwater debris piled up around these oversized ice cubes and when they melted, their imprints remained in these wooded scoops a hundred feet or more across. Kettles are found in many lowland areas in glaciated terrain; where they extend below the water table, there are "kettle ponds." Echo Lake in North Conway is a sandy kettle pond, and there are hundreds on Cape Cod in Massachusetts.

The trail winds along a ridge between kettles on the left and right. The floors and steep sides are well-forested with hardwoods. These formations are more easily viewed through the leafless trees in winter. You climb a bit more, cut through a stand of spruce, and weave along the edge of a deep, steep bowl on the right. At the far end of this kettle the trail squeezes around the trunk of a giant white pine. Beyond the kettles you wind upward over easy terrain with some tall, straight spruces, then you break out into an airy beech glade. More of this mellow snowshoeing brings you to the junction with the Scaur Trail at 1.8 miles.

Turn right here for a steady climb up through the hardwoods. In 0.1 mile you approach spruce-topped ledges on your right. The trail sweeps eastward around the back side of the knob, then swings right (south) and climbs steeply through dense conifers. You may have to slap your snowshoe crampons on the snow to surmount the last pitch, which ends with a scramble up a slot between wooded ledges.

At 2.0 miles you crest the little ridge and swing left and down a few yards to the open ledges. Sunny and sheltered from the cold north wind, this makes a nice lunch spot. The view, obstructed only slightly by a couple of scrubby trees, sweeps nearly 180 degrees to the south, spanning the mountains that ring the upper intervale of Waterville Valley. On the right, looking SW, are Mt. Tecumseh and the trails of the Waterville ski area. With binoculars you can watch skiers and riders swooping down the slopes. If it's cold the resort's snow guns will be spewing out plumes of manmade snow.

The huge bulk of Sandwich Mtn. is an arresting sight to the south. You look into the lower valley of Drakes Brook between sharp Jennings Peak and the broad, double-domed summit of Sandwich, with the bold shoulder

Trail junction on Livermore Road

of Noon Peak thrust out in front. To the right of Jennings the Acteon Ridge, highlighted by the bare Sachem Peak, closes in the Mad River valley. To the left of Sandwich is the long, low ridge of Snows Mtn., with the similar Flat Mtn. sprawling behind. The village of Waterville Valley is hidden by the lower ridge of Snows. To the left (SE) you peer up the valley of Cascade Brook to the mysterious gap known as Lost Pass. The South and Middle Peaks of Mt. Tripyramid tower over the trees on the left. The ridges of The Sleepers are behind. A few yards to the left of the main viewpoint you can look northward to the broad, dark ridge of Mt. Kancamagus.

How did "The Scaur" get its name? Presumably it's a variant spelling of the word, "scar," which is what the rocky outcrop looks like when seen from the south. To confuse the issue, there's also Scaur Peak, a 3605-ft. spur of Mt. Tripyramid, a couple miles east up the ridge, and a mini-range called Scar Ridge five miles to the NW, beyond Mt. Osceola.

You can mull over this nomenclature as you retrace your steps along the Scaur Trail, Kettles Path and Livermore Trail. Use caution going down the first steep pitch. Although a loop back via the lower Scaur Trail and Greeley Ponds Trail looks tempting on the map, and is actually 0.4 mile shorter, be forewarned that this descent route is very steep, with a potentially difficult crossing of Mad River at the bottom.

ADDITIONAL OPTION

Timber Camp Trail *5.8 miles round trip, 1050-ft. elevation gain, intermediate*
Old logging roads provide relatively painless climbing on this snowshoe

venture accessed from the Depot Camp trailhead. After a gentle approach via Livermore and Greeley Ponds Trails, the Timber Camp Trail takes you up to the site of an old logging camp high in the remote basin of Greeley Brook on the east side of Mt. Osceola. There are two good views near the top of the trail.

From the parking area follow Livermore Trail 0.3 mile and turn left onto the ungroomed Greeley Ponds Trail. This route rises gradually along a wide old road lined much of the way with tall hardwoods. Pass a junction with Scaur Trail on the right at 1.0 mile and enjoy scenic snowshoeing alongside the Mad River. The Goodrich Rock Trail leaves left at 1.2 miles. A short distance beyond, at 1.4 miles, the Timber Camp Trail splits off to the left, marked by a sign set back from the junction.

Snowshoe gradually northward up this old logging road, with glimpses right into the valley of Flume Brook and ahead to the south ridge of Mt. Kancamagus. There's a fork at 2.0 miles; go left and uphill on the trail marked "To High Camp." (The trail straight ahead is signed, "To Greeley Brook.")

The Timber Camp Trail climbs more steadily, then eases to a hairpin turn left at 2.2 miles. You soon make a sweeping curve back to the right and head northward again. Swing left at 2.5 miles to an open bank up on the left of the trail. Scramble up the snowy slope for fine views NE to the south ridge of Mt. Kancamagus, spotted with a snowy cliff, and SE to Flume Peak and the three summits of Mt. Tripyramid. It's an unusual vista over a wild nook in the mountains. Northward the outline of Mad River Notch can be discerned through the trees, and if you look up to the NW you'll see the sheer face of Mt. Osceola's Painted Cliff looming above you.

The Timber Camp Trail runs along the base of this open spot (a gravel bank in summer) and continues gently up and west into a high bowl that forms the headwaters of Greeley Brook. The densely wooded headwall rises ahead. At 2.9 miles the trail ends in a windswept clearing, a sort of high mountain pasture left from the days when loggers toiled from this high country camp. There's a fine view back to the Tripyramids and an impressive look up at the Painted Cliff. The actual site of "High Camp" is indicated by a sign tucked in the woods a short distance west of the opening. After taking in the views, enjoy an easy downhill shuffle back to the Greeley Ponds Trail and on to your car.

35. Three Ponds Trail

LOCATION: North of Rumney

DESCRIPTION: A gentle ramble to a pair of remote backcountry ponds with views of surrounding mountains

TRAILS: Three Ponds Trail

DISTANCE: 5.5 miles round trip

STARTING ELEVATION: 1310 ft.

HIGHEST ELEVATION: 1740 ft.

ELEVATION GAIN: 550 ft.

RATING: Beginner/intermediate

USGS MAP: Mount Kineo

TRAILHEAD: Take Exit 26 off I-93 and follow NH 25 west for 7.3 miles (keep straight at the rotary at 4.0 miles). Turn right (north) at a flashing light onto the road leading to Rumney and follow it north through the village. At 4.9 miles from NH 25 keep straight at the foot of Stinson Lake and drive along the shore. At 6.8 miles, after cresting a hill, look for a hiker symbol on the left marking the Three Ponds Trail. The parking area is usually plowed. If it's not, seek a safe roadside parking spot in either direction on this lightly traveled road. Note: The eastern road approach from US 3 via Ellsworth is not plowed all the way through.

WMNF PARKING PASS: Yes

The snowshoe along Three Ponds Trail takes you into one of the most peaceful corners of the mountains, a remote roadless basin enclosed by Mt. Kineo (3313 ft.) and Carr Mtn. (3453 ft.). Two secluded ponds provide nice views up to these wild, wooded ridges. This trip has gentle grades nearly the whole way. It's best done in midwinter cold, as there are several brook crossings and the widest views are found out on the frozen ponds themselves. The area's numerous beaver ponds and meadows also invite exploration. The trail is used by snowmobiles; be alert for oncoming riders. You'll encounter few if any snowmobiles midweek.

From the parking area, enter the woods at the trail sign. After 0.1 mile of easy climbing the Mt. Kineo Trail departs on the right. Continuing ahead, Three Ponds Trail surges up a steeper pitch, then levels and rolls through mixed woods past the Carr Mountain Trail on the left at 0.5 mile. You descend gently past a beaver swamp on the right and skirt a large beaver meadow on the left. The yellow-blazed trail swings left at 1.0 mile and crosses Sucker Brook on a wide snowmobile bridge.

Turn right here and proceed up a gentle old logging road alongside the brook. There's a short steeper pitch, then a 0.2-mile relocation swerves right off the road, meanders beside the brook, and angles left back to the road at the top of the grade. (Snowmobile tracks may lead straight up the road; the relocation was created to bypass a muddy section.) Soon you cross a tributary brook on a snowmobile bridge, then you make your first unbridged crossing of Sucker Brook.

The trail drifts gently upward through open hardwoods, with the stream

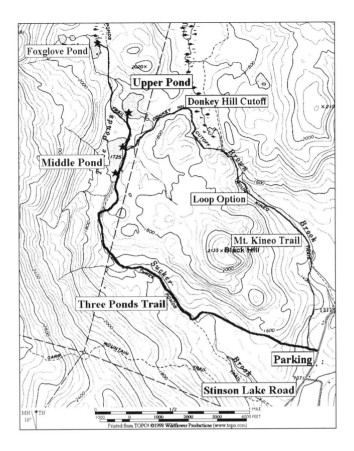

now on your left. At 2.0 miles you cross Sucker Brook again, with another crossing just 200 feet beyond. The trail veers right to higher ground, avoiding an area flooded by beavers. You can sense the opening of boggy, trailless Lower Pond off to the right. After humping over a couple of rises and dips you drop left to the SE corner of the Middle Pond.

The trail tracks along the east shore of this elongated, attractive water body, passing a side trail right that climbs a short distance to the open-front Three Ponds Shelter. The main trail soon reaches a shoreside opening with a pretty vista north to Whitcher Hill and across to the ridge of Carr Mtn., stretching long and high above the west side of the pond. If the pond is well-frozen, this is a good spot to snowshoe out and down the length of the pond to the north, exiting at the far NE corner. (Heed the usual precautions about pond ice.) On a sunny day this is an exhilarating open traverse. From the west side of the pond, near a lone sentinel pine that towers above a shrubby bog, there's a good view NE to the long, dark crest of Mt. Kineo.

A quiet winter day at Middle Pond

If you opt to stick to the landward route, continue north from the view opening on Three Ponds Trail, following along the shore. You make a slight jog to the right, pass the north end of the loop trail up to the shelter, then bear right at a fork and skirt a shrubby swamp. At 2.5 miles a sign marks the junction with Donkey Hill Cutoff. Three Ponds Trail bears left here and makes a precarious crossing of a beaver dam, then hops over a knoll and down to the NE corner of Middle Pond. If you've traversed the pond itself, you'll rejoin the trail here. This spot provides a nice view across the snowy pond to the high ridge of Carr Mtn.

The trail now heads north into the woods, ascending easily to a double blaze and a fork at 2.7 miles. The main trail continues to the left here, but your route is straight ahead on an unmarked spur trail to the Upper Pond. You swing right to a small clearing, then cut left through a fir thicket to a snow-laden boulder at the shore. There's a view of Mt. Kineo here, and by shuffling across the ice to various corners of the dogleg-shaped pond you'll find vistas of Kineo and Carr from different angles. After enjoying the seclusion here, you'll have an easy ramble following your tracks back to the trailhead.

ADDITIONAL OPTIONS

Foxglove Pond Beyond the Upper Pond the Three Ponds Trail proceeds a short distance to where it rejoins the snowmobile track. Adventurous snowshoers might enjoy trekking another 0.5 mile northward along the trail, climbing about 150 feet to Foxglove Pond, located a short distance left (west) of the trail and rimmed with an extensive snag-filled bog. This wild spot is more accessible in winter and is interesting to explore if well-frozen. There are views of Mt. Kineo and Whitcher Hill from the pond, and to the west there are two tiny, hidden beaver ponds tucked in against the north ridge of Carr Mtn.

Loop Option   From the trail junction by the north end of Middle Pond it's possible to loop back to the trailhead via the Donkey Hill Cutoff and Mt. Kineo Trail. This is a 2.8-mile return vs. 2.5 miles directly back along Three Ponds Trail. From the junction, Donkey Hill Cutoff leads NE for about 0.6 mile, then turns SE as it skirts the vast Brown Brook marshes on the left. You'll see views of Mt. Kineo across the swampland. Along the way the trail crosses several low ridges; look carefully for yellow blazes. At 1.1 mile from Three Ponds Trail turn right on the Mt. Kineo Trail at the edge of Brown Brook. For 0.6 mile you follow an old logging road down the west side of the brook, passing a frozen cascade and pool. The trail then swings right off the road and traverses rolling terrain on the south slope of Black Hill, meeting the Three Ponds Trail in another 1.0 mile. Turn left for the 0.1-mile jaunt back to the trailhead.

36. Rattlesnake Mountain

LOCATION: Rumney

DESCRIPTION: A short, fairly steep climb to a summit loop traversing ledges with good views over the Baker River valley

TRAIL: Rattlesnake Mountain Trail

DISTANCE: 2.5 miles round trip

STARTING ELEVATION: 630 ft.

HIGHEST ELEVATION: 1594 ft.

ELEVATION GAIN: 1000 ft.

RATING: Intermediate

USGS MAP: Rumney

TRAILHEAD: The Rattlesnake Mountain Trail starts on Buffalo Road in Rumney. Take Exit 26 off I-93 and follow NH 25 west for 7.3 miles (keep straight at the rotary at 4.0 miles), then turn right at a flashing light on the road leading to Rumney village. At 0.7 mile from Rt. 25 turn left onto Buffalo Road. Follow this road westward, passing parking lots used by rock climbers in summer. In 2.5 miles there's a small plowed parking area for the

Rattlesnake trail on the right, under tall white pines. If you come to the Rumney Transfer Station, you've gone 0.1 mile too far.

WMNF PARKING PASS: Yes

The low, rocky, snow-plastered ridge of Rattlesnake Mountain keeps watch over the Baker River valley and is an unmistakable landmark as you drive west on NH 25 from Plymouth towards Rumney. This southern-most spur of Carr Mountain was burned over many years ago. Its ridgecrest ledges offer excellent views of the valley and surrounding mountains. Though Rattlesnake tops out at less than 1600 ft., you'll huff and puff along the middle section of this climb, where most of the uphill is accomplished. A short loop trail around the broad summit leads to the view ledges.

The yellow-blazed trail starts beside a brook and quickly hops up a bank to the right and climbs gradually eastward through a white pine grove. At 0.1 mile you emerge into young open hardwoods with a small brook on the left and ascend beside it, crossing a branch stream. As the trail drifts away from the brook you push steadily upward along a section of old logging road. The grade eases briefly as you work up a hogback between two drainages, then you surge steeply upward again. Above 1200 ft. broken treetops are evidence of the '98 ice storm that tortured hardwood forests in many places around the White Mountains.

At 0.6 mile the trail swings right and the grade soon relaxes. You shuffle gently upward across the broad ridge through a shattered forest of oak and other hardwoods. At 0.8 mile you reach the crest of the ridge and the signed loop junction.

Swing right onto the west end of the loop for the shortest access to the view ledges. The trail dips and rises southward through sunny, open oak woods, passing a trunk on the right gouged by crow-sized pileated woodpeckers. In places the ice-damaged forest has a ghastly battlefield look. As the climb steepens a bit, look back to the next knob to the north, where skeletal trees bear witness to a fire set by an arsonist in the 1980s.

Soon you mount an open ledge—at the top there's a clear view north to the upper ridges of Carr Mtn. and several distant ridges. An interesting stretch of trail leads you over a hump and along a little ledgy swell, then through a cut beneath a rocky knob on the left. Add layers before you swing left and scramble up to the open summit ledges at 1.2 miles.

During late winter or anytime after a thaw you may find bare metamorphic ledges on these sun-struck exposures. Use caution if the ledges are sheathed in crust or ice. You immediately pass the first southerly outlook on the right, gazing down into the pastoral Baker River valley with its oxbows, snowy fields and the long strip of Rt. 25. Beyond the valley are nearby Plymouth Mtn. (left) and Tenney Mtn. (right), with the white dome of Mt. Cardigan in the distance.

The trail scoots along the front edge of the ledges on this narrow, knobby ridgecrest. You rise NE to a high point, then descend easily along an exposed rocky hogback. This is a premier picnic spot, with views opening northward to Carr Mtn. and its southern ridges, Mt. Kineo, and distant Scar Ridge and Mt. Hancock (marked by a whitened slide). Close by to the NE is the great wooded spread of Stinson Mtn. Eastward is the picturesque village of Rumney with the Squam Range on the horizon. Looking westward you gain glimpses of Mt. Cube and Smarts Mtn., two peaks near the Connecticut River valley.

To complete the loop around the summit area, continue NE down the spine of ledge. At the bottom the trail drops off to the right—use caution here if it's icy—and then turns left to descend into scrubby woods. You pass an outlook east towards Rumney and follow blazes down and left to a dip amidst the mangled oaks. The trail swings out to the east side of the summit, rising to a gentle open area with a good northerly view to Mts. Carr and Stinson.

From here the loop trail descends a bit and follows a rolling, meandering course through the woods, heading north and then west back to the loop junction at 1.7 miles. Continue straight here for the quick 0.8 mile descent to your car.

37. Blueberry Mountain (Benton)

LOCATION: West of Mt. Moosilauke

DESCRIPTION: A mellow climb up a ledgy, piney mountain with views of Mt. Moosilauke and mountains to the south

TRAILS: North and South Road, Blueberry Mountain Trail

DISTANCE: 4.8 miles round trip

STARTING ELEVATION: 1350 ft.

HIGHEST ELEVATION: 2662 ft.

ELEVATION GAIN: 1300 ft.

RATING: Intermediate

USGS MAPS: Warren, East Haverhill

TRAILHEAD: Take NH 25 to the village of Glencliff at the SW base of Mt. Moosilauke. Turn north on High St. (leading to the Glencliff Home for the Elderly) and follow it for 1.0 mile to the junction with the unplowed North and South Road (marked by a sign for the Appalachian Trail) on the left. Park on the side of High St., taking care not to block the entrance to North and South Road. There's a view SW to Webster Slide Mtn. across a field.

WMNF PARKING PASS: No

Blueberry Mountain (2662 ft.) is a gentle, ledgy summit in the low but interesting Benton Range, which extends for several miles north and south on the west side of Mt. Moosilauke and its neighbor, Mt. Clough. After a road walk approach, the Blueberry Mountain Trail takes you up to the ridge at generally easy grades, ideal for snowshoeing. The upper part of the trail leads across sunny, snowy low-angle slabs amidst a scrubby forest of red pine and spruce; in places it requires care to follow. Various spots along this delightful open area provide distant views to the south and unique close-up vistas of Moosilauke. Some western and northern views are available on the west side of the ridgecrest.

This trip starts at the south end of the unplowed North and South Road, which may be packed down by snowmobiles. The road—briefly a part of the Appalachian Trail—descends gently to a gate and a bridge over Jeffers Brook. Just beyond, at 0.1 mile, the Town Line Trail (the southbound AT) leaves on the left. You climb easily northward up the road through hardwoods beside Jeffers Brook, passing the Tunnel Brook Trail on the right at 0.3 mile. The grade is steadier to the start of Blueberry Mountain Trail on the left at 0.7 mile.

Turn left onto the trail, which follows a wide, curving logging road up for 0.2 mile. Here the trail leaves the logging road up a bank on the right—look for yellow blazes. You climb moderately through bright, open hardwoods, crossing the logging road again in another 0.2 mile. You continue to wind upward at pleasant grades. Look in the woods for bear-clawed beeches. Off to the right the great dark bulk of Moosilauke can be seen through the trees.

At 1.6 miles from your car, just after a right turn in the trail, the woods abruptly change to deep spruce. You continue the comfortable ascent along

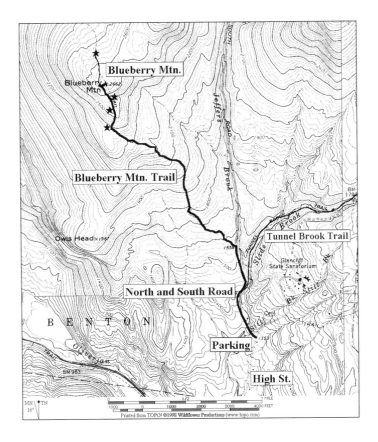

a corridor through the conifers. Red pines and open patches begin to appear. At 1.8 miles the trail swings left and up to the first semi-open ledges. Atop this pitch you get your first view back to the west side of Mt. Moosilauke. You traverse westward across the slope through an expanse of red pines and low blueberry scrub, following blazes on the trees. There are limited southward views to the left.

A right turn at 1.9 miles, marked by an arrow, has you heading north up the ridge over more snowy, pine-fringed ledges. Westerly breezes may sigh through the pine boughs. In a short distance an opening just left of the trail provides a view south to Carr Mtn. The trail passes to the right of a diamond-shaped marker, and 75 feet beyond bends right at a blaze and angles upward in that direction. Soon you dip into woods of spruce and pine and contour gently on the east side of the ridgecrest for 0.1 mile.

Emerging from the woods, you snowshoe more steeply for 0.1 mile up a swath of snow-covered ledges—the steadiest climbing of the day. At the top of this pitch, by a yellow-blazed pine, a side path leads 20 feet left to a perch with a good view south. Sharp-peaked Mt. Kineo and massive Carr Mtn. are to the left. Snow-capped Mt. Cardigan takes center stage in the distance. On the right are two nearby rounded mountains, Mt. Mist and Webster Slide, with part of frozen Wachipauka Pond visible at their base. Bulky Smarts Mtn. rises beyond Mist, and ledgy Cube is seen over Webster Slide.

Beyond the side path the trail climbs more easily, crossing a ledge patch and entering a belt of scrub at its upper right corner. Next you cross a large open area. At 2.3 miles, just past a blazed pine, a gentle east-facing slab on the right offers a dramatic close-up of the west side of Moosilauke. The flattened, snow-topped summit is to the left and the cone-shaped South Peak is on the right. Between them is the great ravine of Slide Brook, streaked with a necklace of whitened slides. The wooded hulk of Mt. Clough can be seen to the left. This is a fine lunch and resting spot, with ample sun on a nice day.

Beyond here the trail continues up through scrub, passing another Moosilauke view, then angles left and up to the crest of the ridge in wild spruce woods. At 2.4 miles a double blaze marks a side path that twists up 0.1 mile to the right to the true summit, where the views are over the trees.

Adventurous snowshoers can continue along the main trail to the NW; markings are minimal save for an occasional large cairn, and following the route can be challenging. The trail meanders across the broad ridgecrest through spruces and across ledges and then starts to descend gradually. About 0.2 mile beyond the summit side path a ledge swath opens a partial view north to Sugarloaf and Black Mtn., two more ledgy summits in the Benton Range. In another 0.2 mile, after crossing a low spot and making a sharp right turn past the "shark fin" rock mentioned in the *AMC Guide*, the trail comes to a spacious opening with views west and NW to the Signal Mtn. Range and the more distant Green Mountains in Vermont. Nearby to the right you see Sugarloaf, Black, and a palisade of cliffs fronting The Hogsback. Beyond here the trail starts to descend more steeply down the west side of the mountain. Proceeding to this point adds 0.8 mile round trip to the hike distance.

The descent back to your car is a snowshoer's delight, with just the right grade. It's especially fun swooping down the ledges into the southerly views along the upper half mile.

ADDITIONAL OPTIONS

Tunnel Brook Notch *6.6 miles round trip, 950-ft. elevation gain, intermediate* Tunnel Brook Notch, the deep gap between Mt. Moosilauke and Mt. Clough, is a fascinating area of beaver ponds and meadows with good views up to the slide-scarred mountain walls. Grades on the Tunnel Brook Trail are easy to moderate. The start is the same as for Blueberry Mtn.—park off High St. by the entrance to North and South Rd. Walk up the latter for 0.3 mile and turn right onto Tunnel Brook Trail.

An old road leads 0.2 mile to an abandoned cabin and a crossing of Jeffers

The west side of Mt. Moosilauke from Blueberry Mtn.

Brook. After one short tricky sidehill you snowshoe gently up along Slide Brook, crossing it twice, to a small reservoir on the right, 1.4 miles from your car. Beyond here the grade increases and you climb steadily through hardwoods high up on the west side of the ravine. The grade eases as you approach the broad height-of-land.

A slight descent leads to Mud Pond, the largest and southernmost in a long chain of beaver ponds, on the right at 2.6 miles. From the shore there is an impressive view up to the South Peak of Mt. Moosilauke and the snowy slides in the upper ravine of Slide Brook. If the pond is well-frozen, you can snowshoe onto it and stand in the middle of the open notch. (Use caution on the ice of the ponds—there may be soft spots where the brook flows in and out, and around the beaver dams.) The trail continues nearly level, running northward through a corridor of firs past several more beaver ponds on the right. At 3.1 miles the route crosses tiny Tunnel Brook and skirts more beaver ponds, with views across to the huge slides on Mt. Clough. The last beaver pond is at 3.3 miles, the turnaround point.

Wachipauka Pond & Mt. Mist *5.8 miles round trip, 1200-ft. elevation gain, intermediate* The Wachipauka Pond Trail, part of the Appalachian Trail, provides access to a scenic pond and an outlook on the side of nearby Mt. Mist. The grades are mostly easy to moderate, with one steeper pitch. The trail starts at a plowed roadside pulloff on the south side of NH 25, 0.6 mile west of Glencliff.

You snowshoe easily southward for 0.5 mile, then a sharp right turn brings a steep ascent up the side of Wyatt Hill. Farther up the climbing becomes easier through nice hardwoods, reaching the high point on the ridge at 1.2 miles. You descend gradually towards Wachipauka Pond, skirting its northern finger. A sideslope traverse and short climb lead to a four-way junction at 2.3 miles. The unsigned trail to the left (east) descends 0.2 mile to the shore of the pond, ending in a clearing beneath a huge white pine. Carr Mtn. can be seen in the distance across the pond. If the ice is solid, you can snowshoe out for a great view up to the cliffs of Webster Slide Mtn. looming close by to the NW. Mt. Mist rises steeply to the SW. Northward in the distance you can see Blueberry Mtn., the cliffs of the Hogsback, Mt. Clough and mighty, snowy Mt. Moosilauke.

Climbing back to the four-way junction, you can turn left (south) on the Appalachian Trail and climb moderately for 0.4 mile to a side path left to a modest outlook (elevation 1850 ft.) on the side of Mt. Mist. You look down on part of Wachipauka Pond and out to Mts. Moosilauke, Cushman, Kineo and Carr. From here retrace your steps along Wachipauka Pond Trail to your car. (*Note*: The Webster Slide Trail, which leads west from the four-way junction, rises 0.7 mile to the summit of Webster Slide Mtn., climbing steeply in its middle section. At the top there are dramatic views straight down to the pond, but the best vantages are tricky and possibly dangerous to get down to in winter.)

38. Mount Moosilauke Trails

The massive bald dome of Mt. Moosilauke (4802 ft.) is the dominant landscape feature in the southwestern sector of the White Mountains. This much-loved and much-climbed mountain boasts a pair of excellent snowshoeing trails that can be used to access lower viewpoints or to scale the windswept summit itself. Moosilauke is crowned with a small alpine zone of about 100 acres. It's not as exposed or potentially dangerous as the upper Franconia Ridge or the Presidentials, but an ascent all the way to the top is suitable only for advanced snowshoers equipped with crampons for the final approach in the open. The trip should only be attempted in favorable weather conditions—clear skies and light winds.

Moosilauke has a long tradition of winter adventure. In the winter of 1869–70, Dartmouth professor J. H. Huntington and his associate, Amos Clough, spent two months living in the summit hotel and recording meteorological observations, including winds over 100 mph—a world record at the time. This has long been "Dartmouth's mountain." The college owns the summit and eastern slopes and operates the Ravine Lodge at the SE base, and since the founding of the Dartmouth Outing Club in 1909, its members have made countless winter treks on Moosilauke. In the 1930s the mountain was an early hotbed for skiing. The first national downhill ski championship was held on the Carriage Road in 1933. (For a full recounting of Moosilauke's skiing annals, see David Goodman's *Backcountry Skiing Adventures: Maine and New Hampshire,* published by AMC Books.)

For snowshoers, two of the best trails on the mountain are the Gorge Brook Trail on the SE and the Glencliff Trail on the SW. Both offer excellent viewpoints below treeline—a chance to enjoy big mountain vistas without much exposure—as well as reasonable routes to the summit itself. Among the mountain's other trails, the Beaver Brook Trail on the north is too steep and icy for comfortable snowshoeing, the Benton Trail from the NW requires a nearly three-mile approach along the unplowed Tunnel Brook Road, and the lower Carriage Road is heavily used by snowmobilers and skiers.

Gorge Brook Trail

There are several snowshoeing options from the major trailhead at the SE base of Moosilauke. Beginners can snowshoe in on the unplowed road to Ravine Lodge and visit an open field with a vista up to the big mountain (*3.4 miles round trip, 500-ft. elevation gain*), with the option to explore easy trails along the Baker River. Intermediates can forge up the Gorge Brook Trail to

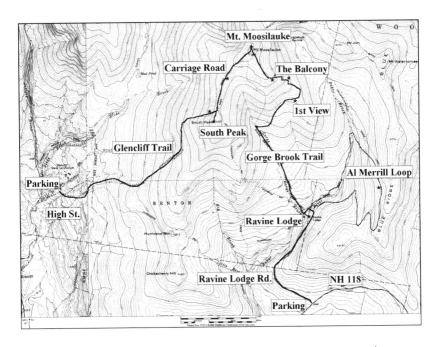

the first vista (*7.8 miles round trip, 1950-ft. elevation gain*). Advanced 'shoers can climb to several higher vantage points culminating in "The Balcony"(*9.8 miles round trip, 2700-ft. elevation gain*) or go all the way to the summit (*10.6 miles round trip, 2900-ft. elevation gain.*) USGS maps for this trail are Mt. Kineo and Mt. Moosilauke.

Access to the Gorge Brook Trail is via the unplowed Ravine Lodge Road, which leaves the north side of NH 118 at a point 7.2 miles west of its junction with NH 112 near North Woodstock and 5.8 miles east of its northern junction with NH 25 near Warren. Be forewarned that NH 118 is a steep, winding mountain highway, often snow-covered and plagued with frost heaves. There is a fairly large plowed area for parking by the entrance to the Ravine Lodge Road; a WMNF parking pass is required. The elevation here is 2100 feet.

Snowshoeing is pleasant up the unplowed Ravine Lodge Road, rising at an easy gradient through nice hardwood forest. At 0.5 mile, recent logging has opened some partial vistas left across the valley and back to Carr Mtn. At 0.7 mile, a sign welcomes you to Dartmouth College land and the road bends right (north.) Views of the great mass of Moosilauke start to appear through the trees; a small powerline runs alongside on the right. At 1.4 miles a service road and the powerline split left to Ravine Lodge. Continue straight here on the main road, passing a steep walkway down to the lodge. The road ends in a cul-de-sac at 1.6 miles (elevation 2500 ft.); continue a short distance ahead for the Gorge Brook Trail. At a kiosk, there's a view left up to the ridge of Moosilauke and the Gorge Brook ravine. In another 200 feet the Gorge Brook Trail descends to the left, then quickly swings left again and angles down to a sturdy footbridge over the rocky Baker River.

If you're out for an easy jaunt you can check out the view of the snowbound stream from the bridge, then follow a side path back up to Ravine Lodge. In a short distance turn right on a road that leads out to an open field in front of the main building. The lodge is a massive log structure built in 1937–38 from large virgin spruce cut nearby. It's open to the public for lodging and meals from May through October. It is closed in winter and visitors should not attempt to access the building or porch. From the snow-covered field, you obtain a nice view up to the South Peak and east shoulder of Moosilauke and the high ridge that connects them. This sunny opening is a nice lunch spot and a fine objective for an easy snowshoe hike.

To continue on Gorge Brook Trail, cross the footbridge over Baker River and turn left on the far bank. (Here the Ridge Trail heads gently upstream for 1.5 miles to the right, offering easy brookside snowshoeing for beginners who want to extend their trip as far as desired.) Snowshoe gently downhill, then up to the right. In 0.1 mile, where Hurricane Trail goes straight, Gorge Brook Trail turns right to follow Gorge Brook up its valley. (The east end of Hurricane Trail, leading 1.0 mile to the lower Carriage Road, is another easy, woodsy snowshoeing trail with a short stretch alongside the river.) The grades are moderate up the often well-packed Gorge Brook Trail, guiding you up along the stream through a pretty forest of birch and fir. In another 0.3 mile (2.3 miles from your car) the trail crosses a bridge left over the brook and passes the junction with Snapper Trail (a connecting route to the Carriage Road.)

You cross back at 2.9 miles on another bridge, and at 3.2 miles there's a sharp right where the trail turns off its former steep, direct route. This inspired relocation, completed about 1990, leads out around the mountain's broad SE spur and has made Gorge Brook Trail a much easier and more pleasant route, with several excellent viewpoints. The trail traverses right through an open salt and pepper forest of birch and fir, then swings left for a moderate climb. At 3.7 miles, you join an old logging road and at 3.9 miles is the first open view, a cleared spot facing south to the sun. Pointed Mt. Kineo (left) and broad-spreading Carr Mtn. (right) are prominent in the foreground, while the distant view includes Mt. Kearsarge and Mt. Cardigan. This spot (elevation 3850 ft.) is a nice objective for an intermediate-level exploration of Moosilauke.

The trail immediately turns left off the old logging road and follows a winding course, climbing steadily back and forth across the slope through lovely high-mountain fir forest where the snow drifts deeply. At 4.4 miles the trail wraps around a small "fir wave" of dead trees with a vista south to Mts. Cushman and Kineo. In another 0.1 mile (elevation 4300 ft.) you come upon two cleared outlooks in succession. The first is somewhat restricted and looks to the southern White Mountains (Osceola, Tecumseh, Sandwich Range). The second, located at a sharp left turn, faces NE to the Franconia Range, the Presidentials, and many other peaks seen over nearby Mts. Jim and Waternomee, eastern spurs of Moosilauke that enclose the upper ravine of Baker River. Part of Jobildunc Ravine, the fine glacial cirque at the head of the Baker, can be seen beneath the wooded dome of Mt. Blue.

Continuing its climb, the trail bends left at 4.7 miles and cuts across the slope through a dramatic semi-open section known as "The Balcony," with magnificent views east over the snow-packed scrub. Ravine Lodge, the Baker River valley and the long east ridge of Moosilauke can be seen below, with many mountains in the Waterville and East Branch regions beyond. Northward are the Franconias, the Kinsmans and Mt. Wolf with Gordon Pond nestled at its base. This is an excellent objective for those who don't want to continue to the exposed summit. Even if the west wind is blowing inhospitably above, this relatively protected 4500-ft. perch is a wonderful spot to soak up views and sun. At the end of "The Balcony," there's a view across Gorge Brook ravine to the large slide on its west side.

Here the trail turns right and runs along the flat crest of the SE spur through a corridor of snow-caked firs. The whitened, wind-whipped summit dome is in sight ahead. At the last pitch of scrub trees, you can decide whether to continue on to the top—on this last 0.2 mile the wind can be brutal and the footing very icy. If the weather is favorable and you're equipped with crampons, the Gorge Brook Trail climbs in the open to the ledgy crest and summit sign. Take care to stay on the marked trail and off the fragile alpine vegetation.

At the very top, a stone wall provides some shelter from the prevailing westerly winds. These ruins are all that remains of the Summit House, a small hotel that stood here from 1860 until it burned in 1942. The summit view is huge in all directions. To the NE and east are range after range of the White Mountains, leading out to the great white beacon of Mt. Washington. All told, 33 New Hampshire 4000-footers can be seen. The New Hampshire Lakes Region spreads out to the SE. Close by, Moosilauke's summit ridge stretches out to the South Peak. To the west is a vast prospect over the Connecticut River Valley, with nearly the entire chain of Vermont's Green Mountains spread across the horizon. Several ski areas can be spotted, including Killington, Sugarbush, and Stowe. On a day of special winter clarity, you may be able to spot several sharp peaks in New York's Adirondacks.

Once below treeline, the moderately graded Gorge Brook Trail is a joy to descend on snowshoes. In fact, backcountry skiers sometimes schuss down its wide, sweeping turns.

ADDITIONAL OPTION

Al Merrill Loop *8.0 miles round trip, 1250-ft. elevation gain, intermediate* An alternate objective for intermediate snowshoers exploring the Ravine Lodge area is a nice vista towards Mt. Moosilauke on the gently graded Al Merrill Loop, which climbs the ridge on the east side of the Baker River valley. This trail is also used by skiers—please do not snowshoe on existing ski tracks, and if the trail is unbroken, snowshoe along one edge of the trail to allow room for a ski track.

From the end of Ravine Lodge Road, continue ahead on the old road past the junction with Gorge Brook Trail. In 0.1 mile, the Al Merrill Loop heads up to the right, passing a side trail left to John Rand Cabin in another 0.4 mile. The trail follows old logging roads at very easy grades, making several long, sweeping switchbacks through a beautiful forest of birch and fir. A deadend side trail departs ahead where the Al Merrill Loop makes a left turn 1.4 miles from its start. (By proceeding 100 yards up this spur and looking back, you can catch views of Mts. Waternomee, Jim, and Blue.)

From the last switchback, you make a long, gentle traverse to the cleared outlook (elevation 3350 ft.) which is dedicated to the Dartmouth soldiers who served in the famed 10th Mountain Division during World War II. Here you'll find a memorable view of Moosilauke's east side, looming massively just two miles away. You look across into the Gorge Brook ravine, scored with slides, and the ice-draped headwall of the Jobildunc Ravine is seen to the right. On the left of Moosilauke there's a distant view out to the Green Mountains in Vermont.

Outlook on the Carriage Road

As an alternative to retracing your steps, you can continue around the loop, rising slightly, then descending gently to the Ridge Trail. This path leads down to the Baker River and crosses over a bridge, then follows it downstream back to the Gorge Brook Trail. Turn left here to climb back to your car. The loop option is 0.3 mile longer than going out and back with an extra 100 feet of climbing.

Glencliff Trail / Carriage Road

The Glencliff Trail ascends Moosilauke from High St. in Glencliff on the SW. It works upward at a steady grade with one sustained, steep pitch as it nears the top of the ridge by the South Peak. This subsidiary summit is a nice objective by itself and is reached by a short side trail. From here, the route to the main summit follows the Carriage Road along the ridge, completely in the open the last 0.2 mile. This route is more exposed to the cold west winds than the Gorge Brook Trail, especially the scrubby upper section of Glencliff Trail and the last stretch of the Carriage Road. There are no real beginner/intermediate objectives on this trail; it's best suited for experienced and fit snowshoers.

To reach the trailhead, take NH 25 to the village of Glencliff and turn north on High St. In 1.2 miles there's a plowed parking area for Glencliff Trail on the right (elevation 1480 ft.). This is on state-owned land and a WMNF parking pass is not required. USGS maps for the trail are East Haverhill and Mt. Moosilauke.

The trail leaves the road a short distance south of the parking area and passes through a gate, crosses a brook, traverses a small field, and climbs through a patch of woods to a farm road. Turn right and follow the road as it curves up the slope through two snowy pastures. On windy days, the traverse of these open fields can be invigorating.

At 0.4 mile, you turn left into the woods from the upper pasture and the Hurricane Trail immediately leaves on the right. You snowshoe upwards at a steady grade on Glencliff Trail, first in mixed woods, then open hardwoods. About a mile farther up, the trail enters the conifer forest zone. In lean snow times there may be a couple of icy spots where springs seep across the trail. At about two miles you slab along the side of the steep slope through thick growth. The trail veers right at 2.5 miles (elevation 3600 ft.) and commences a steeper climb straight up the slope through fine fir forest, with distant views to the west glimpsed through the trees. Wind-drifted snow may swamp the trail in this stretch, making for heavy trail-breaking.

Near the top of the steep climb, you pass a snowy rock talus slope on your right—from here (4300 ft.) there are wide views out to the west and down to the great slides of Mt. Clough. The ascent is more moderate to the South Peak side trail on the right at 3.0 miles (elevation 4460 ft.) and the Carriage Road just beyond.

The side trail to South Peak may be obscured by snow-caked firs, but it's worth the trouble to take this 0.2-mile jaunt across a col and up through open scrub and rock to this barren little summit (elevation 4523 ft.). You'll find unique views up to the white-cloaked dome of Moosilauke and down into Tunnel Brook Notch, with its beaver ponds and slides. There are panoramic vistas west to the Connecticut River valley and Vermont, south to the hills of central New Hampshire, and east to the southern region of the White Mountains. *A round trip to the South Peak is 6.4 miles with an elevation gain of 3050 ft.*

If you're aiming for the main summit of Moosilauke, turn left on the Carriage Road at the top of the Glencliff Trail. The wide trail, which may have both snowshoe and ski tracks, ascends gradually up a corridor through high scrub. (Although snowmobiles are barred by a line of rocks on the Carriage Road 0.1 mile below the Glencliff Trail junction, they sometimes continue on to the summit anyway.) At about 3.4 miles, a short path leads right to an outlook east over the Gorge Brook ravine, with the summit looming off to the left.

Continue beyond here only if the weather is favorable and you're outfitted with crampons. Your exposure to the wind increases as you head up the ridge, and at 3.7 miles, you dip slightly and leave the sheltering scrub behind. For the last 0.2 mile you must scrabble up a mix of snow, ice, and rock to the summit, feeling the full force of the wind. Please follow cairns on the marked trail and avoid trampling fragile alpine flora. *The summit*, a decidedly alpine setting in winter, is reached at *3.9 miles (round trip 7.8 miles) with an elevation gain of 3300 ft.* Add 0.4 mile and 100 ft. for the side trip to South Peak.

As you descend the summit to the south, you have a gorgeous view of the rime-coated ridge stretching away to South Peak. The easy walk across the narrow ridge on the Carriage Road is enjoyable and the steady grade of Glencliff Trail will get you down in a hurry.

39. Blueberry Ledges

LOCATION: Wonalancet, on south side of Sandwich Range

DESCRIPTION: A pleasant climb to gently sloping ledges on the south side of Mt. Whiteface, with a view south to the Ossipee Range

TRAIL: Ferncroft Road, Blueberry Ledge Trail

DISTANCE: 4.0 miles round trip

STARTING ELEVATION: 1140 ft.

HIGHEST ELEVATION: 2150 ft.

ELEVATION GAIN: 1000 ft.

RATING: Intermediate

USGS MAP: Mount Tripyramid

TRAILHEAD: This hike starts at the trailhead known as Ferncroft in the village of Wonalancet, just off NH 113A in the NW corner of Tamworth. From the west, take Exit 24 off I-93 and follow US 3 to Holderness. Turn left on NH 113 and proceed 11.6 miles to Center Sandwich. Turn left here, staying on NH 113 another 3.6 miles to the junction with NH 113A in North Sandwich. Continue straight on NH 113A and follow it 6.6 miles to a sharp right turn by the fields of Wonalancet. Make a left onto Ferncroft Road at the corner and drive 0.5 mile to a plowed parking area on the right. From the east, take NH 113 from NH 16 at the village of Chocorua. In 2 miles turn right on NH 113A and follow it 7 miles to where Ferncroft Road leaves on the right at a sharp left turn. On either approach, allow extra time to negotiate these winding, frost-heaved back roads.

WMNF PARKING PASS: No

This trip introduces you to the pleasures of snowshoeing in the off-the-beaten-path region on the south side of the Sandwich Range. The hamlet of Wonalancet—little more than a post office, a chapel and a handful of homes—has been a hiking center for more than a century. In the 1890s, under the direction of dynamic innkeeper Katherine Sleeper, a network of

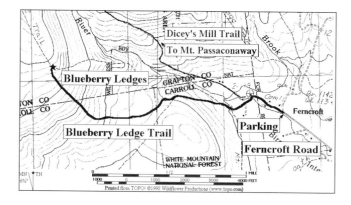

trails was developed to access the high peaks to the north—Whiteface, Passaconaway, Paugus and several outliers. In 1898 Sleeper formed the Wonalancet Out Door Club, which currently maintains over 50 miles in the Sandwich Range and publishes a terrific trail map of the area.

The Blueberry Ledge Trail up Mt. Whiteface was cut in 1899 and remains the most popular route to the spectacular views from the mountain's south summit. The upper part of this trail is rocky and rugged and should be tackled in winter only by trampers proficient with snowshoes and crampons in steep terrain. The lower half, however, is a mellow snowshoe ramble up through attractive woods to the gently sloping, semi-open slabs for which the trail is named. If you're a real view hog, this trip may not be for you, but the partly restricted vista from the top of the slabs is pleasant, and the Blueberry Ledges are just a nice place to be on a sunny winter day. It's also a good choice when it's too cold or windy to trek up to a more exposed perch.

Note: The beginning of this hike is on private land; please respect owners' privacy and do not stray from the road and trail.

From the Ferncroft parking area walk northward up the plowed and sanded Ferncroft Road for 0.3 mile. At a sign for Blueberry Ledge Trail turn left across "Squirrel Bridge." (Dicey's Mill Trail to Mt. Passaconaway continues straight here.) You can put your snowshoes on here. Across the bridge bear right on an unplowed road, passing a couple of summer homes. At 0.5 mile the blue-blazed trail heads into the woods as the main road bears right and another road and the Pasture Path branch off to the left.

The Blueberry Ledge Trail now climbs easily through deep spruce woods, bearing left on an old road at 0.6 mile. In a few yards the Blueberry Ledge Cutoff splits right. Stay ahead on Blueberry Ledge Trail, which quickly enters the White Mountain National Forest and the Sandwich Range Wilderness. The easy spruce-shaded climb continues to a junction with the McCrillis Path on the left at 0.9 mile.

The Blueberry Ledge Trail climbs up across a slope and soon presents an interesting view through the bare hardwoods. To the north is the dark, rounded hump of Mt. Wonalancet, and to the NW is the steep, snowy crest of Mt. Whiteface. In the back you see part of Whiteface's long north ridge, which forms one side of a beautiful glacial cirque known as The Bowl. This secluded basin between Mts. Whiteface and Passaconaway harbors one of the largest old-growth forest stands in the White Mountains. It was protected from logging in the early 1900s thanks to lobbying by Katherine Sleeper and other Wonalancet residents. Today it is a Research Natural Area within the Sandwich Range Wilderness.

Now the trail meanders across a level area of mixed forest, climbs a short pitch through hardwoods, and plunges back into spruce woods. You wind upward at easy to moderate grades, with one steeper pitch that can be icy if the cover is thin (it can be skirted on the left).

At 1.6 miles you turn left for a brief traverse, then right and up to the base of the Blueberry Ledges. Climbing steadily, you soon reach the first wide band of ledge. A short detour to the right here opens framed views eastward across the slanting, snowy ledges to the jagged peak of Mt. Chocorua and the lumpy mass of Mt. Paugus, marked by a break of whitened cliffs.

You proceed upward through a belt of spruce woods, then clamber up through more ledgy patches with limited views. The pleasant pattern of snowy ledge and snow-laden spruce, with a few red and white pines mixed in, continues until you angle right and up to the highest of the Blueberry Ledges at 2.0 miles (elevation 2150 ft.). Near the top of this open area a low-lying sign marks the upper junction with Blueberry Ledge Cutoff.

A few yards to the right you'll find the best views, looking SE down a gently sloping expanse of whitened ledge to the Ossipee Range, split by a tall foreground spruce. Mt. Shaw, highest of the Ossipees, is a pointed peak set back in the center. Ossipee Lake can be seen to the left of the range, and to the right is part of Lake Winnipesaukee, with the Belknap Mountains on the horizon. On a sunny day this is a fine spot for a lunch break.

The return to your car is by the same route down Blueberry Ledge Trail. The descent down the ledges on the upper section is especially enjoyable.

ADDITIONAL OPTIONS

Mt. Passaconaway *9.2 miles round trip, 2950-ft. elevation gain, advanced* The Dicey's Mill Trail leads from Ferncroft to the summit of this attractive 4043-ft. peak. Though the top is wooded, good views will be found. Grades are mostly moderate with some steep pitches approaching the summit. Keep straight where the Blueberry Ledge Trail splits left and cross a field. You climb gradually through open hardwoods up the valley of Wonalancet River, entering the White Mountain National Forest and the Sandwich Range Wilderness at 0.8 mile.

At 2.3 miles the trail crosses the stream and begins a long, slabbing climb up the side of a southern spur of Passaconaway. Much ice storm damage is evident among the hardwoods. There are glimpses of the Wonalancet Range across the valley and the great dome of Passaconaway up ahead. At 3.7 miles you crest the ridge and climb up past the site of a former lean-to called "Camp Rich." The trail zig-zags up the lower part of the summit cone, then attacks a steep, winding pitch, sometimes icy, up through wild conifer forest. At the top you swing right past a partial western outlook to meet the Walden Trail near the summit.

The actual high point, on a short side path right, has an over-the-trees view south to Mt. Whiteface and the lake country, much improved in winter. A short distance ahead on the Walden Trail there's a lofty east-facing perch with a great dropoff below. The view spans the Presidentials, Mt. Paugus, Mt. Chocorua, and around to the lake country. A north outlook, with a 180 degree view of many peaks, is accessed by a 0.3-mile downhill spur path between the summit and the east outlook—add 0.6 mile and 200 feet of elevation gain to the above totals for this side trip. The trip back down the cone can be a fast slide with the right snow.

The *WODC Trail Map and Guide* can be used to plan some enjoyable intermediate snowshoe outings around Wonalancet on trails such as **Old Mast Road, Kelley Trail** (challenging in its upper section), **Cabin Trail, Big Rock Cave Trail,** and **Whitin Brook Trail**.

40. Mt. Israel

LOCATION: Sandwich

DESCRIPTION: Solid climb to an isolated 2630-ft. mountain with superb views of the Lakes Region and the Sandwich Range

TRAIL: Wentworth Trail

DISTANCE: 4.6 miles round trip

STARTING ELEVATION: 930 ft.

HIGHEST ELEVATION: 2630 ft.

ELEVATION GAIN: 1700 ft.

RATING: Intermediate

USGS MAP: Center Sandwich

TRAILHEAD: This trek starts by the Mead Wilderness Base Camp off Sandwich Notch Road. First you must find your way to the town of Center Sandwich. From the west, take I-93 to Exit 24 and follow US 3 to Holderness, then turn left on NH 113 and follow it 11.6 winding miles to Center Sandwich. From NH 16 to the east, take NH 25 for 6 miles to the second junction with NH 113, then turn right and follow Rt. 113 for 6 miles to Center Sandwich, bearing left at the junction with NH 113A.

In Center Sandwich, turn from NH 113 onto Grove St., heading NW— look for signs for Sandwich Notch and Mead Base. In 0.4 mile bear left on Diamond Ledge Rd., which is hilly and narrow, but well-sanded; drive with caution. (Don't go right on the Mt. Israel Road, which won't take you to the trailhead.) In another 2.2 miles the unplowed Sandwich Notch Rd., a snowmobile route, continues ahead while a plowed road bears right through fields toward Mead Base. There's a plowed roadside area to park at this junction. You may be able to park 0.15 mile up the side road at a plowed spot where the Bearcamp River Trail (sign) goes right across the fields. The plowed road continues another 0.1 mile but there is no turnaround at the end. Don't block the road.

WMNF PARKING PASS: No

M t. Israel is an out-of-the-way mountain with an exceptional view of the Sandwich Range to the north, plus good vistas south over the big lakes—Squam and Winnipesaukee. The climb to the views is steady with

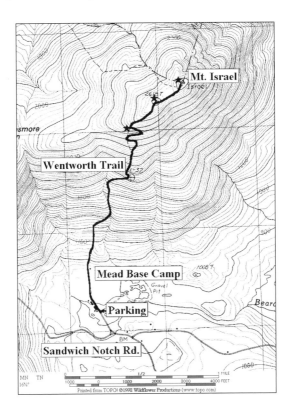

Snowshoers at the summit of Mt. Israel

an occasional steeper pitch. The mountainside forests are an interesting mix of maple, beech, birch, and oak, with some very old trees, shifting to spruce at higher elevations. If you don't mind the convoluted driving, this locals' favorite is a great intermediate snowshoe trip.

The mileage given above starts from the parking spot beside Bearcamp River Trail. The large open fields here are part of the Cook Farm, a 300-acre parcel of conservation land sprawled across the broad Mt. Israel Intervale. Mt. Israel looms large and close to the north with its SW spur, Dinsmore Mtn., to the left. Walk north 0.1 mile up the plowed section of the road—this may be a cold and windy stretch. Strap on your snowshoes and continue another 0.1 mile up the country lane and under a sign for Mead Base. Continue in the same direction to the left of the white house, where the Wentworth Trail (sign) enters the woods. Here also is a sign noting that in 1950 Mrs. George Mead donated a 2443-acre tract to the U.S. Forest Service, including Mt. Israel and the area northward towards Sandwich Mtn. As part of the agreement she requested that one parcel of land be dedicated to youth programs—the Mead Wilderness Base.

The yellow-blazed Wentworth Trail, maintained by the Squam Lakes Association, was opened in 1937 and was partially relocated after the 1938 hurricane. It climbs at easy grades through open hardwoods. At 0.6 mile you swing right and traverse eastward across the slope. Look for stone walls poking out of the snow. This south side of Mt. Israel was mostly pasture in the late 1800s. Moses Sweetser's 1876 guidebook noted that two-thirds of the ascent was made through pastureland. One of the early settlers here was Israel Gilman, who arrived in the 1760s. His name was later given to the mountain that stands guard over the intervale.

Soon you bear left and ascend moderately, then slab up to the right to a shoulder forested with mature oaks. Look right through the trees for views of Squam Lake. At 1.2 miles turn sharp left by a massive oak and cut across a steep slope, then zigzag steadily upward with a few sharp pitches. You'll see many treetops shattered by the 1998 ice storm.

Hardwoods give way to spruces as you switchback higher up the mountain. A final traverse to the left leads past a framed view south to Red Hill. At 1.7 miles the trail makes a right turn at the base of some rough ledges. Here a spur trail leads a few yards left to a sunny viewpoint looking south over the lake country. Snowy Squam Lake is fully revealed with its many bays and islands. A good chunk of Lake Winnipesaukee is visible too. Tower-topped Red Hill rises between the two great lakes. More distant mountains include the Ossipee Range to the SE, the Belknap Range to the south, and Mt. Kearsarge, Ragged Mtn., and Sunapee Mtn. far to the SW.

Beyond the outlook you claw up a short, steep rocky pitch—probably the toughest spot on the trail. Moderate climbing ensues, then the angle eases amidst ridgecrest spruces. There's a nice level section through a corridor of conifers that gives you the illusion of being on a much higher mountain.

At 1.9 miles you mount the open ledges of Mt. Israel's west summit, with the scrubby, slightly higher east summit visible to the right. Gaze northward for your first sprawling view of the Sandwich Range. On the left and closest to you is the huge bulk of Sandwich Dome, showing distinct bands of tree growth on its slopes—open translucent hardwoods below, dark, crowding conifers above. Several beaver ponds can be spotted around its base. A southern shoulder, Black Mtn., is speckled with snow-covered rock.

To the right of Sandwich is the long, even ridge of the northern Flat Mtn. Farther back, behind the cut of remote Lost Pass, are the twin peaks of North and South Tripyramid. (Middle Tripyramid is hidden by the slide-scarred South Peak.) The two wooded domes of The Sleepers join "The Trips" with the double-humped summit of Mt. Whiteface, marked by a cliff on its south face. In front of the West (left) Sleeper is the high plateau that holds Flat Mountain Pond, though the pond itself can not be seen. Below the East (right) Sleeper is the rounded hump of the southern Flat Mtn. The dark cone of Mt. Passaconaway peers over the shoulder of Whiteface, sending step-like ridges cascading to the lowlands of Wonalancet.

This spot is a fine objective in its own right, but the view is even wider at the east summit, 0.2 mile away. From the ledge the trail traverses right (east), then swings left and drops over a three-foot ledge, presenting a mild challenge in both directions. Descend gently to an area of ledge and scrub, where the trail may be hard to follow. Angle right across the opening and exit to the right. The trail soon swings left across a ledge with a partial view of the lakes. Climb a bit through spruces to the junction with the Mead Trail on the left, and continue ahead another 200 feet to the summit rock, topped by a cairn. You've come 2.3 miles from your car.

Down in front a band of crusted ledge provides a panoramic viewing perch. The Sandwich Range is once again front and center, with its two eastern peaks visible on the right—lumpy Mt. Paugus, marked by big blotches of snowy ledge, and the graceful rocky cone of Chocorua ("as sharply cut as the Matterhorn," wrote guidebook editor Sweetser in a bit of 19th-century hyperbole.) Farther east, ghostly and distant on the horizon, is the long ridge of Maine's Pleasant Mtn.

This vantage also opens distant views to the west, taking in Mts. Stinson, Carr, Kineo and Cushman plus the huge bald dome of Mt. Moosilauke—at 4802 ft. the highest point you can see from Mt. Israel.

Because this perch faces north, it often catches the cold prevailing winds. You may need to hunker down in the scrub behind the summit for lunch.

The return route is by the same trail. After plowing your way back to the west summit, the trip down can be accomplished very quickly in good snow conditions!

ADDITIONAL OPTIONS

Flat Mountain Pond *East approach: 8.6 miles round trip, 1400-ft. elevation gain, intermediate/advanced. West approach: 9.6 miles round trip, 1300-ft. elevation gain, intermediate/advanced*   Flat Mountain Pond is a long open swath circled by mountains in a remote corner of the Sandwich Range Wilderness. The pond can be approached on either end of the horseshoe-shaped Flat Mountain Pond Trail in the vicinity of a hamlet called Whiteface Intervale. It is fringed with birch forests that grew up in the wake of a 1923 fire, and at various points around and on the pond there are good views up to the surrounding peaks. Either route provides a fairly long but moderately-graded snowshoe trip to this wild and beautiful place.

Reach Whiteface Intervale by driving along NH 25 to the westerly of its two junctions with NH 113, between East Sandwich and South Tamworth. Follow NH 113 west for about 3½ miles to its junction with NH 113A at North Sandwich. Turn right on NH 113A and drive 2.9 miles north to Whiteface Intervale Rd. on the left. About 0.1 mile down Whiteface Intervale Rd. there is a junction with Bennett St. on the left.

East Approach   From the junction with Bennett Street, stay straight on Whiteface Intervale Rd. for 0.3 mile to the plowed parking area for Flat Mountain Pond Trail on the left. The trail follows a succession of old logging roads across flat terrain for about 0.8 mile—follow arrows and blazes carefully. There's a view of Sandwich Dome across a large beaver meadow about 0.4 mile in. You then scoot along a hemlock ridge, passing a view up to spread-eagled Mt. Whiteface, with a sheer cliff on its south face, at 0.9 mile. This stretch tends to be icy in lean snow times. At 1.6 miles, you drop to the right to cross Whiteface River, which has very large rocks. The former bridge here has been washed out, and this crossing can be difficult if the stream is not well frozen.

Turn left on the opposite bank and follow the trail upstream through hardwoods, passing McCrillis Trail on the right at 1.7 miles and crossing the river's East Branch at 2.0 miles. Grades are easy along the bank of the river, with only an occasional pesky sidehill. Ice storm damage is very evident in places. At 3.1 miles you cross back over the river and climb moderately to the high plateau that holds the pond. After humping over a couple of knolls, you reach the north end of the pond at 4.2 miles. Be wary of thin ice in the boggy NE corner. We once punched through the ice here into shallow water and muck. There are fine views SW to looming Sandwich Dome along the shore here. At the pond's NW corner, the Flat Mountain Pond Trail makes a 90-degree left turn, crosses an inlet brook, and runs along the west side of the northern section of the pond. (If you continue straight ahead at the corner, you can follow an old railroad grade 0.1 mile to an open beaver meadow with an interesting view up to 3311-ft. Flat Mt.—the northern of two ridges bearing that name on either side of the pond. There's also a glimpse north to isolated Lost Pass.) Once you're past the inlet area, if the pond is well-frozen you can snowshoe out on the ice for an exhilarating traverse. If unsure about the ice, I would err on the side of caution—this is a remote area and no place to take an unplanned dip. First you cross the smaller northern pool of the pond, then you push through a narrow strait and onto the long, wide southern part of the pond. It's a unique experience to snowshoe along this open strip of snow and ice. Further south, you'll have views back to Mt. Whiteface, its West Spur, and East Sleeper. At the south end of the pond, 0.8 mile from the north shore, there's a lean-to up on a knoll and a long view up to Sleeper Ridge and Mt. Tripyramid. Avoid the ice by the outlet at the SE corner. If you elect to follow the trail in the woods along the west shore, be prepared for some rough, sidehilly ups and downs. It's 1.1 mile from the north shore to the shelter via the trail. Note: Mileages for traversing the pond or the trail along the shore are not included in the total for the east approach.

West Approach To drive to the trailhead for the west approach, turn left off Whiteface Intervale Rd. onto Bennett St. Follow Bennett St. to a fork at 1.7 miles, where plowing ends. There is usually space for several cars to park here. From here, snowshoe up the unplowed extension of Bennett St. (straight ahead, the left fork) past the summer trailhead parking area. From here, the road becomes the Flat Mountain Pond Trail. At 0.8 mile, turn right on the Bennett Street Trail, which follows Pond Brook at easy grades through attractive woods, with one crossing of a tributary brook. At 1.4 miles, bear left onto Gleason Trail, climbing up to cross a brook and then ascending steadily through the hardwoods to the Flat Mountain Pond Trail at 1.9 miles.

Turn right on Flat Mountain Pond Trail, which follows the old grade of the Beebe River logging railroad—the last line of its kind to be built in the

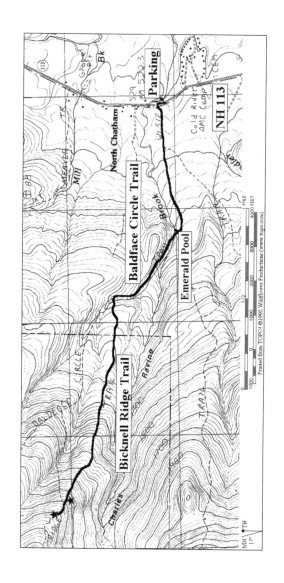

Parking

NH 113

North Chatham

Baldface Circle Trail

Emerald Pool

Bicknell Ridge Trail

Printed from TOPO! ©1998 Wildflower Productions (www.topo.com)

White Mountains. Operations on the 22-mile line began in 1917. In 1923 a huge fire, kindled in the logging slash, consumed 3,500 acres around Flat Mountain Pond. Most of the area regenerated to birch woods. Much of this forest was damaged by the 1998 ice storm, as you'll see when you snowshoe up the railroad grade. Don't be surprised to find a snowmobile track here — riding is allowed up to the pond, but not beyond the south end into the Sandwich Range Wilderness.

There's a steep brook crossing at 2.5 miles, and two more just before a neat hairpin curve by a beaver pond at 3.8 miles. You may have to maneuver across the beaver dam to get by here. The easy grade continues to the south end of Flat Mountain Pond at 4.8 miles. Here the shelter, with a clearing in front that makes a great lunch spot, is found on a side path right while the Flat Mountain Pond Trail splits left to make its circuit around the west shore. Ahead, the railroad grade leads 100 yards to the boggy shore and a fine view up the pond to Whiteface Mtn. and Sleeper Ridge. If you want to traverse the pond or the trail to the north end, add about two miles round trip to the distance listed for the west approach.

41. Bicknell Ridge

LOCATION: Baldface Range, south of Evans Notch

DESCRIPTION: An easy climb to ledges with impressive views of the Baldfaces and the Evans Notch area

TRAILS: Baldface Circle Trail, Bicknell Ridge Trail

DISTANCE: 5.8 miles round trip

STARTING ELEVATION: 520 ft.

HIGHEST ELEVATION: 2100 ft.

ELEVATION GAIN: 1600 ft.

RATING: Intermediate

USGS MAP: Chatham

TRAILHEAD: This trip starts at the plowed parking area for the Baldface Circle Trail, located on the east side of NH/ME 113 in North Chatham, NH, 17.4 miles north of US 302 in Fryeburg, ME. The drive up Rt. 113 has several turns at intersections—follow signs carefully, especially at the right turns at 1.2 and 2.1 miles. Sections of this road are infested with frost heaves. Drive with patience—the Evans Notch area is remote, but worth it! There are some nice mountain views along the way. The trailhead cannot be ap-

South Baldface from Bicknell Ridge

proached from the north in winter—Rt. 113 is unplowed through Evans Notch. There are toilet facilities at the parking area.

WMNF PARKING PASS: Yes

The pair of 3500-foot peaks known as the Baldfaces are a majestic sight when viewed from Rt. 113 in the bucolic Cold River valley to the east. These mountains—the highest in a range that stretches south from Evans Notch along the eastern edge of New Hampshire—were seared by a forest fire in 1903. Their upper ridges are still mostly bare of trees. In winter, when the ledges are blanketed in white, the Baldfaces display an alpine grandeur that belies their modest elevations.

Open-ridge walking and eye-stretching views make the 10-mile circuit over South and North Baldface a popular summer outing, but few hikers venture across these exposed heights in winter. That would be a formidable trip, for experts only, with a tricky climb up icy ledges on the steep side of South Baldface followed by several miles of above treeline travel.

Happily, intermediate snowshoers can experience the beauty and isolation of the Baldfaces in winter with a modest trek up to the first ledges on Bicknell Ridge, a long eastern spur of the range. The climb to this point up the Baldface Circle and Bicknell Ridge Trails is mostly at easy grades through attractive woods. The prize is a sunny south-facing ledge area with an imposing close-up view of South Baldface. Nearby vantages open additional views east to the lowlands of western Maine and north to the mountains around Evans Notch. Because this area is far off the usual hiking circuit, especially in winter, you may find untracked snow here. On a sunny day it's one of the most enjoyable snowshoe ventures in the Whites.

From the parking area, walk out to Rt. 113, turn right, and walk 200 feet north up the road to a hiker symbol and sign for Baldface Circle Trail. The trail climbs up the snowbank to the right of the sign and angles into the woods. In a few yards it bears left and leads you on an easy walk westward through small pines and hardwoods. In about 0.3 mile you enter an area where dozens of hemlock and spruce have been felled by NW winds. Beyond this devastation you make a left turn onto an old road, and more easy walking brings you to Circle Junction at 0.7 mile. Here the South Baldface branch of the Circle Trail splits left and a spur path departs right for Emerald Pool. Continue straight ahead on the North Baldface branch of the Circle Trail.

In 100 yards you swing right to cross Charles Brook, a good-sized mountain stream with plenty of rocks to cross on if it's not frozen over. On the far bank the trail climbs gradually upstream, following Charles Brook and then a northern tributary. The woods are a mix of hemlocks fringing the stream on the left and hardwoods upslope on the right.

At 1.4 miles, at a junction on the brook bank, turn left onto Bicknell Ridge Trail and cross the stream. After a brief stretch through small trees you break out in open hardwoods. The trail, a wide corridor intermittently blazed in yellow, swings right and wanders gradually up and westward, with long views into the forest. Before long you pass the National Forest boundary. (Up to this point the trails have been on private land and a corridor of WMNF land.) You follow old logging roads, then make a jog to the right up a shallow draw—a key turn that is not well-blazed.

You continue a gentle upward meander through these bright, spacious woods. The broad ridge starts to define itself and the pitch slowly increases. The snowy eastern wall of South Baldface shines through the trees up ahead to the left. A lower dark knob, Spruce Knoll, caps a parallel ridge across the valley. White birches mix into the woods as you draw even with the South Baldface ledges. The trail keeps to the left (south) side of the ridge. It's a beautiful stretch of snowshoeing.

At 2.4 miles (elevation 1600 ft.) the trail bends right and angles more steeply NW across the ridge. Look for yellow blazes up the slope. You cross two small streambeds and climb into spruce forest. The ascent is steady, but never truly steep, through these darker, rockier woods. At 2.7 miles you climb up a small patch of snowy ledge with limited views. Huffing a bit, you rise along the left edge of the ridge, then angle up to a sizeable open patch that faces south to the sun.

The view across the deep ravine of Charles Brook to the great snowy mass of South Baldface—seen broadside from base to summit—is one of the more impressive close-ups of a White Mountain peak. The large treeless areas on the ridge, with sunlight glinting off the ice, give the scene a powerful, almost Western look. It's hard to imagine a trail struggling up that steep eastern face—but that's the route of the South Baldface link in the Circle Trail.

To the right, at the head of the ravine, the small snowy cone of North Baldface crowns a steep, spruce-clad headwall. Looking west up the ridge you can see some of the ledges the Bicknell Ridge Trail crosses higher up. To the left of South Baldface, over its col with little Spruce Knoll, is the dark wooded peak of Eastman Mtn. To the SE there's a view over the Cold River valley to distant Pleasant Mtn. in Maine, marked by ski trails on its north end.

This sunny spot, somewhat sheltered from north winds, is a great place for a lunch break. A trailside boulder may provide a dry resting spot. For photos, a wide angle lens will take in the expanse of South Baldface.

Just above this vantage is the signed junction with Eagle Cascade Link, which drops back to the Circle Trail. For additional views, continue past this intersection on Bicknell Ridge Trail. In a short distance the trail angles up to the right (NW) through a scrubby semi-open area—you may spot the tops of cairns poking out of the snow. In 100 yards turn left at a blaze onto a narrow corridor through a belt of scrub. By this corner there's a nice view on the right looking NE to the broad spread of Speckled Mtn. The ledges of Blueberry Mtn. are prominent on the south end of a long ridge. Frozen Shell Pond can be seen to the right of Speckled.

Beyond the scrub patch you clamber up more snow-covered ledges. At the top, only 0.1 mile from the first viewpoint, the trail levels as it enters deep spruce woods. Snowshoe 100 feet right here through open terrain to a roomy ledge area with an excellent view north to the mountains around Evans Notch. On the left (west) side of the pass the rounded tops of West and East Royce peer over a dark, ledgy ridge sloping down from Mt. Meader. On the right (east) side is the square, ledgy top of Caribou Mtn. with wooded Gammon Mtn. on its left and Speckled to the right. By poking around you can find views east to the Deer Hills across the valley and farther afield to Streaked Mtn. and other low Maine ridges.

This is a good turnaround point for an intermediate snowshoe visit to Bicknell Ridge. With favorable conditions, advanced snowshoers can continue another 1.0 mile and 900 vertical feet up Bicknell Ridge Trail, alternating between spruce woods and open ledges with ever-changing views of the Baldfaces, the Evans Notch mountains and western Maine. At the top (3050 ft.) you meet the Baldface Circle Trail on the open, ledgy ridge between North Baldface and Eagle Crag. The prize here is an expansive vista across the remote Wild River valley to the east side of the Carter Range, with deep, cirque-like basins enclosed by long ridges. Round trip to this view is 7.8 miles with elevation gain of 2500 feet.

42. Blueberry Mountain (Evans Notch)

LOCATION: South end of Evans Notch

DESCRIPTION: A short, steep climb to a ledgy summit with good views west and south

TRAILS: NH/ME Rt. 113, Bickford Brook Trail, Blueberry Ridge Trail, Overlook Loop

DISTANCE: 3.8 miles round trip

STARTING ELEVATION: 590 ft.

HIGHEST ELEVATION: 1780 ft.

ELEVATION GAIN: 1300 ft.

RATING: Intermediate

USGS MAPS: Wild River, Speckled Mountain

TRAILHEAD: In winter, NH/ME 113 is not plowed through Evans Notch. From the south it is plowed to the junction with the entrance road to Basin Pond, just north of North Chatham. There is ample room to park here for the hike to Blueberry Mountain. To get there, take NH/ME 113 from US 302 in Fryeburg, ME. Follow signs carefully at several turns and intersections, especially the right turns at 1.2 and 2.1 miles. Be prepared to negotiate numerous frost heaves. About 7 miles from Fryeburg there's a series of fine views left to Kearsarge North and the range of hills north of it. Approaching North Chatham there are impressive views of the Baldfaces to the left. Reach the end of the plowed road and parking on the left at 19.5 miles from Fryeburg.

WMNF PARKING PASS: Yes

Blueberry Mountain (1781 ft.) is a low, ledgy spur at the end of a long ridge extending south from Speckled Mountain in the Caribou–Speckled Mountain Wilderness. The summit area offers outstanding views of the mountains and hills west and south of Evans Notch—well worth the long, bumpy ride up Rt. 113. The climb up the west side of Blueberry is short but steep and could be challenging in crusty conditions. Blazing is sparse on the upper mile, so if no one has made tracks ahead of you, allow some extra time for route finding. Bickford Brook must be crossed at the base of the climb, a potential problem after a major thaw. With good snow and weather conditions, though, this trip is a snowshoer's delight.

The hike starts by following the unplowed Rt. 113 northward from your car. This is a snowmobile route and should have a nice packed track for snowshoeing, but be prepared to yield the trail to passing snowmobilers.

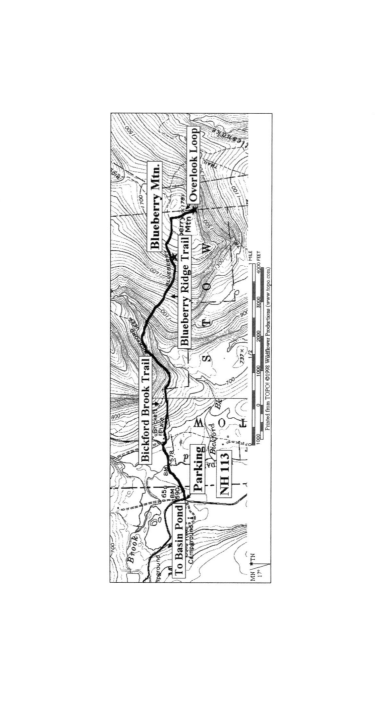

After crossing the state line into Maine you pass a field on the left and traverse a bridge over the Mad River. At 0.2 mile you'll come to the Brickett Place, a red brick house on the right with a snowy crag hanging on the ridge above. The dwelling was built in 1812 by homesteader John Brickett, who exercised Yankee self-sufficiency by firing his own bricks on-site. The house was renovated in the 1930s by the Civilian Conservation Corps and for a time was used as a WMNF ranger station. It's still in fine shape today.

Follow the driveway to the right off Rt. 113 and around to the east side of the house, where you'll see a kiosk and a sign for Bickford Brook Trail. The trail departs to the right and curves upward at a moderate incline through small hardwoods. At 0.5 mile from your car (0.3 mile from Brickett Place) you turn right onto an old road that once serviced a firetower on the summit of Speckled Mtn. The grade is gentle as Blueberry Mtn. looms ahead. The old road swings left to head up the valley of Bickford Brook, passing the boundary sign for the Caribou-Speckled Wilderness and reaching the junction with Blueberry Ridge Trail (sign) at 0.9 mile, amidst open hardwood forest.

Turn right on Blueberry Ridge Trail and descend slightly through hardwoods, then more steeply into hemlocks—look carefully for yellow blazes. At the bottom, 0.1 mile from Bickford Brook Trail, bear left to a junction beside the brook. Side trails lead left to the Upper Bickford Slides and right to the Lower Bickford Slides, a series of waterfalls. Your route is across the brook on Blueberry Ridge Trail. Downstream to the right you can see the small snowy gorge that holds the Lower Slides.

Once across the brook, angle 30 feet left and up to a sign for Blueberry Ridge Trail. The next move here is obscure in winter—this is a Wilderness area and blazes are lacking. The trail continues up the slope in the same direction on a bearing of about 100 degrees (a bit south of east). It soon becomes a fairly obvious corridor leading up the steep slope through open mixed woods. After about 0.1 mile blazes reappear intermittently. If the trail is unbroken, seek out the swath where no undergrowth pokes up through the snow.

About 0.2 mile up from the brook the pitch relaxes briefly. The trail bears slightly right and soon climbs steadily up the slope again through scrubbier trees. Looking back you can glimpses the Royces, Basin Pond and the Carter Range. The ascent is quite steep now, and though blazes are few, the route is obvious. The terrain becomes ledgy and there may be ice beneath the snow in a couple of the steeper spots.

When you've climbed about 0.5 mile from Bickford Brook the trail angles up to the left and lifts you to the first outlook ledge—a sloping expanse of snow with an excellent view to the west. Cut across to the left (north) side and slightly down for the widest vista, taking in the entire Royce–Baldface range.

To the NW, beyond a nearby ridge and Evans Notch, is the massive ledgy wall of West Royce, with the top of East Royce peering over on the right.

West Royce from the west outlook on Blueberry Mtn.

Westward you look into the cirque (a broad glacial valley with a steep head-wall) known as The Basin, with frozen Basin Pond at its mouth and the Carter Range towering beyond the headwall. Left of The Basin is the darkly wooded Mt. Meader, and Meader Ridge runs south to the high, snowy Bald-faces. From this angle South Baldface looks impressively alpine. Eastman Mtn. is to the left of the Baldfaces. At the base of these ridges are the broad fields of the Cold River valley.

Above this vista, following the trail up to the summit plateau may present a challenge if the snow is unbroken. The trail exits this ledgy area at the top left corner and winds up through scrubby spruce and pine. After 100 yards or so it swings right on a ledge with a view back to the Royces, bur-rows through a deep grove of spruces, and eases up to a gentle expanse of ledge and scrub. Go straight here, then around to the left of a high spot, and you'll soon come to the junction with the White Cairn Trail, which enters on the right 0.2 mile from the west outlook.

Continue ahead on Blueberry Ridge Trail across a ledge, through a patch of scrubby woods, and out to another open area near the actual summit of Blueberry Mountain. Look for a sign on the right, "CTA Outlook Loop," attached to a scruffy spruce. Turning right here, you may find this side path difficult to discern in deep snow, but if you follow corridors due south across the semi-open plateau you'll come to the top of the south cliffs of Blueberry in 0.1 mile. You can savor the winter sun and a broad southerly vista here, with snowy Shell Pond nestled in a peaceful wooded hollow be-neath Harndon Hill and Deer Hill. The distant south view is a spread of ponds, fields and low ridges. To the SE are parts of Kezar Lake, with Pleasant Mtn. rising beyond. Far to the SW you can see Black Cap Mtn., Kearsarge North, North Moat Mtn. and the top of Mt. Passaconaway.

From the top of the south cliffs, follow your tracks back down the Blueberry Ridge and Bickford Brook Trails and along Rt. 113 to your car. Enjoy the westerly views on the upper part of the descent.

ADDITIONAL OPTION

Basin Pond and Hermit Falls *4.2 miles round trip, 150-ft. elevation gain, beginner* The gentle snowshoe up the road to Basin Pond and along the Basin Trail to Hermit Falls is an easy and scenic alternative to the Blueberry Mtn. climb. Begin at the same parking space at the end of the plowed section of Rt. 113 north of North Chatham. Snowshoe up the unplowed road leading west, winding gradually upward 0.6 mile to the parking lot beside Basin Pond. Amble out to the edge of the pond for a stunning view into the glacial cirque of The Basin, formed by Mt. Meader on the left, the Basin Rim in the center, and the ridges of West Royce on the right. If the ice is solid (look for recent snowmobile, ski or snowshoe tracks), you can shuffle out on the pond for wider views. Keep off the ice by the high dam at the east end.

You'll find the sign for the Basin Trail at the west side of the parking lot. The yellow-blazed trail runs through the woods above the south shore of the pond. At 0.9 mile from your car, by the bogs and meadows at the west end of the pond, you bear left on an old logging road. After crossing two brooks—the second on a footbridge—the trail meanders gently through a fine beech forest on the broad floor of the cirque. You reach the lower junction with the Hermit Falls loop trail at 1.9 miles. Follow this 0.2 mile to the base of the frozen falls, a quiet scenic spot in a shady ravine. From here follow your tracks back to your car. (*Note*: Above the Hermit Falls loop the Basin Trail becomes progressively steeper, culminating with a difficult pitch up the headwall. This section is not recommended for snowshoeing.)

43. Caribou Mtn.

LOCATION: NE of Evans Notch

DESCRIPTION: A moderate climb to a broad open summit with sweeping views of the Caribou-Speckled Wilderness, Evans Notch, Wild River valley and distant ranges

TRAILS: Bog Road, Caribou Trail, Mud Brook Trail

DISTANCE: 6.8 miles round trip

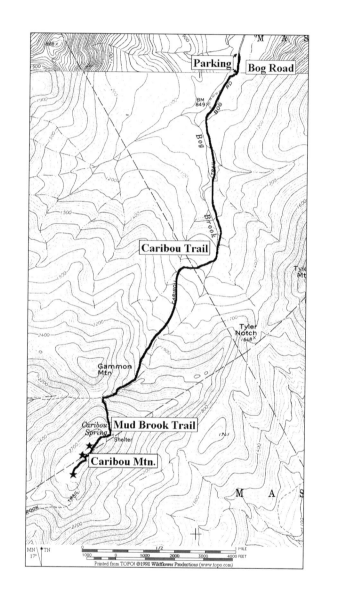

STARTING ELEVATION: 800 ft.

HIGHEST ELEVATION: 2850 ft.

ELEVATION GAIN: 2050 ft.

RATING: Intermediate / advanced

USGS MAPS: Gilead, Speckled Mtn.

TRAILHEAD: This hike uses the north half of the Caribou Trail, starting on Bog Road, a plowed side road off US 2 near West Bethel, ME. The turn-off is 5.1 miles east of the junction with Rt. 113 (the Evans Notch Road, unplowed through the pass in winter) and 1.3 miles west of the post office in West Bethel. There are signs for Bog Rd. and "Pooh Corner Farm" at the junction. The road is regularly plowed at least to the farm at 2.0 miles, and in winter 2000 it was cleared to a turnaround at 2.5 miles, with room for several cars to park. The summer trailhead for Caribou Trail is at 2.8 miles.

WMNF PARKING PASS: Yes (if plowed to turnaround)

The summit of 2850-ft. Caribou Mtn.—an expanse of open rock several acres in extent—is one of the most exhilarating spots in the White Mountains. Relatively few hikers enjoy its alpine aura and astounding views in winter, when the popular loop hike over the summit from Rt. 113 to the west is not accessible by car. (Unless, that is, you're up for 3.2 miles of slogging each way along the unplowed road.) Happily, the northern trail approach can be readily used in winter with just a short road walk at the start. The climb up this end of the Caribou Trail is easy in the lower half and moderately steep in its upper half and along the final segment on Mud Brook Trail. The woods are open and attractive nearly the whole way. Be sure to bring plenty of layers to counter the cold breezes on the exposed summit, and perhaps crampons if you suspect the ledges are icy.

If Bog Rd. is plowed to the turnaround, you'll have just a 0.3-mile snowshoe ahead up the road to the start of the Caribou Trail. (The mileages below are calculated from the turnaround. If the plowing ends just beyond the farm, add 0.4 mile each way.) From the trailhead kiosk continue up the extension of Bog Rd., climbing gradually, and bear left at a fork in 0.2 mile— this turn is marked by an arrow. The road soon curves right and at 0.7 mile, after a gently rising straightaway, the trail leaves the road, continuing ahead where the road swings left.

You dip into a brushy area and pick up an old logging road, quickly crossing a small brook. The snowshoeing is easy and pleasant up this gentle swath through hardwoods and hemlocks. There's one short detour around to the left where the trail skirts a washout, then returns to the road. Farther on you cross a branch of Bog Brook. Just beyond, a spur logging road leads left to an open logging yard; here there's a look left up to the wooded ridge of trailless Tyler Mtn.

Easy going continues to a crossing of Bog Brook at 1.5 miles. Shortly you

Caribou's ledges overlook the Caribou–Speckled Wilderness and Kezar Lake

come to a Forest Service sign cautioning hikers to make the correct turn at the junction of Caribou and Mud Brook Trails (1.3 miles ahead) when *descending* from the summit of Caribou. (Coming down, turn right.) You mush onward at soothing grades, soon breaking out into an open forest of beech, maple and birch. The trail, well-blazed here in yellow, jogs right briefly to follow a small brook, then pulls off to the left for 0.1 mile of stiff climbing. Then you rise at an easy to moderate slant through expansive hardwoods. A spruce-wooded knob of Gammon Mtn. rises up ahead to the right. Looking back through the trees you can see nearby Tyler Mtn. and distant horizons. Look carefully for sometimes-faded blazes in these open woods.

Reaching the base of a slope on the right, the trail eases off through some large old yellow birches, crosses a small brook, and pushes up a lovely hardwood draw. The remote feel of this upper valley is enhanced as you pass the sign marking the boundary of the Caribou-Speckled Wilderness Area at 2.4 miles. At the top of the draw you dip slightly alongside a brookbed on your left. In 200 feet the trail angles up to the right at a fairly steep grade, crossing a feeder brook, and proceeds upward along a bank high above a deep, steep gully on the left. There's one short, mildly challenging sidehill here.

The gully soon becomes shallow and splits into two draws. At this fork the trail swings left and crosses the righthand draw, climbs 50 feet to a double blaze on a big yellow birch, then makes a hard right and shoots steeply up a mini-ridge along the left (south) side of the righthand draw. This is the steepest climb of the day, but short. A brief sidehill section lifts you to the broad, flat col between Caribou and Gammon Mtns. at 2.8 miles.

At a trail sign turn left onto the Mud Brook Trail. (The Caribou Trail continues ahead, descending 3.0 miles to Rt. 113.) You climb easily southward, swinging around to the left (east) side of the ridge. Follow the route carefully as it weaves upward through wonderfully weathered yellow and white birches, keeping east of the crest. At 3.1 miles you pass a clearing on the left marking the site of the former Caribou Shelter.

Here the trail turns right, winds up through spruce and fir, and crosses a shallow hardwood draw. You climb a short steep pitch back into spruce, then make a sharp left and gain the top of the ridge. The grade is easy as you bore through conifers along the crest; the trail may be a bit overgrown in places. At 3.3 miles you emerge on a small, semi-open false summit with a view NW to the Mahoosuc Range. This is a good place to layer up, as the true summit is only a couple of minutes away.

The trail may be hard to pick up in deep snow as it leaves this opening. It drops off slightly to the left and tunnels another 100 yards through conifers to the edge of the summit ledges. A short climb in the open deposits you on the top of Caribou—the northern of two rocky knobs that rise above a barren, scrub-fringed plateau. Please take care not to trample any of the alpine-type plant life around the ledges. Good snowshoe crampons or boot crampons may be handy here. In late winter you might step out onto bare rock.

On a clear day the 360-degree view of remote mountain country from Caribou rivals that from many a higher peak. Perhaps most striking is the panorama SW over the broad valley of Wild River backed by the high, wooded wall of the Carter Range, seen end-to-end from Carter Dome to Shelburne Moriah. Peering over in the back are the alpine crests of Boott Spur, Mt. Washington and the Northern Presidentials—Jefferson, Adams and Madison.

Looking NW there's an expansive view to the rugged Mahoosuc Range and the more distant Pliny and Pilot Ranges, with portions of the Androscoggin River valley in the middle foreground. Far off to the north and NE you can spot landmark Maine peaks such as Baldpate, Sugarloaf, Abraham and Mt. Blue. The tops of Speckled, Kearsarge North, the Baldfaces and East Royce can be seen poking above the rocky south knob of Caribou.

To get the full sweep of views in this direction, a short jaunt to the south ledges is highly recommended (weather and snow conditions permitting). At a sign for Mud Brook Trail by the summit, the route drops to the east to get down off the summit knob, then heads south across the plateau over snow-crusted ledges. At the south end of the crest, you can make your way left to large areas of flat, open ledge with steep dropoffs in front. These perches open stupendous southerly views. To the SW is the rugged cut of Evans Notch winding between the dark masses of Speckled Mtn. and East Royce, with the snowy Baldfaces beyond. In the distance are the Moats and Mt. Chocorua. To the SE you gaze over the broad hardwood basin of the West Branch of Pleasant River, a little-known area enclosed on the south by the long ridge of Butters and Redrock Mtns. The north slope of Butters is a steep slope of pure open hardwood, with a whitened, ghostly look in the snow. Kezar Lake and Pleasant Mtn. can be seen in the distance over Butters.

Back at the north knob (the true summit), follow the same route back to your car, turning right on Caribou Trail in the Caribou-Gammon col. The upper 1½ miles of the descent is a snowshoer's delight in favorable snow conditions.

44. Mts. Starr King and Waumbek

LOCATION: Jefferson

DESCRIPTION: A moderate climb to a Presidential view, a winter wonderland ridge, and a 4000-foot peak.

TRAIL: Starr King Trail

DISTANCE: 7.8 miles round trip

STARTING ELEVATION: 1450 ft.

HIGHEST ELEVATION: 4006 ft.

ELEVATION GAIN: 2850 ft.

RATING: Intermediate / advanced

USGS MAP: Pliny Range

TRAILHEAD: The short road to the summer trailhead parking area is not usually plowed. Winter parking is found at a plowed pulloff on the south side of US 2, 0.1 mile west of the side road that leads to the summer trailhead, and a short distance east of the junction of US 2 and NH 115A in Jefferson. This walk adds 0.3 mile each way to summer trail mileages.

WMNF PARKING PASS: No

The trek up the Starr King Trail to Mts. Starr King and Waumbek is one of the easier snowshoe ascents of a 4000-foot peak. The grades are moderate with hardly a steep pitch on the entire trip. Along the way, you pass through bright, open hardwood stands and Christmas-card fir forests. From a clearing atop Mt. Starr King (3907 ft.), there's a fine panorama south to the snow-capped Presidentials and distant horizons. A mile's snowshoe along a lovely fir-clad ridge bags you the 4006-ft. summit of Mt. Waumbek, where the views are limited but better than in summer. Up to Mt. Starr King the trail is often well-packed by snowshoers. These two mountains are the high-

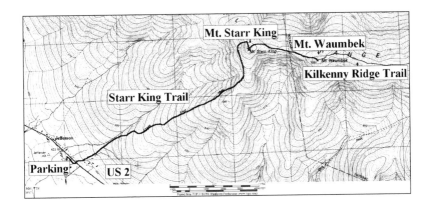

est peaks in the Pliny Range, a semi-circular ridge that borders the Kilkenny region in the northern section of the White Mountain National Forest.

From the parking pulloff on the south side of US 2, walk 0.1 mile east along the highway and cross to the north side at the hiker symbol and sign for Starr King Trail. Walk up the road, bearing left to avoid private driveways. In 0.2 mile, a short spur bears right to the unplowed summer trailhead parking area.

Snowshoe ahead up the road, which is soon joined by a trail coming in from the summer parking area. You climb easily up the old roadbed above a small brook on the left. About 0.7 mile from your car, the trail bears right onto another old roadway, and then right again at 1.1 mile.

For the next 0.6 mile, you snowshoe at a steady grade up the broad SW ridge of Mt. Starr King through a beautiful open forest of mature hardwood, with some large specimens of sugar maple, yellow birch, and beech. At 1.7 miles (2900 ft.) the trail swings left to begin a long traverse on the NW side of the ridge. The character of the forest abruptly changes to a shady, snow-dappled corridor of fir and white birch. A deep valley drops off to the left, and you have glimpses of a parallel ridge on the far side. The grades are moderate through here, perfect for snowshoeing. You pass a sign marking a spring at 2.4 miles. Farther up, you cut through a blowdown area and climb through the open fir forest typical of the Pliny and Pilot ranges.

At 2.8 miles you swing right off the traverse and wind upward to the summit of Mt. Starr King at 2.9 miles. The actual high point is wooded and affords almost no view in summer, but winter's deep snows lift you enough for partial views north and NE to Terrace Mtn, Mt. Cabot, Mt. Weeks, and distant Maine peaks, and west towards Vermont. Continue across the flat summit to the first of two open outlooks on the south side. A raised snowy ledge to the right offers the best viewing perch.

The panorama of the Presidential Range to the SE will have you digging for your camera. Craggy and snowy, they march across the skyline beyond the valley of the Israel River: Madison, Adams, Jefferson, Clay, Washington, Monroe, Franklin, Eisenhower, Pierce, Jackson, and Webster. There's an especially good look into the wild maw of Castle Ravine between Mts. Adams and Jefferson. The nearer Mt. Dartmouth crouches under the Southern Presidentials. To the left of the Presys, you see the Moriah summits and parts of the Carter Range spread out beyond Mt. Pliny, and close by up the ridge is the double wooded summit of Mt. Waumbek.

To the right of the Presys are Mt. Deception and the shapely Cherry Mtn. in the foreground, and the Willey Range, Bretton Woods Ski Area, the Twin Range, Mt. Garfield, the Franconia Range, the Kinsmans, and Mt. Moosilauke beyond. To the SW and west, the view sweeps over the sprawling lowlands of Jefferson and Whitefield, a patchwork of snowy fields and dark woods. Cherry Pond and Little Cherry Pond stand out as white splotches on the broad plateau. On clear days, Vermont's Green Mountains can be seen on the horizon.

The trail turns left at this viewpoint and in a few yards, comes to a good-sized clearing with a stone fireplace and chimney at the upper edge, all that remains of a shelter that once stood at this site. Here you get a second look at that great south view, though a bit more restricted in front. If you stop here for lunch, a bold Gray Jay may join you seeking a handout.

The mountain you're standing on was named for Thomas Starr King, a Unitarian minister from Boston whose 1859 book, *The White Hills: Their Legends, Landscape, and Poetry,* inspired thousands of Gilded Age tourists to visit and appreciate the White Mountains. Although there's no record of him climbing his namesake mountain, Starr King was eloquent in his praise of the view from Jefferson Hill at the base of the peak, calling it the "ultimate thule of grandeur in an artist's pilgrimage among the New Hampshire mountains, for at no other point can he see the White Hills themselves in such array and force." Another minister and mountain enthusiast, Julius Ward, gushed about the view from Mt. Starr King in his 1890 book, *The White Mountains: A Guide to their Interpretation*: ". . . the Presidential Range from this point is grander and more inspiring than from any other quarter in the west or north."

The continuation of the trail to Mt. Waumbek leaves the clearing behind the old fireplace and chimney. It descends briefly NE, then swings east along the broad ridge, losing elevation gradually. The snowshoeing is beautiful through open, lichen-draped fir forest. The snow lies deep, and the actual trail may be hard to follow if there is no track. You dip to the col a bit on the south side, then meander back and forth along the ridge crest until a final moderately steep pull of 0.2 mile lifts you to the wooded summit of Mt. Waumbek at 3.9 miles.

The views are limited here, but better in winter. There's one partial vista south to the Presidentials, and by poking around on the north side, you can find peeks at Terrace Mtn., Mt. Cabot, The Horn, and distant mountains in

*At the summit
of Starr King*

New Hampshire's North Country and western Maine. Woodsy Waumbek
has a northwoods feel with several feet of snow blanketing the ridge. Once
we encountered a large flock of restless, chattering redpolls—one of several species of "winter finches" that descend on New England from northern Canada. This summit, the highest in the Pliny Range, was once known
as "Pliny Major," but the name was changed to "Waumbek" sometime in
the late 1800s. The name derives from the Native American terms "waum-
bik" or "white rocks," and "waumbekket-methna," meaning "white or
snowy mountains."

If you want to experience even more deep-snow beauty, you can continue east along the ridge from the summit of Waumbek on the Kilkenny
Ridge Trail, snowshoeing nearly a mile with little elevation loss, and passing
through an unrelentingly beautiful ridgetop fir forest. About 0.2 mile east of
the summit, the trail climbs over a little knob where there's a glimpse
northward to Mt. Cabot, displaying the great white talus field on its south
face, and the slide-marked south peak of Terrace Mtn.

Mt. Cabot   The western approach to 4170-ft. Mt. Cabot via the Mt. Cabot Trail was going to be a featured snowshoe hike in this book until access over a section of private land was closed off in February 2000. Mt. Cabot is the highest peak of the Pilot Range and is one of the snowiest spots around, and the Mt. Cabot Trail has excellent, moderate grades for snowshoeing. Although the summit itself has no view, there are two excellent vistas on the way up. From Bunnell Rock (3350 ft.) there's a nice look across Bunnell Notch to Terrace Mtn, and out to Mt. Moriah on the left and Starr King/ Waumbek, the Twin Range, Franconia Ridge, and Cannon to the right. About 0.4 mile below the summit there is a cabin with a wood stove, maintained by the Jefferson Boy Scouts and Pinkerton Academy Outing Club and open to public use. Just beyond is a clearing at the site of an old firetower. To the east you look over the Kilkenny Region with the sharp summit of The Horn dominating, and beyond to the Mahoosucs and many other Maine mountains. Westward, there's a wide view towards Vermont, with the Presidentials peering over the trees to the south.

With the western trailhead unavailable, Cabot-climbers will find the shortest approach from the end of York Pond Road on the east (see Rogers Ledge hike description for directions.) This route follows the York Pond Trail for 0.2 mile, the obscure Bunnell Notch Trail for 2.9 miles, and the Kilkenny Ridge Trail for 1.7 miles to Mt. Cabot. The round trip is 9.6 miles, with a 2500-ft. elevation gain. If the Mt. Cabot Trail approach is re-opened, that route is 7.8 miles round trip with a 2700-ft. elevation gain. Consult the *AMC White Mountain Guide* for details.

Mt. Prospect   *3.2 miles round trip, 650-ft. elevation gain, beginner*   Little 2077-ft. Mt. Prospect, located in Weeks State Park just north of the White Mountains, affords grand views from two outlooks along an unplowed road that winds up to the summit. It's an excellent snowshoe climb for beginners. The auto road, built in 1911 and designated a New Hampshire scenic byway, leaves the east side of US 3 at the top of a hill about 3 miles south of Lancaster and 6 miles north of Whitefield. Park at a plowed pulloff on the west side of the highway just north of the road entrance. There are good views north and south here. Use caution when crossing the highway.

The road climbs at easy grades through attractive birches, crossing the Around-the-Mountain Trail at 0.1 mile, then swings right and traverses southward across the slope. At 0.6 mile, the road begins a big loop around to the left, reaching a viewpoint at 0.7 mile looking west to the nearby Blood Pond and Martin Meadow Pond. You now slab NE to the magnificent eastern viewpoint at 1.1 mile. The panorama here spans from Mt. Cabot on the left to Mt. Lafayette on the right, with Mt. Washington and the Presidentials as the centerpiece.

Continuing up the road, you come to a hairpin curve left at 1.3 miles and swing up to the summit at 1.6 miles. Here there's a stone lookout tower and the impressive 1912-vintage summer home of Congressman John W. Weeks, who sponsored legislation in 1911 that led to the creation of National Forests in the east, including the White Mountain National Forest. All of the summit buildings are closed in winter, but the lawn area in front of the mansion provides good views in several directions, including west to the Connecticut River valley and Vermont.

Cherry Mountain *3.8 miles round trip, 1900-ft. elevation gain, intermediate*
The 3573-ft. summit of Cherry Mountain (once known as Mt. Martha), just north of the town of Twin Mountain, commands good views east and SW from cleared outlooks. The Cherry Mountain Trail provides a relatively short but steep route to the top. The trailhead is located on the east side of NH 115, 1.9 miles north of its junction with US 3. The parking area is above the highway opposite the junction with Lennon Rd. and is often unplowed. Adequate roadside parking can usually be found around the intersection. The trail climbs on a logging road up through a log yard and stays straight at a fork at 0.5 mile. Narrowing to a trail, it keeps a fairly easy grade for a bit, then makes a long, stiff climb to the crest of the ridge at 1.7 miles. At a T-junction, the trail turns left and follows a snowmobile-packed track to the summit in another 0.2 mile. (Snowmobiles come up from Cherry Mountain Road via the wide, graded east end of Cherry Mountain Trail.)

The flat summit, which once bore a firetower, features two fine cleared outlooks around its edges. To the east, you admire the snowy sweep of the Presidentials—this is one of the finest angles for viewing the big range. To the SW and south is a panorama of peaks in and around the Pemigewasset Wilderness with some twenty-two 4000 footers visible from this one spot. Mt. Lafayette is especially prominent, and there's a nice view into the Zealand Valley and a unique glimpse of the deep gap of Crawford Notch.

45. Rogers Ledge

LOCATION: Kilkenny region, west of Berlin
DESCRIPTION: An all-day venture into remote birch forests, leading to a spectacular clifftop viewpoint
TRAILS: Mill Brook Trail, Kilkenny Ridge Trail
DISTANCE: 8.4 miles round trip
STARTING ELEVATION: 1550 ft.

HIGHEST ELEVATION: 2965 ft.

ELEVATION GAIN: 1500 ft.

RATING: Advanced

USGS MAP: West Milan

TRAILHEAD: From NH 16 in Berlin, take NH 110 west, following signs carefully as it makes several turns through the city streets. In 7.1 miles turn left on York Pond Road, marked by a sign for the Berlin Fish Hatchery. Drive 4.8 miles down this road, which is plowed but tends to be icy in places, to a gate at the entrance to the hatchery. In recent years the gate has been open through the winter. (If it's closed, park at a pulloff on the left before the gate. This will add 0.4 mile each way to the trip distance.) Drive 0.2 mile beyond the gate, turn right on a side road (sign for Mill Brook Trail), follow it 0.2 mile to its end, and park in a designated area to the left of a gray stone building. The Mill Brook Trail starts to the left of and behind the building.

WMNF PARKING PASS: Yes

The Kilkenny region is one of the most remote and beautiful corners of the White Mountains, especially in winter. Burned by a vast forest fire in 1903, it has largely regrown to parklike paper birch forests. Though this area took a hard blow from the January '98 ice storm, with thousands of treetops broken, The Kilkenny continues to enchant.

The prize at the end of this trek is Rogers Ledge, a great granite cliff that overlooks the Kilkenny uplands, the Pilot and Mahoosuc Ranges, and beyond to the sawtooth skyline of the Presidentials. This trip offers adventure and solitude aplenty. Since the area is lightly traveled, there's a good chance you'll be breaking trail most or all of the way, and your route-finding skills may be put to the test.

To find the Mill Brook Trail, follow a roadway curving left behind the hatchery building. Just before the road ends, bear sharp right at a sign for Mill Brook Trail nailed to a white birch. In 100 feet, as you draw even with a small building and dam, make a sharp left onto an old logging road leading into the woods. In another 100 yards bear left at an arrow where an older road diverges right. The road fades away to a trail as you climb gently up the valley of Cold Brook, through deep mixed woods at first, then through ice-damaged hardwoods. The trail is blazed in yellow for the first half mile, but is unblazed beyond, and in places you'll have to focus carefully on following the route.

For the first 1.3 miles the going is easy alongside the brook, then you climb away from the stream through mixed woods with some nice fir and spruce. At 1.5 miles there's a post on the left marking the Milan/Berlin town line. You dip back to brook level and follow the stream closely again through a long open corridor that is grassy and marshy in summer. At about 2.1 miles the trail swings up to the right and ascends a slope high above the

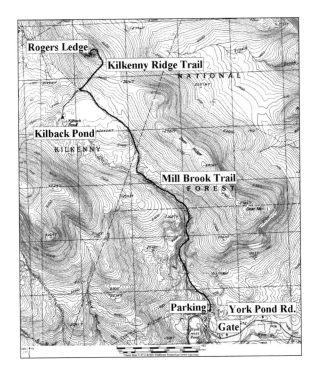

brook. There are a few sidehill sections here that may require finesse in crusty conditions. The woods are mostly birch now. Soon you level out along the edge of the ravine and dip slightly.

You continue along the side of the valley just above a small brook, climbing gradually with more potentially pesky sidehilling. At 2.9 miles you emerge onto a fairyland plateau of white birches—endless ranks of them rising from the snow. The meander across this tableland is a spectacular stretch of snowshoeing with a wonderful feeling of remoteness—the essence of The Kilkenny. At 3.3 miles you dip off the plateau into an open salt-and-pepper forest of birch and fir, and after a gentle descent you meet the Kilkenny Ridge Trail at 3.6 miles.

Turn right here on the yellow-blazed Kilkenny Ridge Trail (a link in the 150-mile Cohos Trail) and head north for the 0.6-mile ascent of Rogers Ledge. You climb steadily through dreamy birch glades, passing a side trail right to a backcountry campsite in 0.1 mile. After a couple of zigs and zags you turn right and tackle a short steep pitch. At the top you turn left and traverse 100 yards along the base of a steep ledge, passing a curiously placed trail sign. Then you swing left again up the north side of the peak for the steepest climb of the day. Look back through the trees for glimpses of the great cliff of Square Mtn. to the NE. After 0.1 mile of stiff climbing you

Snowshoers take in the Kilkenny views from Rogers Ledge

abruptly reach the wooded crest of Rogers Ledge, where the Kilkenny Ridge Trail turns right.

The true summit of this 2965-ft. peak, named for Major Robert Rogers of Rogers' Rangers fame, is just up to the left and has a small view ledge in front. The best views, however, are found a few yards to the right along two short spurs. The first side path leads out to a pair of ledges at the brink of the cliff that are somewhat protected from cold westerly winds. A few yards farther west a second path cuts out to a flat perch just behind the expansive table-flat slab atop the main cliff face. There's a five-foot ledge step to get down onto the big rock shelf, so the view is most safely enjoyed from above.

At your feet is the high plateau of the northern Kilkenny, enclosed on the left by gentle Deer Ridge and on the right by a lofty wooded swell known as "Unknown Pond Ridge," with The Horn, The Bulge and a shoulder of Mt. Cabot peering over its crest. Several whitened beaver ponds can be spotted on the birch-wooded upland, including hidden Kilback Pond in a splash of conifers at the base of Unknown Pond Ridge. Farther to the right is the long, wild chain of wooded summits on the trailless Pilot ridge, culminating in the sharp peak of Hutchins Mtn. Far to the left, beyond a slice of the city of Berlin, there's a great broadside view of the Mahoosuc Range, marked by the prominent spire of Goose Eye Mtn.

Twenty miles to the south, beyond the low Crescent Range, gleam the mighty Presidentials, with the Northern Peaks taking center stage. Left to right you see Mts. Madison, Adams, Washington, Jefferson, Monroe, Franklin, Eisenhower and Pierce. Binoculars draw you in for a closer look at the maw of King Ravine on the side of Mt. Adams. Left of the Presys are the three Moriah summits and all the peaks of the high Carter Range. The U-shaped gouge of Carter Notch is distinct, with Wildcat to the right.

When you've absorbed these premier views, return to the main trail and retrace your tracks. After the initial steep descent the snowshoeing is mostly an easy downgrade, spiced by those occasional sidehills, back to your car.

ADDITIONAL OPTIONS

Kilback Pond   Ambitious explorers can extend the Rogers Ledge trek with a side trip on the southbound Kilkenny Ridge Trail to tiny Kilback Pond, nestled amidst spruces on the plateau south of the cliff. Back at the junction of Mill Brook and Kilkenny Ridge Trails, snowshoe south on the latter trail, climbing for 0.1 mile past a small brook and then meandering through a remote, enchanting birch and conifer forest. In 0.6 mile you come to the shore of the pond, rimmed with a necklace of spiring spruces. From its frozen surface there are views north to the sheer pink face of Rogers Ledge and SW to looming Unknown Pond Ridge. The diversion to this wild, remote spot adds 1.2 miles round trip and only a slight bit of climbing to the day's itinerary.

Unknown Pond *6.6 miles round trip, 1550-ft. elevation gain, advanced*   Unknown Pond is one of the gems of The Kilkenny, cupped on a high shelf between Unknown Pond Ridge and The Horn. In winter the York Pond Road is plowed and can usually be driven, with care, to its end. The Unknown Pond Trail starts at a sign 2.0 miles beyond the fish hatchery gate, which has been kept open throughout the winter in recent years. There is a plowed parking area on the right about 100 yards beyond the trail sign.

The Unknown Pond Trail may be hard to follow through recently logged areas near the start—look carefully for blazes and arrows. It soon hops aboard an old railroad grade, passing a view to Terrace Mtn. Then you start to climb alongside the outlet brook from Unknown Pond, crossing it twice and a tributary once. Farther up the grade steepens and there is some serious sidehilling that can be difficult in crusty snow. The pond, a serene and secluded place, is reached at 3.3 miles. From its frozen surface there is a picturesque view of The Horn, a pyramid crowned with snowy ledges, rising to the SW. (This open, rocky 3905-ft. summit is 2.0 miles away via the Kilkenny Ridge Trail and a side path, with an 800-ft. elevation gain.) To the north rises a set of cliffs on Unknown Pond Ridge, an enticing goal for snowshoe bushwhacking enthusiasts, with a superb view over the pond, The Horn and the distant Presidentials. Tiny "Bishop's Pond," tucked in at the base of The Horn, is another interesting off-trail objective. The snow lies deep in the open birch and fir woods hereabouts, an ideal setting for snowshoe exploration.

Snowshoeing at Touring Centers

With the recent boom in the popularity of snowshoeing, most touring centers have opened at least some of their cross-country ski trails to snowshoers. As a general rule, snowshoers are allowed only on trails that are "skate-groomed" (rolled flat for skating skiers), or along the skate-groomed middle sections or ungroomed edges of double-tracked trails. Snowshoers should never walk on set ski tracks and should yield to passing or descending skiers. A few areas have trails exclusively for snowshoe use. Pets are allowed on designated trails only, or not at all.

A trail fee is required for all use of trails at the White Mountain touring centers listed below. Most have lightweight snowshoes available for rent. If you enjoy snowshoeing on smooth, groomed trails—and who doesn't?—you'll find many scenic and enjoyable outings at these locations. It's always best to call ahead for current rates, hours, conditions and availability of rentals. In 2000, trail fees ranged from $6–$15 and snowshoe rentals from $10–$15 per day.

The information below was provided by the touring centers, including special features and recommended snowshoeing trails.

Bear Notch Ski Touring Center

Route 302, Bartlett; west of village and Bear Notch Road.
603–374–2277 • *www.bearnotchski.com*
65 km open for snowshoeing
Snowshoe rentals available
Located in Saco Valley, with many scenic trails along Saco River and Albany Brook. Trailside scenery also includes fields, waterfalls, beaver bogs and varied forests. Guided nature tours for snowshoers on weekends. Yates Ledge Trail offers a "superb backcountry snowshoe experience"—recommended as a guided tour.

Bretton Woods Cross Country Ski Resort

Route 302, Bretton Woods, on grounds of Mount Washington Hotel.
603–278–3322 • *www.brettonwoods.com*

100 km open for snowshoeing
Snowshoe rentals available
   Three trails systems in spectacular setting at base of Presidential Range. Cross-country center is located in the majestic, historic Mount Washington Hotel—now open in winter. Trails around golf course area offer awesome views of Presidentials, Willey Range, Dartmouth Range and the red-roofed hotel. Trailside scenery also includes Ammonosuc River, northwoods forests, and beaver ponds. Warming yurt on Ammonoosuc trail system. High mountain cabin with wood stove available by reservation on Stickney trail system. Mountain Road trail is lift-serviced—ride up and snowshoe several miles down!

Great Glen Trails

Route 16, Pinkham Notch, near base of Mt. Washington Auto Road.
603–466–2333 • *www.mt-washington.com*
40 km open for snowshoeing
Snowshoe rentals available
   Magnificent setting at eastern base of Presidentials. Outstanding views of Mts. Madison, Adams and Washington on west side and Carter Range on east. There's also a variety of river, pond, swamp and meadow scenery. Especially recommended are the 5-km Aqueduct Loop with Northern Presidential vistas and the snowshoe-only 3-km Starfire Ridge loop with Carter Range views. A unique option is to snowshoe up the snowcat-groomed Mt. Washington Auto Road to treeline, where there is a small warming hut. A snowcat shuttle service is available for those who just want to snowshoe down. Beautiful timber frame base lodge. For lean snow times, Great Glen also has snowmaking on some trails.

Jackson Ski Touring Foundation

Main Street, Jackson
603–383–9355 • *www.jacksonxc.com*
7 km groomed, 30 km backcountry open for snowshoeing
Snowshoe rentals available
   New Hampshire's largest touring center, located in the picturesque village of Jackson. Several backcountry trails available for snowshoeing in Carter Notch Road/Prospect Farm area, including route to Perkins Notch. Some groomed trails open for 'shoeing around village center. For details inquire at JSTF office in Jackson village.

Loon Mountain Cross-Country Center

Route 112, Lincoln, 2 miles east of town.

603–745–8111 • *www.loonmtn.com*

30 km open for snowshoeing

Snowshoe rentals available

Trail system offers snowshoeing along the wide, scenic East Branch of the Pemigewasset River and up on the ridge to the south, with an occasional scenic vista. Especially recommended are the 3-mile Black Mountain Trail / Serendipity loop in the East Ridge system, with delightful riverside snowshoeing along the East Branch and Hancock Branch, and the 2-mile Spur Line / J. E. Henry loop in the West Ridge system, which also has nice riverside scenery. Loon plans to expand its snowshoeing trail system in the near future.

Mt. Washington Valley Ski Touring and Snowshoe Center

Based at Ragged Mountain Equipment, Rt. 16 / 302, Intervale.

603–356–9920 • *www.crosscountryskiNH.com*

65 km open for snowshoeing

Snowshoe rentals available

Trail system maintained through cooperative efforts of 20 businesses and landowners. Trails connect villages of Intervale, Kearsarge, and North Conway, offering unique possibilities for "inn-to-inn" snowshoeing. Largest trail system is in "Whitaker Woods" near downtown North Conway. The Vista Trail here has a beautiful view of Mt. Washington. The Lower East Branch trail network is ideal for beginners with views of the Saco and East Branch Rivers. The Intervale Trail opens a 360-degree view of the Saco Valley. Snowshoe clinics are regularly offered—no charge with trail pass.

Sunset Hill Nordic Center

At the Sunset Hill House, Sunset Hill Rd. off Route 117, Sugar Hill.

603–823–5522 • *www.sunsethill.com*

30 km open for snowshoeing

Snowshoe rentals available

Located at the Sunset Hill House, where there are unmatched views of the Franconia Range and the Presidentials. The Sunrise Trail and Golf Course Loop offer particularly good vistas. Deer are often sighted along the Orchard Trail. There are plans to expand the network in the near future.

Waterville Valley Nordic Center

Located at Town Square, Waterville Valley, off Route 49.

603–236–4666 • *www.waterville.com*

70 km open for snowshoeing

Snowshoe rentals available

One of the largest trail networks in the Whites, in a picturesque mountain-ringed setting. You can also connect with many ungroomed WMNF trails, such as Greeley Ponds Trail, Livermore Trail and Fletcher's Cascade Trail. The Red Feather Trail is a snowshoe-only route. An easy trip leads along the Osceola Trail to wide mountain views at Bob's Lookout, a large clearing. Another gentle route follows Village Trail along Snows Brook and Mad River to the Waterville Valley Campground. The outlying groomed trails provide a good variety of rolling terrain and some scenic vistas.

Recommended Reading

"How to" Snowshoeing / Winter Hiking Books

Winterwise: A Backpacker's Guide, by John M. Dunn, 1996. Lake George, NY: Adirondack Mountain Club. Solid guide oriented to Northeastern mountains.

Don't Die on the Mountain, by Dan H. Allen, 1998. New London, NH: Diapensia Press. Packs a lifetime of Northeastern trail wisdom into its pages. Has especially good sections on route finding and decision-making.

Winter Camping, by Stephen Gorman, 2nd edition, 1999. Boston, MA: Appalachian Mountain Club Books. Excellent guidebook for snow-season travel and camping.

Snowshoeing, by Gene Prater, edited by Dave Felkley, 4th edition, 1997. Seattle, WA: The Mountaineers. The classic guide, written by one of the designers of the modern "Western" snowshoe.

Snowshoeing: A Trailside Guide, by Larry Olmsted, 1997. New York: W. W. Norton. Snazzy, solid guide generously illustrated with color photos.

Basic Essentials: Snowshoeing, by Phil Savignano, 2000. Guilford, CT: Globe Pequot Press. Lots of info distilled into an affordable guide.

Snowshoeing—Outdoor Pursuits, by Sally Edwards & Melissa McKenzie, 1995. Champaign, IL: Human Kinetics. Good basic guide with color photos.

The Essential Snowshoer, by Marianne Zwosta, 1998. Camden, ME: Ragged Mountain Press. Excellent beginner's guide with good section on choosing snowshoes.

Snowshoeing, by Steven A. Griffin, 1998. Mechanicsburg, PA: Stackpole Books. Another solid entry-level guide.

The Winter Wilderness Companion, by Garrett & Alexandra Conover, 2000. A very different kind of guide to traditional winter outdoor skills.

Trail Guidebooks
(See also "Maps" in Introduction, page 32)

AMC White Mountain Guide, edited by Gene Daniell and Jon Burroughs, 26th edition, 1998. Boston, MA: Appalachian Mountain Club Books. The "hiker's Bible" covers all 1,200 miles of trail in the Whites, with complete set of trail maps.

White Mountains Map Book, by Steve Bushey and Angela Faeth, 2000. Stowe, VT: Map Adventures. Compact guide to 76 hikes with winter info and excellent waterproof map.

Scudder's White Mountain Viewing Guide, by Brent E. Scudder, 2000. Littleton, NH: Bondcliff Books. Panoramic sketches of the views from 43 summits, including several covered in this snowshoe guide.

Backcountry Skiing Adventures: Maine and New Hampshire, by David Goodman, 1999. Boston, MA: Appalachian Mountain Club Books. Vivid descriptions of remote backcountry ski routes with excellent practical and historical info.

Winter Trails—Vermont and New Hampshire, by Marty Basch, 1998. Guilford, CT: Globe Pequot Press. Covers over 40 trails for snowshoeing and cross-country skiing across the two states.

Winter Trails—Maine, by Marty Basch, 1999. Guilford, CT: Globe Pequot Press. Describes 40 snowshoe & ski trips, including the Deer Hills in Evans Notch and Goose Eye Mtn. in the Mahoosucs.

50 Hikes in the White Mountains, by Daniel Doan and Ruth Doan MacDougall, 5th edition, 1997. Woodstock, VT: Backcountry Publications.

50 More Hikes in New Hampshire, by Daniel Doan and Ruth Doan MacDougall, 4th edition, 1998. Woodstock, VT: Backcountry Publications. These two classics have been guiding White Mountain hikers since the 1970s.

Ponds & Lakes of the White Mountains, by Steven D. Smith, 2nd edition, 1998. Woodstock, VT: Backcountry Publications. More snowshoe trip ideas can be gleaned from the "winter" tips for each pond.

Waterfalls of the White Mountains, by Bruce, Doreen and David Bolnick, 2nd edition, 1999. Woodstock, VT: Backcountry Publications. Mostly easy trips with lots of historical info.

Hiking New Hampshire, by Larry Pletcher, 1995. Helena, MT: Falcon Publishing. Fine guide in the 50 Hikes motif.

Hiker's Guide to the Mountains of New Hampshire, by Jared Gange, 1997. Huntington, VT: Huntington Graphics. Good overview of Granite State trails.

Nature Hikes in the White Mountains, by Robert N. Buchsbaum, 2nd edition, 2000. Boston, MA: Appalachian Mountain Club Books. Lots of easy hikes described with natural history highlights.

Let's Take a Walk: Family Hikes in the White Mountains, by Michele Cormier, 1999. Describes 75 easy/moderate hikes.

History and Narratives

The White Mountain Reader, edited by Mike Dickerman, 2000. Littleton, NH: Bondcliff Books. Excellent anthology of White Mountain writings from a wide variety of authors and eras.

Forest and Crag, by Laura and Guy Waterman, 1989. Boston: Appalachian

Mountain Club Books. Authoritative and thoroughly engaging history of Northeastern hiking.

Not Without Peril, by Nicholas Howe, 2000. Boston: Appalachian Mountain Club Books. Gripping stories relating 150 years of misadventure on the Presidential Range.

The White Mountains: Names, Places, Legends, by John T.B. Mudge, 2nd edition, 1995. Etna, NH: Durand Press. Good source for White Mountain history and nomenclature.

Place Names of the White Mountains, by Robert & Mary Julyan, 2nd edition, 1993. Hanover, NH: University Press of New England. Over 600 entries on area nomenclature.

Mount Washington, Narratives and Perspectives, edited by Mike Dickerman, 1999. Littleton, NH: Bondcliff Books. Fine compilation of pieces written about the Northeast's highest peak.

Logging Railroads of the White Mountains, by C. Francis Belcher, 1980. Boston, MA: Appalachian Mountain Club Books. Recounts the colorful era of the lumber barons.

J. E. Henry's Logging Railroads, by Bill Gove, 1998. Littleton, NH: Bondcliff Books. Fascinating history of Zealand and Pemigewasset Wilderness areas.

The Moosilaukee Reader, Vols. I and II, edited by Robert W. Averill, 1999. Warren, NH: Moose Country Press. Varied collection of writings about Mt. Moosilauke.

A Guide to Crawford Notch, by Mike Dickerman et al., 1997. Littleton, NH: Bondcliff Books. Handy compilation of history, hiking, nature info.

History of the White Mountains, by Lucy Crawford, 1846. New edition 1999. Etna, NH: Durand Press. Reprint of the classic history of the famed Crawford family.

Along the Beaten Path, by Mike Dickerman, 2nd edition, 2000. Littleton, NH: Bondcliff Books. Entertaining collection of pieces on hiking the Whites.

Why I'll Never Hike the Appalachian Trail, by Mike Dickerman, 1997. Littleton, NH: Bondcliff Books. More mountain nuggets from a White Mountain tramper.

Backwoods Ethics, by Laura & Guy Waterman, 1993. Woodstock, VT: Countryman Press. Thoughtful and humorous writing about low-impact hiking and other backcountry issues.

Wilderness Ethics, by Laura & Guy Waterman, 1993. Thought-provoking book considers how to preserve the "spirit of wildness."

Nature

A Guide to Nature in Winter, by Donald Stokes, 1976. New York: Little, Brown & Co. Excellent coverage of snow, trees, birds, weeds, animal tracks and more—will greatly enhance your appreciation of winter.

Animal Tracks of New England, by Chris Stall, 1989. Seattle, WA: The Mountaineers. Handy illustrated pocket-size guide.

Tracking and the Art of Seeing, by Paul Rezendes, 2nd edition, 1999. New York: Harper Resource. Beautifully illustrated book by master tracker.

North Woods, by Peter J. Marchand, 1987. Boston, MA: Appalachian Mountain Club Book. A very readable treatise on forest ecology in northern New England.

Life in the Cold, by Peter J. Marchand, 1996. Hanover, NH: University Press of New England. Thorough introduction to winter ecology.

Useful Websites and Phone Numbers

Trail Information

Views from the Top—Northeast. *www.lexicomm.com/whites/index.html* The "Trail Conditions—New Hampshire" section carries reports submitted by hikers—a great way to check up on snow depth and conditions.

White Mountains Info Server. *www.cs.dartmouth.edu/whites* David Metsky's site is a terrific resource for White Mountain hiking.

Weather

Mt. Washington Observatory. *www.mountwashington.org* Excellent site includes weather report, live summit camera, avalanche danger, snow depths and conditions at Pinkham Notch, Crawford Notch and other locations.

National Weather Service. *iwin.nws.noaa.gov/iwin/nh/zone.html* Gives zone forecasts for New Hampshire. *iwin.nws.noaa.gov/iwin/nh/public.html* Gives forecast for higher summits of White Mountains.

General Information

White Mountain National Forest. *www.fs.fed.us/r9/white*

WMNF Supervisor's Office, Laconia, N.H.	603–528–8721
Ammonoosuc Ranger District, Bethlehem, N.H.	603–869–2626
Androscoggin Ranger District, Gorham, N.H.	603–466–2713
Pemigewasset Ranger District, Plymouth, N.H.	603–536–1310
Saco Ranger District, Conway, N.H.	603–447–5448

Appalachian Mountain Club. *www.outdoors.org*

Pinkham Notch Visitor Center, Gorham, N.H.	603–466–2721

Randolph Mountain Club. *www.randolphmountainclub.org*

Wonalancet Out Door Club. *www.wodc.org*

ABOUT THE AUTHOR

Steve Smith has been exploring White Mountain trails for over twenty years and started snowshoeing them in 1983. He is the author of the guidebook *Ponds and Lakes of the White Mountains* and has been a co-author of two other guidebooks. He owns the Mountain Wanderer Map and Book Store in Lincoln, New Hampshire, specializing in New England outdoors and travel. Steve and his wife, Carol, reside in Lincoln.